SCM STUDYGUIDE TO

SCM Studyguides

SCM Studyguide to Theological Reflection
SCM Studyguide to Christian Ethics
SCM Studyguide to Old Testament
SCM Studyguide to The Books of the Old Testament
SCM Studyguide to New Testament Interpretation
SCM Studyguide to Biblical Hermeneutics
SCM Studyguide to Christian Doctrine
SCM Studyguide to Christian Mission
SCM Studyguide to Pastoral Theology
SCM Studyguide to Science and Religion
SCM Studyguide to Early Christian Doctrine and the Creeds
SCM Studyguide to Church History
SCM Studyguide to The Sacraments
SCM Studyguide to Anglicanism
SCM Studyguide to The Psalms
SCM Studyguide to Preaching
SCM Studyguide to Practical Skills for Ministry
SCM Studyguide to Christian Spirituality
SCM Studyguide to Liturgy

SCM STUDYGUIDE TO PREACHING

Peter K. Stevenson

scm press

© Peter K. Stevenson 2017

Published in 2017 by SCM Press
Editorial office
3rd Floor, Invicta House,
108–114 Golden Lane,
London EC1Y 0TG, UK

Hymns Ancient & Modern® is a registered trademark
of Hymns Ancient and Modern Ltd

SCM Press is an imprint of Hymns Ancient & Modern Ltd (a registered charity)
13A Hellesdon Park Road, Norwich,
Norfolk NR6 5DR, UK
www.scmpress.co.uk

Except where indicated, scripture quotations are from the New Revised Standard Version of the
Bible, Anglicized Edition, copyright © 1989, 1995 by the Division of Christian Education of the
National Council of the Churches of Christ in the USA. Used by permission. All rights reserved.
Other Bible versions used are:
The Good News Bible, published by The Bible Societies/HarperCollins Publishers Ltd UK ©
American Bible Society, 1966, 1971, 1976, 1992.
The Holy Bible, New International Version, 2011 edition. Copyright © 1973, 1978, 1984, 2011
by Biblica (formerly International Bible Society). Used by permission of Hodder & Stoughton Ltd,
a member of the Hodder Headline Group.
The Holy Bible, Today's New International VersionTMTNIV® Copyright© 2001, 2005 by the
International Bible Society®. All rights reserved worldwide. TNIV Thinline Copyright©2005 by the
Zondervan Corporation.
The New Testament in Modern English by J. B. Phillips copyright © 1960, 1972 J. B. Phillips.
Administered by The Archbishops' Council of the Church of England. Used by permission.

British Library Cataloguing in Publication data

A catalogue record for this book is available
from the British Library

978 0 334 04374 4

Typeset by Regent Typesetting
Printed and bound by
CPI Group (UK) Ltd

Contents

Part 5 The Preaching Life

Acknowledgements

The experience of changing jobs and moving from one capital city to another has meant that this book has had a much longer period of gestation than originally planned. On the plus side, that delay has provided space for continuing learning about preaching.

I am grateful to Natalie Watson for the invitation to prepare this Studyguide and for her patience as new duties and responsibilities delayed progress. I also appreciate the way David Shervington has recently picked up the baton and helped me get across the finishing line.

Many people have helped to shape the ways I go about the business of preaching. In my early days of Christian ministry in Bedford, I benefitted greatly from the imaginative biblical preaching modelled by the Revd Peter Ledger. The invitation from the Revd Dr Michael Quicke, to design and teach a module in preaching at Spurgeon's College in London, helped stimulate a deeper interest in preaching and in the growing body of homiletical literature. The experience of teaching and writing about preaching with my Spurgeon's colleague, the Revd Dr Stephen Wright, ensured that the learning process continued. I also gained a great deal from lively conversations about preaching with Professor Mike Graves during his visits to teach in London, which have provoked further thinking about narrative preaching.

It has been a privilege to share my enthusiasm for preaching with generations of students at Spurgeon's College and more recently at the South Wales Baptist College in Cardiff. Many of the ideas in this Studyguide have been road-tested with them, and I am grateful for the feedback they have given along the way. My Cardiff colleague, the Revd Ed Kaneen, has provided valuable advice on aspects of biblical interpretation and has kindly allowed me to draw on some of his lecture material in Chapter 10.

While no longer in local church ministry, I continue to preach regularly and am grateful for the churches who invite me to preach, and sometimes invite me back.

Living in a two-preacher household, my deepest gratitude goes to Susan, my partner in marriage and ministry, for her ongoing love, patience and encouragement.

Introduction

Getting ready for a family holiday in northern Spain, we not only booked the ferry and the accommodation but also ordered a guidebook and some detailed local maps. They proved a good investment, as they alerted us to things to look out for on the way.

This Studyguide is a kind of guidebook or road map for the preaching journey, for the process of preparing and delivering a sermon is always a journey of discovery.

To begin with, preachers embark on a journey of discovery as they venture into the strange world of the Bible as explorers of the different 'worlds' of the text. On behalf of the congregation, the preacher explores the biblical terrain carefully and prayerfully in order to discern what God may want to say through the ancient text to people today. Such an engagement with Scripture helps to remind the Church of its core identity and its place within the mission of God, so that it can better resist the temptation to be squeezed into the world's mould.

The process of moving from the biblical text to a sermon that connects with the contemporary context is one that presents certain challenges. With that in mind, Chapters 2 and 3 offer some strategies for using the Bible in preaching.

Paying careful and prayerful attention to the biblical text is not, however, the final stage of the preaching journey, for if the sermon is to connect with the concerns of people today, then it is also important to interpret the context in which it will be delivered. Conscious that good preaching is not only biblical but also local and contextual, Chapter 4 affirms the importance of interpreting context and taking time to understand the different kinds of people within a particular congregation.

The hope is that a clear message begins to emerge from this process of exploring both the worlds of the text and the congregation. This leads on to the next stage of the preaching journey, which involves designing the sermon.

It is clear that the Bible contains many different kinds, or genres, of material. For example, interpreting the Psalms will demand different hermeneutical strategies from those needed when interpreting passages from the book of Revelation. Similarly, no one way of designing sermons will necessarily be a good fit for sermons based on different parts of the Bible. A sermon structure that functions well when used with a narrative passage from the Gospels may not be the best fit for a sermon based on one of Paul's epistles.

With that in mind, this Studyguide does not impose one method of designing sermons, rather in Chapters 5 to 8 it offers several strategies that can be used. Working through this material may lead to the conclusion that one of these ways of structuring sermons is the natural, instinctive way you approach the preaching task. However, alongside discovering a default approach that feels comfortable, it is also helpful to be aware of other approaches that can enrich your preaching repertoire. Perhaps you will want to experiment with preaching four sermons, using each of the approaches outlined in Chapters 5 to 8.

Let the words of my mouth and the
meditation of my heart
be acceptable to you,
O LORD, my rock and my redeemer.

Psalm 19.14

Taking those few short steps from my seat to the pulpit or the lectern means that the moment of truth has come when I need to share what I have discovered with the congregation. Although there are times when a little voice within may whisper that this sermon is not worth preaching, the preacher's continual prayer is that God will take our limited human words and somehow use them to convey his living word to people. The good news is that it does not all depend on us.

Desiring to be workers who have 'no need to be ashamed, rightly explaining the word of truth' (2 Timothy 2.15), we want to cooperate with God by preparing thoroughly for the preaching event. Some practical suggestions for the task of preparing and delivering sermons are outlined in Chapters 9 and 10.

Portraying preaching as a journey of discovery hints at more than just the step-by-step process of preparing and delivering a sermon. That process is indeed a journey of discovery for the preacher, who then invites others to join in journeying deeper into God's Word. In addition, though, such a portrayal also alludes to the personal journey of faith that is involved in developing the preaching life.

Over the years my own preaching journey has provided opportunities to preach to congregations large and small, in several countries. Preaching in all sorts of different places has been stretching and demanding, and has underlined the importance of understanding the preaching context. For me, preaching is still a journey of discovery because with every sermon I am learning more about preaching and the Bible, and am being drawn into a deeper relationship with God.

Whatever stage you have reached on your own preaching journey, I hope this book can serve as a friendly guide that will both encourage you to press further along the road, as well as supply you with some useful resources to help you on the way.

Alongside the Studyguide there is also a website containing additional materials. There you will find a short video introduction for each of the book's 11 chapters. Further materials will be uploaded to the website from time to time.

Part 1

Preaching Matters

1

Why Bother with Preaching?

For a video introduction to Chapter 1 visit studyguidepreaching.
hymnsam.co.uk

Have I drawn the short straw?

When the warm glow of being invited to write a book dies down, reality begins to bite. For who is going to want a book about preaching?

After all, there are plenty of voices arguing that preaching has had its day. At a time when there is growing interest in pioneer ministry and fresh expressions of church, surely preaching is part of that discredited Christendom mindset that the Church needs to leave behind?

Why write a *Studyguide to Preaching* when people are asking: 'Why bother with preaching at all?'

Preaching under fire?

Always on the lookout for something to illustrate talks and lectures, it was the 'heavy postcards' in the display case in the museum gift shop at Tenby that caught my eye. Not heavyweight, expensive cards printed on high quality paper, but 'heavy postcards' in the form of ceramic figures crafted by a local artist.

Several of the brightly coloured figures had religious overtones, such as the singer in the church choir whose halo was perched at a rather drunken angle.

However, it was the heavy postcard of the preacher leaning over the front of the pulpit that caught my eye. Gripping the edge of the pulpit with his left hand, the red-headed preacher points menacingly down with his right index finger towards the congregation cowering below.

This ceramic image of a preacher grabs the attention and conveys energy and passion. Perhaps it could be generously interpreted as a picture of 'preaching on fire', or maybe of someone who has a 'passion for the truth'.

Now, when I asked some colleagues about the titles they might choose if they were putting this heavy postcard of a preacher up for sale, their blunt suggestions painted a less than attractive view of preaching:

- Six feet above contradiction …
- Ranter …
- Anger …
- Yesterday's preacher …
- Sinners in the hands of an angry God …

My friends' suggestions chimed in with the sombre title the artist had given this creation, for on the disturbing label underneath the figure in the display cabinet was: '*Damnation*'. Such a provocative title sends a chill down the spine, painfully reminding us that for many people beyond the bounds of the Church, words such as 'preachers' and 'preaching' conjure up negative and toxic feelings.

In an age suspicious of all forms of authority, it is not surprising that many people today view preaching as an outdated, authoritarian attempt to impose unwelcome ideas on people. Indeed, such criticisms are nothing new, for as far back as 1857 we find the novelist Anthony Trollope poking fun at preachers.

> There is, perhaps, no greater hardship at present inflicted on mankind in civilised and free countries, than the necessity of listening to sermons. No one but a preaching clergyman has, in these realms, the power of compelling an audience to sit silent and be tormented.[1]

Caught in friendly fire?

Similar concerns about the relevance of preaching also emerge from within the Church. At one end of the spectrum, concerns are voiced about boring monologues; as Thomas Long observes: 'for many people the words *boredom* and *sermon* are a proper pair, like *horse* and *carriage*'.[2]

A much weightier criticism is that, far from equipping God's people for works of service, sermons delivered by religious professionals disable the laity, reducing their ability to read the Bible and take responsibility for their own faith development. From this angle, as one critic puts it: 'preaching as it is practised in modern churches is extra-biblical, a poor form of communication, and creates dependency'.[3]

PAUSE FOR THOUGHT

Take time to reflect on the criticisms of preaching you are aware of, and then give some thought to ways preachers might best respond to those criticisms. It may be helpful to ask other people for their ideas and opinions.

- What do you believe to be the most serious criticisms of preaching today?
- In what ways can preachers best respond to those criticisms?

Space here forbids a step-by-step response to all of the important questions being raised about preaching. The aim is not to enter the fray on the side of the angels but to offer some biblical and theological perspectives on the theme that might help to position this discussion in a larger context.

In thinking theologically about preaching, it is relevant to ask, first, whether preaching is primarily about Christian education or encountering God.

Poor educational practice?

Some criticisms of preaching are reminiscent of educational debates about *teacher-centred* versus *learner-centred* approaches to learning. In terms of preaching, the argument might be that for optimum learning to take place within the congregation, a preacher needs to be less the 'sage on the stage' pouring out information, and more of a 'guide by the side' enabling people to learn for themselves.

Such comments oversimplify complex debates about the learning process, for how helpful is it to draw such a stark contrast between the transmission of knowledge and the transformation of the learner? Even the most limited exposure to classroom reality suggests that even if an ideal learning environment is created, there is no guarantee students will automatically want to learn for themselves. Often teachers need to supply essential knowledge about a topic first, before students are able to learn effectively. At other times students will need space to learn for themselves and at their own pace.

Clearly many preachers could benefit from thinking a bit more about how people learn, and how congregations experience sermons. However, the criticism that monologue preaching is a poor way of educating a mixed-ability congregation builds on the often unacknowledged assumption that preaching is primarily to be understood through the lens of education.

But is preaching primarily an educational event?

> Sermons are not first of all to educate us or tell us how to behave. That may be part of the matter. First of all, however, they are to enable us to see the glory of God in the face of Jesus as did those disciples on the mount of transfiguration.[4]

Education or encounter?

From the outset, this Studyguide takes a different tack. It assumes that preaching needs to be viewed primarily as something that takes place – and needs to be understood – within the framework of Christian worship.

At a very basic level this is partly because most preaching actually takes place within the context of worship. Rather than seeing the sermon as an outdated form of educational practice, it is more appropriate to view preaching as one part of the rich diet of the Church's public worship.

Seen from this angle, preaching can be understood as an encounter with God taking place within a full-bodied worship experience. It plays its part in a worship event where words, music, colour and action make their combined appeal to the emotions, imagination and intellect of the worshippers.

The link between worship and preaching can be traced back a very long way, especially if Jesus' sermon in the synagogue in Nazareth, recorded in Luke 4.16–21, can be seen as the prototype of Christian preaching.

When [Jesus] came to Nazareth, where he had been brought up, he went to the synagogue on the sabbath day, as was his custom. He stood up to read, and the scroll of the prophet Isaiah was given to him. He unrolled the scroll and found the place where it was written:

> 'The Spirit of the Lord is upon me,
> because he has anointed me
> to bring good news to the poor.
> He has sent me to proclaim release to the captives
> and recovery of sight to the blind,
> to let the oppressed go free,
> to proclaim the year of the Lord's favour.'

And he rolled up the scroll, gave it back to the attendant, and sat down. The eyes of all in the synagogue were fixed on him. Then he began to say to them, 'Today this scripture has been fulfilled in your hearing.'

Luke 4.16–21

Luke's account of Jesus delivering his 'Nazareth Manifesto' is set within the context of a service in the synagogue that normally included a sermon. So far from preaching being 'extrabiblical', there are grounds for suggesting that Christian liturgy inherits, from its roots in synagogue worship, the practice of sermons based on biblical texts.

The present passage is the oldest account of a synagogue service. After private prayer on entry to the building by the worshippers, there was a public confession of the Jewish faith in the Shema (Dt. 6.4–9; 11.13–21), followed by prayers, including the Tephillah and the Shemoneh Esreh. Then came the centre of the worship, the reading of the Scriptures. A passage from the Pentateuch was read, according to a fixed scheme of lections, by several members of the congregation in turn, with an Aramaic paraphrase. There was also a lesson from the prophets; in later times this too was according to a fixed lectionary, but it is a matter of dispute whether this system existed in the first century, and, if so, what form it took. It is safest to assume that there was at least some freedom of choice of prophetic reading in the first century. Following the readings was a prayer, and then came the sermon, if there was somebody competent present to give one. Finally the Qaddish prayer was recited. The readers for the day were appointed before the service began ... Possibly Jesus had informally requested permission to read before the service began, and Luke has not gone into the details of the arrangement.[5]

Now the provocative comments of Jesus in the synagogue that day are so brief that some might question whether it is realistic to call this a *sermon*.

It seems reasonable to see Jesus' message in that light because the comments recorded in Luke's Gospel could plausibly represent a summary of what Jesus said, or perhaps give a flavour of his opening remarks. Whether short or long, Jesus' sermon had a much more dramatic impact on his hearers than many sermons since!

In a classic analysis of the Nazareth sermon, Yngve Brilioth highlighted three primary elements in Jesus' preaching at Nazareth, which root preaching in the context of worship and underline its biblical dimensions.

1 *The liturgical element*: Jesus' sermon was delivered within the context of the Jewish service. The sermon was an accepted, traditional, and prescribed part of this service, even though it was not obligatory.
2 *The exegetical element*: Jesus spoke from a text, the question of whether it depended on his own choice or not being of no consequence. Gradually the freedom of choice in the synagogue was limited more and more by a developing order of prescribed pericopes. We can observe a similar development within the church. This development, however, is less significant

than the essential principle that the edifying discourse have its roots in the exposition of a text, and that the sermon, after ceasing to be a direct commentary on a text, continue to have as its starting point a word of Scripture. One of the most essential guarantees of the sermon's religious content is found in this rootage.

3 **The prophetic element**: 'Today this scripture has been fulfilled in your hearing.' The content of Jesus' preaching was summed up in this prophetic declaration, which retained the characteristic crisp, lapidary style of the oracles. The sermon was prophetic in the deepest sense, inasmuch as it is the essential nature of prophecy to speak to the present with divine authority and to transform the historical revelation into a contemporaneous, divine reality.[6]

Recognizing some of the historic, biblical roots of Christian preaching does not answer all of our contemporary questions. However, placing debates about preaching into this liturgical perspective may prompt us to ask different kinds of questions.

It may suggest that the key issue is not simply whether a particular sermon was educationally appropriate for this diverse congregation. A more relevant question would be about whether this complete act of blended worship, including the sermon, contained sufficient nourishment to cater for the various personality types and spiritual needs within the congregation.

PAUSE FOR THOUGHT

Take time to reflect on the role preaching plays within the worship of the church you are most familiar with.

- Reflect on the last service of worship you attended.
- What role did preaching play in that service?
- How well did the sermon fit into the service?
- To what extent had the service been planned to fit the sermon?
- To what extent did the service cater for the needs of a range of people?
- In what ways did the worship event appeal to people's thinking, feeling and imagining?

Preaching in worship

Some valuable reflections on the relationship between preaching and worship, offered by Chris Ellis, can help us explore things further. In a reflection on the place of Scripture within worship in the British Baptist tradition, Ellis points to three key aspects of what is happening when people gather for worship.[7] While there is no set liturgy within this tradition, Ellis argues that when people come together for worship there is a sense that they are:

- Gathering to Hear God's Word;
- Gathering to Speak God's Word;
- Gathering to Meet God in God's Word.

These concerns are not unique to one single denomination, but they provide useful lenses for viewing the role preaching plays in the way many Christians understand public worship.

Gathering to Hear God's Word

Historically the desire to hear God's word when believers gather for worship is clearly visible in the prominence accorded to pulpits within Nonconformist church buildings.

That longing to hear a message from God, which will transform lives and situations, is also evident in the songs and hymns used in worship. A hunger for hearing God's word is expressed clearly in the contemporary hymn, 'Speak, O Lord, as we come to You'. This song was written to encourage people to expect to hear God speaking through the sermon.

> Speak, O Lord, as we come to You
> To receive the food of Your holy word.
> Take Your truth, plant it deep in us;
> Shape and fashion us in Your likeness,
> That the light of Christ might be seen today
> In our acts of love and our deeds of faith.
> Speak, O Lord, and fulfil in us
> All Your purposes, for Your glory.[8]

The confidence that in worship believers do not simply gather to listen to human opinions but to a message that comes from God can also be seen in a classic hymn drawn from the Anabaptist tradition:

> Our Father God, Thy name we praise,
> To Thee our hymns addressing,
> And joyfully our voices raise
> Thy Faithfulness confessing;
> Assembled by thy grace O Lord,
> We seek fresh guidance from Thy Word;
> Now grant anew thy blessing.
>
> Touch Lord the lips that speak for Thee;
> Set words of truth before us,
> That we may grow in constancy,
> The light of wisdom o'er us.
> Give us this day our daily bread;
> May hungry souls again be fed;
> May heavenly food restore us.[9]

Gathering to Speak God's Word

Ellis notes that:

> Baptist worship has been dominated, not by the word of God but by the preaching of the word of God. Far more time is spent by the preacher expounding and applying the word then ever is given to simply reading the word.[10]

With this in mind, he presses on to make two affirmations.

First, he asserts that 'The essence of preaching is indeed proclamation … and the primary purpose of the discourse is not so much to explain as to announce.'[11] This insight chimes in with the advice a Presbyterian teacher, Anna Carter Florence, gives new preachers. Year by year she stresses to those starting out on the preaching journey that:

their job is not to make the text understandable, or logical, or relevant, or fun. Their job is quite simple, really. It is to *preach the text*, because there isn't anything more interesting or sensible than that. Preach the text, offer it in all its thickness and inscrutability, and trust that it will speak better than we could to the competing worlds of consumerism and militarism and individualism and anxiety that plague our people.[12]

The Bible itself suggests that the power of the word of God does not ultimately depend on our human ability to explain it. Preachers can proclaim the word reassured that underneath our fumbling human attempts to find the right words, the good news is that God's living word has the power to make things happen.

> For as the rain and the snow come down from heaven, and do not return there until they have watered the earth, making it bring forth and sprout, giving seed to the sower and bread to the eater, so shall my word be that goes out from my mouth; it shall not return to me empty, but it shall accomplish that which I purpose, and succeed in the thing for which I sent it.
>
> Isaiah 55.10–11

Second, alongside this emphasis on proclamation, Ellis affirms that 'preaching is a rich event-in-time in which both the congregation and the preacher play their respective parts'.[13]

For me the experience of preaching for many years to multicultural congregations in south London has underlined the significant contribution congregations can and do make to the preaching event. Some calls for more dialogue and less monologue in preaching can perhaps overlook this. For example, within the Black Preaching tradition[14] it has long been assumed that when it comes to the sermon, there will be a dynamic and audible dialogue between preacher and congregation. In other contexts, that rhythm of call and response may not be audible but the dimension of dialogue can be awakened as the preacher employs word pictures and open-ended questions, stirring people's imaginations and teasing their minds into active thought.

Gathering to Meet God in God's Word

Ellis argues that 'Christian worship is a gathering of the church in the name of Jesus Christ in order to meet God through scripture, prayer, proclamation and sacraments and to seek God's kingdom.'[15]

Within that larger framework he reinforces the idea that:

> the primary purpose of preaching is not to explain but to enable an encounter with the living Christ … We gather around the word in order to seek God, and while all preaching should contain elements of teaching, or doctrine, the hearers need to be transformed by an encounter with God and not simply with the intellect of the preacher.[16]

This emphasis on the importance of an encounter with God resonates with some bold claims about preaching made by Paul Scott Wilson.

> In the best sermons, Christians not only learn something but also feel renewed hope, stronger faith, and recommitment to mission or Christian living. Simply stated, they experience God. Thus one may claim that preaching is an event in which the congregation hears God's Word, meets their Savior, and is transformed through the power of the Holy Spirit to be the kind of community God intends. Preaching is an event, an action; something happens in the lives of the hearers by way of a divine encounter. Christ commissioned preaching. Since this encounter is a salvation event, it effects an end to the old ways, reconciliation with God, and empowerment for ministries. All of this is part of the purpose of preaching.[17]

By speaking of preaching in such terms, Scott Wilson is setting the bar for preaching at a high level, viewing it as a saving encounter with God.

Reading such comments may prompt a voice within to say: 'It's not like that at our church.' Or we may be tempted to say: 'He wouldn't call preaching an encounter with God if he'd heard the sermon I had to endure last week!'

PAUSE FOR THOUGHT

'Preaching is an event, an action; something happens in the lives of the hearers by way of a divine encounter ... Since this encounter is a salvation event, it effects an end to the old ways, reconciliation with God, and empowerment for ministries.'[18]

- Do you believe that preaching is an event of encounter with God?
- What difference would such a belief make to the way you prepare to preach?
- What difference might such a belief make to how you preach?

By describing preaching in this kind of way, both Chris Ellis and Paul Scott Wilson are suggesting that preaching has a sacramental character.

Sacramental preaching?

Talk about preaching as an event that involves 'an encounter with God' encourages us to see preaching within the context of a sacramental paradigm. It is not being claimed here that preaching is a divinely appointed sacrament like baptism and Holy Communion, rather that there is a sacramental dimension to it.

In other words, it suggests that in the activity of preaching, the living God is able to take and use our faltering human speech to mediate and communicate his living word to human beings.

Some years ago Donald Coggan wrote about the 'joyful tyranny' of preaching. Those words remind us that preaching regularly can be a demanding and costly calling. Seeing preaching within a sacramental paradigm does not mean all sermons will be heavenly experiences but it is a reminder of preaching's potential. Working from this perspective means preachers can embark on the challenging task of designing and delivering sermons, confident that God is able to take our human words and use them to mediate his love to others. Such a sacramental understanding of preaching both raises our expectations and also takes some of the weight off preachers' shoulders.

The basis for believing that God can take such created things as human words and use them to mediate his reality to us is rooted in the incarnation. The confession that 'the Word became flesh and lived among us' (John 1.14) bears witness to the God who takes ordinary flesh and blood and uses it to reveal his love and truth to human beings.

Preaching as a sacrament

Stephen Wright is another who advocates seeing preaching as a kind of sacrament. For him this is rooted in the conviction that:

> The world itself is sacramental of God's presence, love and power, and Christ himself as the supreme sacrament, the defining centre through which we encounter God. Not only the classically defined 'sacraments' of baptism and Eucharist, therefore, but also Scripture and preaching, may then be seen, in a derived way, as events, places, moments through which we encounter God. Crucially, though, they do this not *independently* of Christ, nor of the created universe, Rather they do this *insofar as* they are signs and pointers to Christ and to his rule over all things.[19]

Human beings are capable of playing this sacramental role in part because they have been created in the image of God and are thus intended to 'image' God through their words and lives shaped by love. None of this, however, means that the preacher is in control of the divine encounter. God has:

> given us Scripture, he gathers congregations of disciples, he calls individuals to a particular role in speaking out his word. But none of these realities *guarantees* that he will reveal himself in any particular place, event, time or person … Our preaching is always just a 'gesturing to the Word'.[20]

Thus in relation to preaching, sacramental language highlights both the potential and the limitations of the human words used in preaching.

Portrait of a preacher ...

> Greet all the brothers and sisters with a holy kiss. I solemnly command you by the Lord that this letter be read to all of them.
>
> 1 Thessalonians 5.26–27

In his study *Preaching Like Paul*, James W. Thompson invites preachers to consider what can be learnt from reflection on the preaching of the apostle Paul.

If the Apostle to the Gentiles were preaching today there would be a wealth of recordings and scripts for students of Paul's preaching to pore over. Although that kind of material is not readily available, Thompson claims that it is possible to overhear something of Paul's preaching 'voice' by paying close attention to his epistles.

Part of the reason this is possible is because the apostle dictated his letters to a secretary and then entrusted them to someone who could read the letter aloud, as a monologue, to believers gathered together for worship. This claim that there is such a 'close relationship between Paul's oral address and his letters is suggested by the fact that he, like other writers of antiquity, dictated his letters to an amanuensis'.[21]

> As he dictated his letters, he undoubtedly envisioned the community of listeners before him. Like preachers who prepare their sermons as they envision concrete situations and personalities, Paul prepared his letters with specific listeners and situations in mind. The process of dictation allowed Paul to speak to the gathered community at a distance. One may assume that the arrangement of his thoughts approximated his normal mode of presentation. His torrential style, passion, and involved sentences bear the mark of the spoken rather than the written word. E. P. Sanders portrays the writing process as part of a ferocious debate in which the harassed and distraught apostle paced the floor, 'dictating, sometimes pleading, sometimes grumbling, but often yelling'.[22]

This begins to paint an intriguing picture, made all the more fascinating because it is also possible that the person commissioned by Paul to deliver his letter would have been coached by the apostle, not only to deliver it by hand but also to present it orally.[23]

Thompson's main thrust, however, is not to argue for more monologue sermons. On the assumption that we can to some extent overhear the 'voice' of the apostle Paul in his epistles, Thompson suggests that we can see how Paul engages in pastoral preaching that challenges 'the congregation to ask the moral questions and to discuss them in the light of the gospel of Christ'.[24]

He also suggests that Paul's preaching can be understood as a public act of theological reflection.

> Theological reflection is a vital dimension of preaching ... While Paul's letters are all pastoral communication ... they are also examples of faith seeking understanding. The modern reader is likely to be amazed at the lengthy arguments that punctuate the letters that were meant to be read in the assembly. These arguments reflect Paul's high expectations for his listeners. He undoubtedly assumes his listeners will follow his intricate argumentation. His theological reflection is not, however, abstract and irrelevant. As much as his letters may offer detailed theological argument, Paul never offers treatises on the great doctrines of the Christian faith in a comprehensive and systematic way. He never offers a comprehensive sermon on the incarnation or atonement. His theological discourse appears in the context of questions that have been raised in his congregations or the issues that threaten the identity of the church. Paul's theological discourse is interwoven with his pastoral communication. The issues that he faces are ultimately theological in nature.[25]

Although I argued earlier that preaching should not be seen primarily through an educational paradigm, Thompson makes a strong case for seeing preaching as a form of practical theology.

Preaching is a way of doing theology – with and on behalf of a community of believers – that seeks to discern God's saving presence in the midst of a hostile and often confusing world. The preacher functions as a community theologian who draws on the Bible and the resources of the Christian tradition to help people see the connections between faith and life.

In the early stages of Christian discipleship, I imbibed a privatized understanding of faith that had a rather limited understanding of theology. With time and experience that view of theology kept growing and developing so that I came to see that 'Theology is the enterprise of relating all human knowledge, as well as all our everyday activities, to God's self-disclosure in Christ.'[26]

At a time of widespread religious illiteracy, in society generally and also within the Christian Church, preaching has a role to play within the larger curriculum of Christian education. If preaching is a form of practical theology, then its challenging task is in some way to help relate 'all human knowledge, as well as all our everyday activities, to God's self-disclosure in Christ'. Barbara Brown Taylor paints a vivid picture of the challenges facing the preacher seeking to carry out such a daunting and inspiring task.

Watching a preacher climb into the pulpit is a lot like watching a tightrope walker climb onto the platform as the drumroll begins. The first clears her throat and spreads out her notes; the second loosens his shoulder and stretches out one rosin-soled foot to test the taut rope. Then both step out into the air, trusting everything they have done to prepare for this moment as they surrender themselves to it, counting now on something beyond themselves to help them do what they love and fear and most want to do. If they reach the other side without falling, it is skill but it is also grace – a benevolent God's decision to let these daredevils tread the high places where ordinary mortals have the good sense not to go.

No other modern public speaker does what the preacher tries to do ... All the preacher has is words. Climbing into the pulpit without props or sound effects, the preacher speaks – for ten or twenty or thirty minutes – to people who are used to being communicated with in very different ways. Most of the messages in our culture are sent and received in thirty seconds or less and no image on a television screen lasts more than twenty, yet a sermon requires sustained and focused attention. If the topic is not appealing, there are no other channels to be tried. If a phrase is missed there is no replay button to be pressed. The sermon counts on listeners who will stay tuned to a message that takes time to introduce, develop and bring to a conclusion. Listeners, for their part, count on a sermon that will not waste the time they give to it.[27]

So what is preaching? Before setting out in the following chapters to explore the preaching process, it is helpful to ask some questions about the nature of preaching.

PAUSE FOR THOUGHT

- What do you believe are the most important things about preaching?
- Write a short paragraph outlining the heart of your theology of preaching.

A working definition ...

The working definition of preaching that underlies this book can be summed up like this:

Discovering the word of the Lord from the Bible, for this group of people, at this particular time, and then delivering that word in the power of the Spirit, in ways that people can understand, so that they can respond in worship and service.

Chapters 2 and 3 will explore some of the thinking behind the claim that the preaching process starts with *discovering the word of the Lord from the Bible.*

The reflections in Chapter 4 consider some of the contexts within which preaching takes place, and the different kinds of people who listen to sermons. This alerts us to the importance of designing sermons for a specific *group of people, at a particular time.*

Chapters 5 to 8 move on to take a look at different approaches to designing sermons.

In Chapters 9 and 10 the focus turns to some basic guidelines for effective communication so that the sermon can be delivered *in ways that people can understand, so that they can respond in worship and service.*

Lord, still me,
Let my mind be enquiring, searching.
Let my heart be open.
Save me from mental rust.
Deliver me from spiritual decay.
Keep me alive and alert.
Teach me, that I may teach them.
Lord, give me the gifts,
to make this gift to you.

A prayer of St Augustine before preaching

Further reading

Kate Bruce, *Igniting the Heart: Preaching and the Imagination* (London: SCM Press, 2015).

David Day, Jeff Astley and Leslie J. Francis (eds), *A Reader on Preaching: Making Connections* (Aldershot: Ashgate, 2005).

David Heywood, *Transforming Preaching: The Sermon as a Channel for God's Word* (London: SPCK, 2013).

Thomas G. Long, *The Witness of Preaching*, 3rd edn (Louisville, KY: Westminster John Knox Press, 2016).

Michael J. Quicke, *Preaching as Worship: An Integrative Approach to Formation in your Church* (Grand Rapids, MI: Baker Books, 2011).

Barbara Brown Taylor, *The Preaching Life* (Cambridge, MA: Cowley, 1993).

William H. Willimon, *How Odd of God: Chosen for the Curious Vocation of Preaching* (Louisville, KY: Westminster John Knox Press, 2015).

Stephen I. Wright, *Alive to the Word: A Practical Theology of Preaching for the Whole Church* (London: SCM Press, 2010).

Notes

1 Anthony Trollope, *Barchester Towers* (Oxford: Oxford University Press, 1953), p. 52.

2 Thomas G. Long, 'Why sermons bore us', *Christian Century*, 6 September 2011, p. 31.

3 David Allis, 'The Problem with Preaching', *Baptist – Magazine of the Baptist Churches of New Zealand* 123:6 (July 2007).

4 Colin E. Gunton, *Theology Through Preaching: The Gospel and the Christian Life* (London: T. & T. Clark, 2001), p. 95.

5 I. H. Marshall, *The Gospel of Luke*. The New International Greek Testament Commentary (Exeter: Paternoster Press, 1978), pp. 181–2.

6 Yngve Brilioth, *A Brief History of Preaching* (Philadelphia, PA: Fortress Press, 1965), pp. 8–10.

7 Chris Ellis, 'Gathering around the Word: Baptists, Scripture and Worship', in Helen Dare and Simon Woodman (eds), *The "Plainly Revealed" Word of God? Baptist Hermeneutics in Theory and Practice* (Macon, GA: Mercer University Press, 2011), pp. 101–21.

8 'Speak, O Lord', words and music by Keith Getty and Stuart Townend, Copyright © 2005, Thankyou Music.

9 From the sixteenth-century *Anabaptist Ausbund*, trans. E. A. Payne, in *Baptist Praise and Worship* (Oxford: Oxford University Press, 1991), p. 151.

10 Ellis, 'Gathering around the Word', p. 109.

11 Ellis, 'Gathering around the Word', pp. 113–14.

12 Anna Carter Florence, 'Put Away Your Sword: Taking the Torture out of the Sermon', in M. Graves (ed.), *What's the Matter with Preaching Today?* (Louisville, KY: Westminster John Knox Press, 2004), pp. 93–108 (99).

13 Ellis, 'Gathering around the Word', p. 114.

14 See, for example, Cleophus J. LaRue, *The Heart of Black Preaching* (Louisville, KY: Westminster John Knox Press, 1999); Cleophus J. La Rue, *I Believe I'll Testify: The Art of African American Preaching* (Louisville, KY: Westminster John Knox Press, 2011); Timothy George, James Earl Massey and Robert Smith, Jr., *Our Sufficiency is of God: Essays on Preaching in Honor of Gardner C. Taylor* (Macon, GA: Mercer University Press, 2010); Joe Aldred (ed.), *Preaching with Power: Sermons by Black Preachers* (London: Cassell, 1998).

15 Ellis, 'Gathering around the Word', p. 116.

16 Ellis, 'Gathering around the Word', pp. 117–18.

17 Paul Scott Wilson, *The Practice of Preaching*, rev. edn (Nashville, TN: Abingdon Press, 2007), p. 5.

18 Wilson, *Practice of Preaching*, p. 5.

19 Stephen I. Wright, *Alive to the Word: A Practical Theology of Preaching for the Whole Church* (London: SCM Press, 2010), pp. 119–20.

20 Wright, *Alive to the Word*, pp. 120–1.

21 James W. Thompson, *Preaching Like Paul: Homiletical Wisdom for Today* (Louisville, KY: Westminster John Knox Press, 2001), p. 28.

22 Thompson, *Preaching Like Paul*, pp. 28–9.

23 Thompson, *Preaching Like Paul*, pp. 30–1.

24 Thompson, *Preaching Like Paul*, p. 106.

25 Thompson, *Preaching Like Paul*, p. 109.

26 Howard Peskett and Vinoth Ramachandra, *The Message of Mission* (Leicester: InterVarsity Press, 2003), pp. 22–3.

27 Barbara Brown Taylor, *The Preaching Life* (Cambridge, MA: Cowley, 1993), pp. 76–7.

Part 2

Preparing to Preach

2

A Journey into Three Worlds

For a video introduction to Chapter 2 visit studyguidepreaching.hymnsam.co.uk

Biblical preaching

Meeting with the leadership team of a church that was considering inviting me to become their next minister, I was understandably asked all sorts of questions. The time then came for me to ask what kind of minister they were searching for. The first response, 'Someone like you', was very flattering but not all that helpful. As the conversation continued, someone commented that they felt the church needed a minister who would provide good Bible teaching.

It is hard to know exactly what that person was looking for because there are so many different ideas about what good biblical preaching looks and sounds like. What I do know is that wrestling with the Bible in preparation for preaching week by week, both to that congregation and many others, has formed a significant part of my ministry over the years. Indeed, that regular discipline of engaging with the Bible has not only been an essential dimension of my preaching life but is something that has shaped and enriched my spirituality in many ways.

For me, preaching and the Bible have been two sides of the one coin. So it is not surprising that much of this Studyguide is devoted to exploring the use of the Bible in preaching. However, to what extent is that link with the Bible an essential dimension of preaching? Or is it more a matter of personal preference or churchmanship? How important is it to retain an umbilical cord between the Bible and preaching, at a time when the Bible's relevance is contested and ideas about preaching are rapidly changing?

Questioning the Bible's role in preaching

One of the values of experiential learning events is the opportunity to learn the unexpected. Our expectation that participants would readily turn to the Bible as a shared text proved faulty. A number of concerns about using the Bible were raised.[1]

A group of Christians gathered to explore connections between faith and work. Some were ordained ministers serving in church or chaplaincy roles, others worked in a range of institutions. All were able to describe situations they faced that took them out of their professional comfort zones.

Having identified issues arising from those situations, the event's organizers encouraged participants to move on to exploring connections with the Bible. It was at that point that many expressed their hesitations about using the Bible in such discussions.

For some, the legacy of historical explorations of the world behind the text was a sense that 'they could not be expected to have the necessary knowledge and skill to use scripture in theological reflection'.[2] Others working in secular settings voiced their 'doubts about the relevance of the Bible'[3] to the world and its concerns. Those who worked with marginalized groups were suspicious of the Bible 'as a text that has been used to oppress women and minorities'.[4]

Depictions of the God of the Bible as misogynist, homophobic and racist are present in the popular literature of the new atheists. That some practices of some churches fall short of socially accepted norms of equality and inclusion is evident and frequently represented in the media. An attempt to represent God as loving and inclusive was not felt to be assisted by the 'texts of terror' found within the books of the Bible.[5]

While these concerns about the Bible were raised in the context of discussions about practical theology, they may reflect a wider lack of confidence about using Scripture felt by some within the Church.

The working definition of preaching outlined at the end of Chapter 1 begins by suggesting that preaching involves '*discovering the word of the Lord from the Bible*'. Such a definition unashamedly places the Bible in the foreground of the theology and practice of preaching. If, however, some Christians feel a degree of unease about handling the Bible, what questions does this raise about the wisdom of giving such prominence to wrestling with Scripture in the preaching process? When it comes to the task of developing relevant, contemporary forms of preaching, to what extent is the Bible a resource or a liability?

The normative form of Christian preaching

One of the foundations on which this Studyguide has been built is the assumption, expressed clearly by Thomas Long, that 'biblical preaching is the *normative* form of Christian preaching'.[6]

Historical studies, such as Brilioth's work mentioned in Chapter 1, demonstrate that the sermon's rooting in Scripture has been a constant feature throughout Christian history. So 'when Jesus preached in the synagogue at Nazareth (Luke 4), he spoke from a text, and for the most part Christian preachers ever since have done the same'.[7]

In drawing attention to this, Long is not only claiming that biblical preaching has been the normal practice over the years but is also arguing that it is the norm, or standard, against which all preaching should be evaluated.

> Biblical preaching is also normative in the second and more vigorous meaning of the norm. Preaching that involves significant engagement with a biblical text is the standard over against which all other types of preaching are measured. If we ask about a particular sermon, 'Is that a Christian sermon?' we are really asking if it bears true and faithful witness to the God of Jesus Christ, and answering that question inevitably takes us to the biblical story through which we know and encounter the God of Jesus Christ ... So, we are claiming that biblical preaching is 'normative' in both ways. Faithful engagement with

Scripture is a standard by which preaching should be measured, and the normal week-in, week-out practice of preaching should consist of sermons drawn from specific biblical texts. Biblical preaching in this strict sense should be the rule and not the exception.[8]

PAUSE FOR THOUGHT

- How do you respond to Long's claim that biblical preaching should be the rule and not the exception?
- What questions do you want to ask?
- What do you understand by the term 'biblical preaching'?

It is hard to dispute the fact that preaching from a biblical text has been standard practice throughout Christian history. However, continuing with such habits simply because 'We've always done it this way' is not always the wisest strategy, especially in times of rapid and discontinuous change. So what other factors need to be taken into account when thinking about the value of the Bible in the preaching process?

A brief theology of revelation

One of the reasons for maintaining a strong link between preaching and the Bible has to do with questions about divine revelation. While 'No one has ever seen God' (John 1.18), the faith of the Church is that in and through Jesus Christ the truth about God has been revealed. Within such an understanding of divine revelation, the Bible plays a crucial role because it bears witness to the Christ who reveals the truth about God.

This perspective was expressed with characteristic clarity by Colin Gunton, who explained:

the creation may reveal the glory of God, but 'scarcely one in a hundred' recognises it for what it truly is. There has, then, to be a distinction between a general revelation in nature, which is indeed there, and the human capacity to appropriate it. The need for what is called special revelation is that, for various reasons, we often do not see what is there before our eyes … That is the point of Calvin's view that without the Bible as a pair of spectacles, we are unlikely to be able to recognise even general revelation for what it is.[9]

> Just as old or bleary-eyed men and those with weak vision, if you thrust before them a most beautiful volume, even if they recognize it to be some sort of writing, yet can scarcely construe two words, but with the aid of spectacles will begin to read distinctly; so Scripture, gathering up the otherwise confused knowledge of God in our minds, having dispersed our dullness, clearly shows us the true God.[10]

Such an understanding of divine revelation implies that it is not possible to uncover the truth about God's character on the basis of human reason alone. Left to our own devices, people like us can generate all sorts of interesting ideas about the nature of God. Viewed in the light of biblical revelation, however, many of those popular images of the deity turn out to be misleading caricatures.

Amid the competing views of God and spirituality currently on offer, biblical preaching has a continuing relevance, for the task of preaching is to proclaim the biblical story, which narrates and reveals the character of God. In fulfilling this role, the preacher is to some extent inheriting the mantle of biblical prophecy.

Inheriting the prophet's mantle

In an early foray into Old Testament studies, I tackled writing an essay focusing on the work of pre-exilic prophets such as Amos and Hosea. The gist of the question was to explore to what extent such prophets were religious innovators or guardians of the tradition.

It was only some years later, when I was quarrying for material for lectures on the book of Amos, that I began to realize what that essay question was really inviting me to consider. The penny finally dropped as I discovered James Limburg's description of the prophetic task.

For many people the image of the Old Testament prophet is of a rather unusual but courageous character, lobbing verbal hand grenades at priests and kings. Limburg suggested that the prophet's calling involved a much broader range of activities.

> The prophetic task has been described as concerned with the future (fore-telling), addressing the present (forthtelling), and recalling the past (retelling). Telling the story of God's mighty acts remains an aspect of the tasks of both preaching and teaching. In hearing this story and discovering it as their own story, a people of God can rediscover who they are. They are reminded of what God has done for them and will be motivated to respond in acts of love.[11]

In a variety of ways the contemporary preacher inherits each of those three tasks of *foretelling*, *forthtelling* and *retelling*.

Foretelling

Preaching takes place in a context where continual reports of wars and rumours of wars can create a feeling of hopelessness. Indeed, one contemporary writer about mission claims that we are living in a '*post* postmodern' context 'character-ized by the chill of anxiety and fear'.[12]

In response to such hopelessness, the preacher's calling is not to indulge in speculation about the timing of the end of the world but to proclaim a living hope founded on the resurrection of Christ. For Tom Wright, the biblical hope of 'life *after* "life after death"',[13] and the vision for God's coming kingdom, inspire believers 'to build *for* the kingdom' now, in the confidence that in the Lord our labour 'is not in vain' (1 Corinthians 15.58).[14] Christians build for God's coming kingdom, believing that 'all we do in faith, hope and love in the present, in obedience to the ascended Lord and in the power of the Spirit, will be harvested, enhanced and transformed at his appearing'.[15]

Forthtelling

Walter Brueggemann has the task of forthtelling in mind when he suggests that the role of prophetic ministry is to subvert,[16] undermine or *dismantle* the royal, imperial world view that maintains an unjust status quo that reinforces the power of the religious and political elite.

He is not, however, advocating outbursts of blind rage about the ills of society, because for Brueggemann, prophetic ministry not only *dismantles* unjust world views but also seeks to *energize* the development of an alternative community. This brand of *forthtelling* does not mean random acts of prophetic protest but offers a way of life, and a pattern of ministry, that embody and communicate a vision of a different kind of world. So Brueggemann suggests that:

> prophetic ministry does not consist of spectacular acts of social crusading or of abrasive measures of indignation. Rather, prophetic ministry consists of offering an alternative perception of reality and in letting people see their own history in the light of God's freedom and his will for justice.[17]

Retelling

One sometimes overlooked dimension of the prophet's task in Old Testament times was to retell the story of the Covenant between Yahweh and the people of Israel. By retelling this story, the prophet sought to remind the Israelites of the narrative that shaped their identity as God's people.

Living in an age of widespread biblical illiteracy, both in society and, sadly, also within the Church, there is still the need to retell the old, old story so that God's people can remember and discover who they truly are. In such a context, biblically based preaching has a part to play by inviting and enabling people to enter into the biblical narrative in such a way that they can begin to own it as their story too.

To suggest that preaching involves *retelling* the biblical story that shapes the Christian community is another way of saying that the preacher functions as a community theologian. Preachers seeking to help people live authentic Christian lives amid changing and challenging times will invest in retelling God's story, so that the people of God can be reminded of the kind of contrast society they are called to be.[18]

Thus far this chapter has argued that biblical preaching deserves to be seen as the normative form of Christian preaching. In support of this claim, reference has been made to the Bible's unique role in bearing witness to the Christ who reveals God to humanity. Strong biblical foundations are also essential if preaching is to have a prophetic dimension. For it is the biblical narrative that both paints a picture of an alternative view of reality and also helps to shape the character of the believing community.

Having argued for the importance of biblical preaching, it is necessary now to ask two further questions:

1   How does the preacher select biblical texts from which to preach?
2   Having chosen the scriptural passage, what is involved in interpreting it so that we can begin the journey from text to sermon?

Choosing a text

As a theological student it was possible for me to preach the same sermon in a number of different places and, I hope, to refine and improve it gradually along the way. Adjusting to a settled ministry in which I needed to preach regularly to the same congregation brought a whole new set of demands. To begin with, I have to confess wasting a great deal of time each week simply deciding which biblical passage on which to preach, before getting around to the demanding process of discerning what to say.

Within some traditions, preachers have the freedom to choose their own biblical texts from which to preach. This can have the advantage of allowing the preacher to respond to whatever issue is facing the church week by week. On the other hand, for those on the early stages of the preaching journey it can prove a time-consuming process. Increasingly, I find it much more satisfying to be asked to preach on a particular passage because this request forces me to pay serious attention to a range of biblical texts.

Many preachers find it helpful to plan series of sermons exploring different parts of the Bible. Often during the summer months, with fewer church-related meetings to attend, I have made time to get to grips with a biblical book – or books – in order to plan a series of sermons for the autumn. There are many good ways of designing sermon series, but reflecting back over the years leads me to suspect that a series unfolding over four to six weeks may be sufficient for both preacher and congregation to sustain.

Preaching from a lectionary

Within many traditions the choice of texts Sunday by Sunday is provided by a cycle of readings or lections contained in a lectionary. The three-year cycle of readings – with some variations – that is used by several mainstream denominations is the Revised Common Lectionary. For each Sunday, following the rhythm of the Christian year, the lectionary offers three recommended readings: an Old Testament reading; a Gospel reading; plus one from the Epistles or another part of the New Testament. Matthew, Mark and Luke are read in successive years, while selections from John's Gospel are woven into the programme at some point during each of the three years.

No lectionary includes every possible passage from the Bible. However, the value of submitting to the discipline of following the lectionary is that it can help to deliver both preacher and congregation from being subjected to sermons on a small number of favourite texts over and over again. It can also function as a helpful spiritual discipline, encouraging preachers to explore and preach on texts they would never otherwise have chosen.

LECTIONARY CASE STUDY

The lectionary can be found in many standard service books. Sometimes I find it useful to refer to an online lectionary site that provides both the set readings for a particular Sunday as well as an overview of the readings being used during that season of the Christian year.

> The Revised Common Lectionary can be found online at
> http://lectionary.library.vanderbilt.edu.

Even a quick glance at the readings suggested by the Revised Common Lectionary reveals that it offers a rich source of materials and ideas for preaching.

For example, in preparing a service of worship to be broadcast on the fourth Sunday after Pentecost in Year A of the three-year cycle, I checked and found the following set of readings.

Season after Pentecost Year A	First reading and psalm	Alternate First reading and psalm	Second reading	Gospel reading
Proper 9 (14) fourth Sunday after Pentecost 6 July 2014	Genesis 24.34–38, 42–49, 58–67; Psalm 45.10–17 or Song of Solomon 2.8–13	Zechariah 9.9–12; Psalm 145.8–14	Romans 7.15–25a	Matthew 11.16–19, 25–30

Step 1

An initial reading of the suggested texts for the fourth Sunday after Pentecost raised a number of possibilities.

I was drawn instinctively to the Gospel reading where Jesus issues the invitation: 'Come to me, all you that are weary and are carrying heavy burdens, and I will give you rest' (v. 28).

A few weeks earlier I had been door-stepped by someone who had asked me a lot of questions about the person of Christ. That conversation reminded me that many people today do not have a very clear understanding of who Christ is. So maybe that is why I also noticed the startling statement in verse 27 that points towards the unique relationship between the Son and the Father: 'All things have been handed over to me by my Father; and no one knows the Son except the Father, and no one knows the Father except the Son and anyone to whom the Son chooses to reveal him.'

Step 2

Reading the 'First' reading from the Old Testament on this occasion, I wondered if the designers of the lectionary might have intended a link between the Genesis narrative and the Gospel reading.

Reading in Genesis 24 about Abraham's servant being sent to find a wife for Isaac led me to the conclusion that there probably was not a direct link. I concluded that a degree of homiletical ingenuity would be needed to suggest a parallel between the invitation to Rebekah to travel to meet and marry Isaac, 'Will you go with this man?' (Genesis 24.58) and the invitation of Jesus who says 'Come, follow me.'

I was relieved later to read the explanatory notes attached to the lectionary, which explained that:

> 'First' OT readings follow major stories/themes, read mostly continuously, beginning in Year A with Genesis and ending in Year C with the later prophets. *Italicized readings, complementary to the standard reading, may be used with, or in place of it.*[19]

In this case the 'italicized' readings were Psalm 45.10–17 or Song of Solomon 2.8–13. Both of those readings could be used to complement a sermon based on the Genesis passage, for we see a royal wedding in the background to Psalm 45 and the verses from the Song of Solomon are part of a poetic book that celebrates the gift of love in explicit and sensual ways.

While Genesis 24, Psalm 45 and the Song of Solomon chapter 2 could contribute positively to a sermon exploring aspects of love and marriage, they did not seem to contribute directly to a sermon that focused on the words of Jesus from Matthew's Gospel.

Step 3

The footnotes went on to explain that '"Alternate First" OT readings follow the historical tradition of thematically pairing the OT reading with the Gospel reading. *Italicized readings, complementary to the standard reading, may be used with, or in place of it.*'[20]

With this in mind it is easier to detect a possible connection between the 'Alternate First' reading, from Zechariah 9.9–12, and the Gospel reading. A Christian reading of Zechariah 9 interprets the passage in messianic terms, offering insights into the long-awaited leader and deliverer that Israel was hoping for. The king who comes in the vision of Zechariah 9 is one who will be 'humble and riding on a donkey'; and that brand of humility is embodied in Jesus, who says 'I am gentle and humble in heart' (Matthew 11.29).

Step 4

The series of 'Second readings' suggested for the season after Pentecost in Year A of the lectionary draws mainly from Paul's letter to the Romans. Anyone wanting to develop a sermon series on Romans would have plenty to choose from, because on 16 of the Sundays during this season the 'Second' reading comes from that letter. Such a series could fit well into the rhythm of the Christian year, as many preachers will want to focus on the life and witness of the Church in the weeks following Pentecost.

The suggested reading for the fourth Sunday after Pentecost was Romans 7.15–25a. This passage has been vigorously debated over the years. Is the apostle writing autobiographically to describe his own experience? Is he depicting a state of spiritual struggle preceding or following conversion to Christ? Or is this an example of a 'speech-in-character' describing the struggle of God-fearing Gentiles or Jews who know the law but still find themselves unable 'to free themselves from passion and desire through works of the law'?[21]

In terms of developing a sermon, it might be possible to explore some links between the struggle described in Romans 7 and the invitation of Jesus in Matthew 11. For Jesus appears to be offering rest to people who were struggling under the burden of an exhausting form of religion, which tired people out with an endless list of demands.

On this occasion I was seeking to discover the word of the Lord from the Bible for a group of people listening to the radio at 7.30 a.m. on a Sunday morning. With the limited time available in that context I concluded that I would be over-complicating matters if I tried to do justice both to the struggle within Romans 7 and the great invitation in the Gospel reading.

Step 5

Having 'lived' with these passages for a while, it felt right to focus my attention on part of the Gospel reading. That extract from Matthew 11 is theologically rich, for it not only includes the intriguing invitation from Jesus but also sheds light on the one who is the eternal Son of the eternal Father. There is more than enough there to inspire several sermons.

If you would like to see the sermon that emerged from this process, you can find it in Appendix 1.

Resources for working with the lectionary

One useful resource for lectionary-based preaching is the *Feasting on the Word* commentary series published by Westminster John Knox Press. The 12-volume series provides comments on the set readings for each Sunday in the three-year Revised Common Lectionary.

PAUSE FOR THOUGHT

Working with the lectionary

- Find the lectionary readings for next Sunday (or for a Sunday when you are preaching).
- You may find the following website useful: http://lectionary.library.vanderbilt.edu.
- Read all of the set readings for that Sunday.
- Which reading do you feel most drawn to?
- In terms of the Christian year, how well do the passages seem to fit?
- What connections, if any, do you think exist between the different readings?
- On which of those passages would you like to design a sermon?
- What kinds of things would you like to include?

Choosing texts for sermons

'There are strengths and weaknesses to any method of choosing texts to preach. We preach from the Bible to ensure that God's Word is proclaimed, and the lectionary provides an excellent safeguard against preaching only one's favourite texts. Unless preachers are careful, however, lectionary preaching can lead to a diminished ability to speak prophetically on specific topics, current issues or general doctrines. To counter this danger, preachers might address important topics as they arise, preach doctrines as they are found in the texts at hand, and occasionally depart from the lectionary (in those denominations where preachers have this liberty) perhaps at regular intervals through the year to preach a topical or doctrinal sermon or sermon series.'[22]

- Think about how you go about the task of choosing a biblical text for a sermon.
- What issues does Paul Scott Wilson highlight about choosing texts?
- What implications might this have for the way you 'choose' texts for your sermons?

Learning to read the Bible again

Built into the notion that preaching involves discerning a spiritual message from the Bible is the necessity for engaging in a careful reading of the text. Such a 'close reading' of the chosen passage marks the first stage of the preaching process. For the first and greatest commandment directed to the would-be preacher is 'Read the Text'; and the second is like unto it, 'Read the Text Again'.

With all the demands on our time there is plenty to distract us from paying such prayerful and careful attention to the text. It is helpful at this point to underline the value of initially reading and reflecting on the set text or texts *before* consulting the wisdom of biblical commentaries, or the notes in the latest study Bible.

One way of slowing down sufficiently to pay attention to the text may be to read the passage in several different translations. Reading the text aloud a number of times might be another way of helping you 'hear' it in different ways.

In Chapter 3 the ancient Christian practice of *Lectio Divina* will be offered as another way of immersing ourselves in a biblical passage.

It is my hope that initial exposure to the text will help you identify a range of questions and ideas, some of which might turn out to contain the seeds of a potential sermon. Having harvested those initial ideas, the next stage is to explore the text in greater depth. For, on behalf of the body of Christ, preachers are called to embark on a journey of biblical and theological exploration so that they can then act as witnesses to what they have discovered.

Moving on to the next stage of the process, there is then great value in drawing on the insights of others who have reflected on these passages before us. Engaging with perspectives offered by biblical commentaries can enrich our understanding of a passage in a variety of ways. It does so by alerting us to things we might otherwise overlook, which may help to answer some of the questions raised by our initial reading of the text. This process of exposing ourselves to the opinions of others may also at times be unsettling when it challenges long-held ideas about the meaning of the text.

One of the challenges facing the contemporary preacher seeking to venture into the world of the ancient text[23] is to develop good habits of handling and interpreting the biblical materials.

The difficulty of interpreting the Bible is felt not only in secular culture but also in the Church at the beginning of the twenty-first century. Is the Bible authoritative for the faith and practice of the Church? If so, in what way? What practices of reading offer the most appropriate approach to understanding the Bible? How does historical criticism illumine or obscure Scripture's message? How are premodern Christian readings to be brought into engagement with historical methodologies, as well as feminist, liberationist and postmodernist readings?[24]

Part of the challenge here is that any textbook on biblical hermeneutics can easily overwhelm us with a long list of different styles of biblical interpretation. The good news is that I do not need to have an exhaustive understanding of all these hermeneutical approaches before I can be permitted to read the Bible for myself.

Stepping back from the many approaches on offer, one way of getting to grips with the different strategies for interpreting the Bible is to see three broad families of approaches.

A journey into three worlds

In a helpful overview of this topic, W. Randolph Tate[25] writes first about 'author-centred approaches to meaning', referring to those styles of interpretation that concentrate their attention on '*the world behind the (biblical) text*'. In other words, such approaches focus on how the text came to be. The historical-critical approach to biblical studies, with its interest in things such as source criticism and form criticism, exemplifies such an 'author-centred' approach.

He also describes 'text-centred approaches to meaning', which concentrate their energies on exploring '*the world within the text*'. Here the focus of attention falls on asking what is the content of this particular text. In part such approaches note that once a text leaves an author's hands, the writer loses control of its 'meaning' because people will find different kinds of meaning within it. Focusing on 'the world within the text' also means paying more attention to the final form of the text, taking note of its literary features. Recognizing that the Bible contains different genres of material, for example, suggests that no one interpretative strategy is likely to suit all passages. It is clear that reading Hebrew narrative requires a different set of hermeneutical skills from those required when interpreting apocalyptic passages such as the book of Revelation.

Tate also points to 'reader-centred approaches to meaning', which remind us that 'different readers interpret a text differently'.[26] The growth of feminist, liberationist and postcolonial readings of biblical texts in the last few decades is an acknowledgement that how we each read the Bible is influenced by things such as culture, context, class and gender. In such approaches to hermeneutics, the focus of attention is more on '*the world in front of the text*'.

Synchronic, diachronic and existential

Another helpful perspective is provided by Michael Gorman, who argues that:

> Exegesis may be defined as the careful historical, literary, and theological analysis of a text. Some would call it 'scholarly reading' and describe it as reading in a way that 'ascertains the sense of the text through the most complete, systematic recording possible of the phenomena of the text and grappling with the reasons that speak for or against a specific understanding

of it'. Another appropriate description of exegesis is 'close reading', a term borrowed from the study of literature. 'Close' reading means the deliberate, word-by-word and phrase-by-phrase consideration of all the parts of a text in order to understand it as a whole. Those who engage in the process of exegesis are called exegetes.[27]

Viewing exegesis as investigation, conversation and art, he suggests that there are 'perhaps three basic approaches to exegesis', which he labels as '*synchronic, diachronic*, and *existential*'.[28] While Gorman is using different terminology from Tate, he is similarly alerting readers to the need to take text, author and readers into account when working with the Bible. In contrast to Tate's 'reader-centred approaches to meaning', Gorman's existential form of exegesis gives more weight to the idea that readers consciously engage with biblical materials for the purpose of transformation.

Such discussions could sound rather remote from the task of the individual preparing a sermon. Something of the potential value for the preacher of these different approaches can be seen in Gorman's suggestions outlined below. In this example he suggests some of the questions users of these three approaches might ask when they turn their focus on the Sermon on the Mount in Matthew's Gospel.

Hermeneutical approach	**Questions this could raise**
Synchronic 'This approach looks only at the final form of the text, the text as it stands in the Bible as we have it.' World within the text.	• What are the various sections of the Sermon, and how do they fit together to make a literary whole? • What does the narrator of this gospel communicate by indicating the setting of the Sermon, the composition of the audience before and after the Sermon, and the audience's reaction to it? • What is the function of the Sermon in the gospel's portrayal of Jesus and of discipleship? • How would a first-century reader/hearer understand and be affected by this Sermon?

Hermeneutical approach	Questions this could raise
Diachronic 'Focuses on the origin and development of a text, employing methods designed to uncover these aspects of it … As a constellation of methods, this approach is often referred to as the *historical-critical method*, and it was the approach of choice by many, if not most, biblical scholars of the twentieth century.' World behind the text.	• What written or oral sources did the evangelist (gospel-writer) adopt, adapt, and combine to compose this 'Sermon'? • What are the various components of the Sermon (beatitudes, prayers, parables, pithy sayings, etc.), and what is their origin and development in Jewish tradition, the career of the earthly Jesus, and/or the life of the early church? • What does the evangelist's use of sources reveal about his theological interests? • To what degree do these teachings represent the words or ideas of the historical Jesus?
Existential 'We may describe this approach to exegesis as self-involving: readers do not treat the text as a historical or literary artefact, but as something to engage experientially – something that could or should affect their lives. The text is taken seriously.' World in front of the text.	• To what kind of contemporary faith and practice does the Sermon call contemporary readers? • How might the text about 'turning the other cheek' be a potential source of difficulty or even oppression for the politically or socially downtrodden? • Does love of enemies rule out the use of resistance or violence in *every* situation? What does it mean *practically* to embody the teachings about nonviolence in the Sermon? • What spiritual practices are necessary for individuals and churches to live the message of the Sermon in the contemporary world?[29]

Benefitting from three worlds

For the preacher there are clear benefits in exploring all three of these 'worlds'. By listening to the contribution each of these three approaches to interpretation makes, our understanding of the passage deepens and insights are uncovered that can help shape effective sermons.

The world behind the text

For example, the opening verse of the book of the prophet Haggai explains that his ministry took place 'In the second year of King Darius, in the sixth month, on the first day of the month' (Haggai 1.1). As this 'king was Darius I Hystaspes who seized the throne of Persia after Cambyses' death (522–521 BC)',[30] it places Haggai's first message to the people in the year 520 BC.

In other words, this prophet's ministry takes place in the period after the devastating experience of the Babylonian Exile following the destruction of Jerusalem in 587 BC. After the balance of power in the Ancient Near East shifted, a new regime emerged that permitted some of the exiles to return. On their return from exile, many of their hopes were dashed as they discovered a homeland in ruins. After a series of failed harvests and with the cost of living rising steeply, the task of rebuilding the life of the nation was both overwhelming and demoralizing.

Understanding something of that painful world behind this particular text helps bring this passage alive for both preachers and congregations. Appreciating how God spoke through the prophet to people facing such difficult circumstances, we can begin to hear a message of hope from God for demoralized believers today who may feel at times that the odds are stacked against them.

Preachers turning to the familiar New Testament parable of the Good Samaritan in Luke 10.29–37 similarly need to know about the world behind a text that bristles with the ethnic and religious tensions that kept Jews and Samaritans apart. From the standpoint of the Jewish teacher of the law, the Samaritan was a heretic. Within the parable, however, it is the Samaritan who turns out to be the one who is obedient to the law of God.

The world within the text

Paying careful attention to the text itself is also vital, because a close reading of the passage often helps the preacher notice essential clues to its meaning. This is amusingly evident in the way the story of Jonah unfolds. For the repetition of the verb 'to go down' in the opening sections of the Jonah narrative (1.3, 5; 2.6) subtly but powerfully communicates the message about the way life goes seriously downhill when people turn their backs on God.

Verse 3 emphasizes that Jonah's disobedience is a *descent* from the Lord by repeating the verb *yārad*, 'to go down': 'And he went down to Joppa ... and he went down on it (the ship) to go with them to Tarshish....' The verb will then recur in verse 5, 'But Jonah went down to the hold of the ship ...,' and in 2:6, 'I went down ...' Jonah, in his disobedience, is descending vertically from the presence of the Lord, and in the poem of chapter 2 that descent is down toward Sheol, the place of the dead. The author of this story is therefore using word symbols to portray the terrible implication of Jonah's disobedience. To flee from the Lord means death. In good storyteller fashion, that is not spelled out for us at the beginning but is revealed gradually as the narrative proceeds.[31]

The world in front of the text

John Drane describes an experience that forced him to question the assumptions shaping his reading of a familiar biblical text. His hermeneutical preconceptions were upended when he shared in a Bible study on the parable of the Good Samaritan, led by a teenage girl on the Smokey Mountain rubbish dump in the Philippines. The turning point came when the group leader asked the question: 'Now who are you in this story?'

I took it for granted that I knew the answer to that as well. At least, I knew who I would like to be. That was easy. I recognized the possibility that I might be the priest or the Levite, who passed by the wounded man and left him on the roadside. I knew I would really like to be the Samaritan, who did good by taking the robbers' victim to a place of safety – though in my heart of hearts I had the sneaking suspicion that (in common with many western people) maybe I was more like the innkeeper, who would do good but only when someone else paid him for it. Anyway, when we were given the opportunity to share our thoughts with one another, I had no difficulty knowing what I was going to say. It was just as well that I was not invited to speak first, for I soon realized that I was responding quite differently from everyone else who was there. For them, there were no agonizing choices as they sought to identify with the characters in the story. They all knew precisely who they were: the person beaten up and left for dead by the roadside. I realised in an instant what was happening. Though I had debated within myself who I might be, in reality my options were strictly limited because I had taken it for granted that, whoever I was, I would be one of the authority figures in this story. It simply never occurred to me that I might be poor and powerless like the man on the roadside. As I realized what I had done, I could hardly believe it. I thought of myself as globally aware and politically correct – yet, even surrounded by the sights and smells of such obvious poverty, I still unconsciously read into this Bible story the imperialistic assumptions of my culture, assuming that if I was in there at all, then I would have to be in control of somebody.[32]

Becoming more aware of the assumptions we bring to the Bible can help preachers in a number of ways. For one thing, it alerts me to the danger of thinking that my reading of the text is the one and only valid interpretation. On the other hand, it also encourages me to bring to the biblical text the questions and concerns arising from the world I inhabit every day.

Perhaps most significantly, an awareness of *the world in front of the text* opens up the possibility of my biblical understanding being enriched by the insights of others. For at a time when the majority of the world's Christians live in the Global South, listening to how people in other parts of the world read the Bible can open up fresh perspectives on familiar texts. Philip Jenkins argues that 'it can be a surprising and humbling experience to try to understand how parts of the Bible might be read elsewhere in the world', and suggests that 'any number of texts offer surprises'.[33]

> Read Ruth, for instance, and imagine what it has to say in a hungry society threatened by war and social disruption ... Or read Psalm 23 as a political tract, a rejection of unjust secular authority. For Africans and Asians, the psalm offers a stark rebuttal to claims by unjust states that they care lovingly for their subjects – while they exalt themselves to the heavens. Christians reply simply, 'The Lord is my shepherd – you aren't!' Adding to the power of the psalm, the evils that it condemns are at once political and spiritual, forces of tyranny and of the devil. Besides its political role, Psalm 23 is much used in services of healing, exorcism and deliverance.[34]

Such global perspectives can be valuable resources for preachers seeking to break through the overfamiliarity with Psalm 23, associated in many people's minds with providing comfort at funerals.

Developing an integrated theological reading of the text

It seems clear that preachers can gain valuable insights from all of these approaches, and Tate argues for employing an integrated approach to meaning that brings his three families of approaches into conversation. His proposal is 'that meaning results from a conversation between the world of the text and the world of the reader, a conversation informed by the world of the author'.[35]

Some ways of categorizing these hermeneutical families might perhaps list the theological interpretation of Scripture as a 'reader-centred' approach to meaning. There are grounds, however, for seeing a theological reading of Scripture as an integrative approach that draws insights from all three approaches while consciously reading the Bible in accord with the faith of the Church.

In Chapter 1 it was suggested that preaching is a form of practical theology whose aim is to relate 'all human knowledge, as well as all our everyday activities, to God's self-disclosure in Christ'.[36] This depicts preaching as a way of 'doing theology' or a form of 'faith seeking understanding', which gladly enters into that three-way conversation involving the world behind the text, the world within the text and the world in front of the text.

Thus we find Daniel J. Trier arguing that:

theological interpretation of Scripture uses multiple lenses along the way but tries to integrate these various perspectives into a coherent vision of who God is and what that calls us to become in Christ. This is the widest-angle lens, and it puts biblical interpretation into proper perspective. Historical and literary details may then appear in a different light; furthermore, some of those matters, while fine for scholarly specialists to pursue, may not be materially central for understanding and communicating the message of the texts. For we are studying the Scriptures to know God, not necessarily to sketch the entirety of Paul's social work or to make occasionally impossible choices between subjective and objective genitives.[37]

CASE STUDY: A JOURNEY INTO THE THREE WORLDS OF MATTHEW 5.38–48

In preparation for a sermon on Matthew 5.38–48, what help might we find by engaging in conversation with the three worlds of the text?

1 The world in front of the text

The place to start is where we as readers sit in front of the text, and there is value in reflecting on the assumptions we bring to the text.

It is also helpful to consider the questions we want to ask about this text, as well as some of the questions people in our congregation are likely to be asking about it.

For example, faced with the disturbing call to love our enemies, we may find ourselves asking questions such as:

- Was Jesus really serious about his followers loving their enemies?
- Surely this is totally impractical in a world like ours?
- Does loving our enemies and forgiving people mean turning a blind eye to evil and violence?
- What on earth would this look like today?

2 *The world behind the text*

Thinking about the world behind this passage might provoke questions such as:

- Was begging a common practice at that period?
- Which groups were seen as neighbours and who were the enemies?
- What kinds of coats and cloaks did people wear?

When probing behind the text, valuable information can be found in up-to-date biblical commentaries. Some information can be drawn from one of the following one-volume commentaries on the whole Bible.

- Tokunboh Adeyemo (gen. ed.), *Africa Bible Commentary* (Grand Rapids, MI: Zondervan: 2006).
- John Barton and John Muddiman (eds), *The Oxford Bible Commentary* (Oxford: Oxford University Press, 2007).
- D. A. Carson, R. T. France, Alec Motyer and Gordon J. Wenham (eds), *New Bible Commentary: 21st Century Edition* (Nottingham: InterVarsity Press, 1994).

Brief but helpful reflections on the text can be found in Tom Wright's *New Testament For Everyone* series, which provides two short commentaries on Matthew's Gospel.

- Tom Wright, *Matthew For Everyone, Part 1: Chapters 1–15* (London: SPCK, 2012).

Preachers investigating biblical passages will benefit significantly from drawing on more detailed commentaries:

- Craig E. Evans, *Matthew*. New Cambridge Bible Commentary (Cambridge: Cambridge University Press, 2012).
- Douglas Hare, *Matthew*. Interpretation: A Bible Commentary for Teaching and Preaching (Louisville, KY: Westminster John Knox Press, 1993/2009).
- Cynthia A. Jarvis and E. Elizabeth Johnson (eds), *Matthew, Volume 1, Chapters 1—13*. A Feasting on the Word Commentary: Feasting on the Gospels (Louisville, KY: Westminster John Knox Press, 2013).

Exploring more deeply into the world behind this particular text from Matthew's Gospel leads us to ask questions about the historical sources and roots of the Sermon on the Mount of which this passage forms a part. In thinking about the events that lie behind the text, many scholars suggest that both Matthew and Luke drew some of their material from a source (Q) no longer available to us as a separate source. In the Lukan version of this sermon, usually known as the Sermon on the Plain (Luke 6.17–49), the assumption is that Luke simply includes the material from the Q source without much more editorial work.

As the Sermon on the Mount in Matthew's Gospel is longer than the Lukan version, this leads many writers to assume that Matthew has taken the opportunity to gather together other examples of the teaching of Jesus and to mould all this material into a more comprehensive account of the heart of Jesus' teaching. Hence we discover that:

> In the sixteenth century John Calvin had already taught that the sermon expresses the intention of the evangelist 'of gathering into one single passage the chief headings of Christ's teaching, that had regard to the rule of godly and holy living ...'[38]

Thinking about the world behind the text also reminds us that Jesus lived and worked in a country occupied by a hated, foreign army. Imperial soldiers could command citizens to carry their baggage for one mile, whether they liked it or not. So the teaching of Jesus did not originate from a centrally heated study but from a land subject to the rigours of military rule.

The statement 'You have heard that it was said' in verses 38 and 43 points behind the text to the Jewish nature of the audience addressed by Jesus. Without further explanation it assumes that his hearers, and the first readers of this Gospel, will be familiar with the provisions of the Old Testament law.

3 The world within the text

It is also vitally important to pay attention to the world within the text; or to put it another way, it is essential to pay attention to the actual text of Matthew's Gospel. As we move to consider the content of the text more carefully, another series of questions might come to our minds:

- Who is being addressed?
- Why is this teaching being given?

- What is the significance of the refrain 'You have heard that it was said ... but I say to you'?
- How does this passage connect with the rest of the Sermon on the Mount?
- How is this passage related to the larger 'text' of Matthew's Gospel?
- What echoes of Old Testament passages can we detect here?

It is clear that the Sermon on the Mount is part of the larger 'text' of Matthew's Gospel. It plays a strategic role within the Gospel as a whole, and clues to its meaning are visible in other parts of the Gospel. For example, in Matthew 4.23 it is stressed that Jesus went throughout Galilee 'teaching'. Then at the end of the Gospel in Matthew 28.16–20, the disciples are sent into all the world to teach new believers to obey all that Jesus had taught.

There are five occasions in this Gospel when:

> Matthew concludes a major speech of Jesus with almost identical formulae, 'Now when Jesus had finished saying these things' (7:28, NRSV, cf. 11:1; 13:53; 19:1; 26:1). The formula acts not merely as a conclusion, but as a transition, pointing back to the completed speech and forward to the continuing narrative, relating Jesus' words to his deeds and binding speech and narrative together.[39]

Matthew 5.38–48 is part of the Sermon on the Mount, which forms the first of those sustained 'speeches' in Matthew's Gospel. M. Eugene Boring notes that 'Already in the second century Matthew was regarded as structuring his Gospel in five "books" in imitation of the Pentateuch and as an alternative to the Jewish understanding of Law.'[40]

Such an idea fits with the suggestion that Matthew is presenting his material about Jesus in such a way as to draw a parallel between Moses, who received the Law on Mount Sinai, and Jesus (the new Moses?), who proclaims a new (or renewed) Law as he goes up another mountain to deliver his Sermon on the Mount.

For those with eyes to see, the refrain, 'You have heard that it was said ... but I say to you ...' contains an implicit Christology. For this 'formula points to the unparalleled authority of Jesus',[41] whose radical interpretation of the divine law demonstrated an authority exceeding that of Moses. If no one on earth was greater than Moses, then who must this Jesus be?

Three overlapping worlds?

This preliminary reading of Matthew 5.38–48 suggests that these three worlds are not totally separate, hermetically sealed units. There is clearly a degree of overlap between the questions and issues raised by these three families of approaches. However, this example suggests that there is great value for the preacher in viewing biblical texts through these three lenses.

PAUSE FOR THOUGHT

Graham Stanton identified a number of questions that, over the years, people have asked about the Sermon on the Mount.

Read through the following five questions Stanton asks about how to interpret it.

Thinking about each question in turn, which of the three 'worlds' do you think these questions are about?

- The world behind the text?
- The world within the text?
- The world in front of the text?

1 Does Jesus simply interpret or clarify the Law of Moses? Or does he present radically new teaching? Is Jesus portrayed as the 'new Moses' who 'goes up on the mountain' (Matt. 5.1) in order to present on a 'new Mt Sinai' a 'new law' for a 'new people'?

2 What is the relationship between Matthew 5—7 and Paul's gospel of grace? Is the Sermon (as Law) intended to make the readers or listeners aware of their need of grace? Or does the Sermon *presuppose* God's forgiveness and acceptance of the sinner and therefore set out demands for true discipleship?

3 To whom is the Sermon addressed? To men and women in general, or to those committed to the way of Jesus? ... While many parts of the Sermon seem to set out an 'ethic of Christian discipleship', the final verses of the whole gospel imply that the teaching of Jesus is to be part of the message taken to 'all nations' (Matt. 28.18–20).

4 Are all parts of the Sermon to be interpreted literally, as some have claimed? Or do some sayings (such as Matt. 5.22, 39, 43) contain hyperbole? Does the Sermon set out a *code* of ethics, or principles or attitudes appropriate for 'members of the kingdom'? …

5 To what extent are individual sayings dominated by the expectation (either of Jesus or of Matthew) of the approach of the end-times (i.e. eschatology)? For example, does Jesus commend a casual attitude to food and clothing in Matthew 6.25–34 because of the approach of the end-times or simply because this is the right attitude regardless of when the end-times come?[42]

Conclusion

A useful model for discussing hermeneutics, the interpretation of scripture, is to identify three locations from which that interpretation might take place. One is 'behind the text', that is exploring the world of the author, to examine issues such as who the book was written by, its intended audience, the historical context, the geographical setting and the purpose of the book. Another is 'within the text' examining such concerns as the original language of the book, its genre, its structure and use of literary devices. The final location is 'in front of the text' focusing on the perspectives and concerns which the reader brings to the text.[43]

For some perhaps, it is difficult to see many connections between their academic study of the Bible and the task of standing in front of a congregation to preach. Thinking about biblical interpretation as a journey into three worlds is one way of demonstrating how a serious study of the text can enable and enrich preaching. It illustrates one of the ways the sermon preparation process can be enriched by the resources of biblical scholarship.

In the next chapter we shall look at some other ways of listening to the Bible as we seek to discern the message we want to communicate. Before moving on, however, it is necessary to explain that an emphasis on biblical preaching does not mean all sermons looking and sounding the same. This Studyguide is not suggesting that biblical preaching means that all sermons must take the shape of a 45-minute, verse-by-verse, running commentary on a biblical passage. For as David Day indicates, biblical exposition can come in many different forms.

> [T]he word 'exposition' is ambiguous. It is often used in a restricted sense and taken to mean a verse-by-verse analytical commentary on the text. I make no such assumption. By exposition I mean *any* process which will ensure that the essential meaning of and force of the text is communicated. The means by which this is done will vary considerably. Indeed, faithful exposition may not always be recognizable as a sermon … Nevertheless a biblical text will lie at the bottom of any truly Christian communication … It is thus my hope that preaching will normally consist of the exposition of a passage.[44]

As we shall see in Chapters 5 to 8, many different ways of designing sermons can be employed as we seek to preach with the grain of Scripture. In addition, as Chapter 5 will suggest, the preacher's task is not to dump every bit of information about a biblical passage on an exhausted bunch of listeners. It is rather to discern the particular message from this chosen text that God wants this particular group of people to hear on this occasion.

Notes

1 Helen Cameron, John Reader, Victoria Slater, with Christopher Rowland, *Theological Reflection for Human Flourishing: Pastoral Practice and Public Theology* (London: SCM Press, 2012), p. 74.

2 Cameron et al., *Theological Reflection for Human Flourishing*, p. 82.

3 Cameron et al., *Theological Reflection for Human Flourishing*, pp. 83–4.

4 Cameron et al., *Theological Reflection for Human Flourishing*, p. 85.

5 Cameron et al., *Theological Reflection for Human Flourishing*, p. 85. The phrase in quotation marks refers to Phyllis Trible, *Texts of Terror: Literary-Feminist Readings of Biblical Narratives* (Philadelphia, PA: Fortress Press, 1984).

6 Thomas G. Long, *The Witness of Preaching*, 3rd edn (Louisville, KY: Westminster John Knox Press, 2016), p. 51.

7 Long, *Witness of Preaching*, p. 51.

8 Long, *Witness of Preaching*, pp. 51–2.

9 Colin E. Gunton, *A Brief Theology of Revelation* (Edinburgh: T. & T. Clark, 1995), p. 61.

10 John Calvin, *Institutes of the Christian Religion*, I.vi.1.

11 James Limburg, *Hosea—Micah*. Interpretation: A Bible Commentary for Teaching and Preaching (Atlanta, GA: John Knox Press, 1988), p. 93.

12 Ann Morisy, *Bothered and Bewildered: Enacting Hope in Troubled Times* (London: Continuum, 2009), p. 3.

13 N. T. Wright, *Surprised by Hope* (London: SPCK, 2007), p. 163; emphasis in original.

14 Wright, *Surprised by Hope*, pp. 218–44; emphasis in original.

15 Wright, *Surprised by Hope*, p. 157.

16 Walter Brueggemann, *The Word Militant: Preaching a Decentering Word* (Minneapolis, MN: Fortress Press, 2007); see e.g. ch. 10, 'Preaching a Sub-Version'.

17 Walter Brueggemann, *The Prophetic Imagination*, 2nd edn (Minneapolis, MN: Fortress Press, 2001), pp. 116f.

18 See also: Peter K. Stevenson, 'Where Have All the Prophets Gone?', *Ministry Today* 56 (2012), pp. 5–15.

19 See the online lectionary site hosted by Vanderbilt Divinity Library: http://lectionary.library.vanderbilt.edu; italics in original.

20 See http://lectionary.library.vanderbilt.edu; italics in original.

21 Stanley K. Stowers, 'Romans 7.7–25 as a Speech-in-Character (προσωποποιία)', in Troels Engberg-Pedersen (ed.), *Paul in his Hellenistic Context* (Edinburgh: T. & T. Clark, 1994), pp. 180–202.

22 Paul Scott Wilson, *The Four Pages of the Sermon: A Guide to Biblical Preaching* (Nashville, TN: Abingdon Press, 1996), p. 37.

23 Sidney Greidanus, *The Modern Preacher and the Ancient Text* (Grand Rapids, MI: Eerdmans; Leicester: InterVarsity Press, 1988).

24 Ellen F. Davis and Richard B. Hays, 'Learning to Read the Bible Again', *Christian Century*, 20 April 2004, pp. 23–4.

25 W. Randolph Tate, *Biblical Interpretation: An Integrated Approach*, 3rd edn (Peabody, MA: Hendrickson, 2008), pp. 1–7.

26 Tate, *Biblical Interpretation*, p. 4.

27 Michael J. Gorman, *Elements of Biblical Exegesis: A Basic Guide for Students and Ministers*, rev. edn (Grand Rapids, MI: Baker Academic, 2010), p. 10. Gorman quotes from Wilhelm Egger, *How to Read the New Testament: An Introduction to Linguistic and Historical-Critical Methodology*, ed. H. Boers, trans. P. Heinegg (Peabody, MA: Hendrickson, 1996), p. 3.

28 Gorman, *Elements of Biblical Exegesis*, p. 13.

29 Gorman, *Elements of Biblical Exegesis*, pp. 15–20.

30 R. L. Smith *Micah–Malachi*. Word Biblical Commentary, Vol. 32 (Dallas, TX: Word, 1998), p. 152.

31 Elizabeth Achtemeier, *Minor Prophets 1*. New International Biblical Commentary (Peabody, MA: Hendrickson, 1996), p. 260; emphasis in original.

32 John Drane, *Evangelism for a New Age: Creating Churches for the Next Century* (London: Marshall Pickering, 1994), pp. 37–9.

33 Philip Jenkins, 'Liberating Word: The Power of the Bible in the Global South', *Christian Century*, 11 July 2006, p. 25.

34 Jenkins, 'Liberating Word', pp. 25–6.

35 Tate, *Biblical Interpretation*, p. 5.

36 Howard Peskett and Vinoth Ramachandra, *The Message of Mission* (Leicester: InterVarsity Press, 2003), pp. 22–3.

37 Daniel J. Trier, *Introducing Theological Interpretation of Scripture: Recovering a Christian Practice* (Nottingham: Apollos, 2008), p. 203.

38 M. Eugene Boring, 'The Gospel of Matthew', in Leander E. Keck et al., *The New Interpreter's Bible, Vol. 8* (Nashville, TN: Abingdon Press, 1995), p. 172.

39 Boring, 'The Gospel of Matthew', p. 111.

40 Boring, 'The Gospel of Matthew', p. 112.

41 Donald A. Hagner, *Matthew 1—13*. Word Biblical Commentary, Vol. 33a (Dallas, TX: Word, 1998), p. 116.

42 Graham Stanton, 'Sermon on the Mount/Plain', in Joel B. Green et al., *Dictionary of Jesus and the Gospels* (Leicester: InterVarsity Press, 1992), p. 740.

43 Cameron et al., *Theological Reflection for Human Flourishing*, p. 81, quoting from 'H+ Making Good Sense of the Bible', a Bible Society course published in 2011 that aimed to train people who would then run workshops in churches helping others make sense of the Bible.

44 David Day, *A Preaching Workbook* (London: Lynx, 1998), p. 15; emphasis in original.

3

Looking for Trouble

For a video introduction to Chapter 3 visit studyguidepreaching.
hymnsam.co.uk

Running from trouble

Each year at theological college I had the opportunity to preach in the sermon class. Week by week the session followed a standard format. One of the students led a short service of worship and preached a sermon. The next act of the drama involved staff and students providing feedback on the sermon, with suggestions about ways to improve the sermon next time around.

In my second year I had chosen to preach on Psalm 139, which was and is one of my favourite parts of the Bible. In designing the service, I had noticed that the hymn book used in college chapel included a selection of verses from the psalm arranged as a congregational reading. So I decided to encourage congregational participation by inviting everyone to share in reading this well-known passage.

In their wisdom, the editors of the hymn book had decided to omit verses that contained the angry outburst: 'O that you would kill the wicked, O God.' Perhaps they felt that such painful sentiments did not fit naturally into acts of Christian worship. I have to confess I was not overly anxious about the exclusion of those verses from the reading, for they did not really fit with the message I wanted to communicate. Omitting those verses seemed such a good idea at the time, until the feedback session when the Principal spoke up and said: 'Mr Stevenson, why did you leave out verses 19 to 21 from the reading?'

Reading the feedback sheets later I noticed that one of my peers had also perceptively commented about this blind spot:

What about the end of the Psalm?
This is human experience.
This would've 'rooted' it a bit more maybe.
Seeing God at work in the midst of the human anger and weakness …
Still they are very hard verses …

On the day I had great difficulty answering the Principal's important question. My stumbling attempt to reply simply revealed that I found those angry verses disturbing and did not know how to handle such troubling passages in the context of preaching.

I recalled that painful episode roughly a decade later, while meeting with musicians and worship leaders to plan upcoming services. 'Next Sunday', I explained, 'I shall be preaching from Psalm 139 and I was wondering if you'd any thoughts or ideas I might bear in mind while preparing the sermon.'

Their response was both surprising and very refreshing, for their instinctive and immediate reaction was: 'Can you help us understand that bit of the psalm that says "O that you would kill the wicked, O God"?'

Those kinds of experiences helped me begin to see that it was a mistake to avoid those troubling Bible passages rather than face the difficulties head on. Experience over the years since has convinced me that when preachers wrestle with such troubling texts, more often than not it arouses attention and injects energy and interest into sermons. So it was not surprising to find that one of the sermon series that aroused greatest interest in that church was one focusing on the 'Hard Sayings of Jesus'.

Looking for trouble

With that experience in mind it was interesting to find one teacher encouraging preachers to go looking for 'trouble' in the text. Eugene Lowry, whose work we shall encounter again in Chapter 7, writes in a playful manner about the demanding process of preparing sermons.[1] He wryly observes that:

preaching a sermon is relatively easy. Preparing one worth preaching is what is difficult. Like Elijah in the cave, we wait for the Divine voice. We look everywhere for the Word. Often, the more we look the less we find.[2]

He reiterates the advice that 'the first task in sermon preparation is to *listen to the text*'.[3] That is why it is important to listen to the biblical text for ourselves, maybe reading it aloud before turning to the expert help contained in scholarly commentaries.

He suggests that in our careful listening to the biblical text, '*We can look for trouble*':

> What is there about the text that does not seem to fit? Is there anything strange here? 'Ideological suspicion' does not always feel comfortable for us, particularly when we are included in its object. But 'suspicion' in its positive sense of *probing uncertainty* is precisely what can be helpful here. *Trouble*, in, around, with, and about the text is often the occasion for a fresh hearing. In leading lectionary workshops, I often ask the participants to gather in small groups and look for what is *weird* in a passage. Anything is helpful at this point if it breaks us loose from the usual, the easily accepted, the routine and timid truth that will not change lives.[4]

Facing the trouble in Psalm 139

Returning to the psalm that caused me some difficulty in the early stages of my preaching journey, it is possible to see how facing the trouble head-on can help to unearth material that is very useful to the preacher.

Christian readers of Psalm 139 find it difficult, if not impossible, to imagine Jesus praying: 'O that you would kill the wicked, O God.' However, while such sentiments run contrary to the call to 'love your enemies', that on its own is not sufficient justification for omitting verses 19–22 from worship and preaching.

Before looking at some of the questions the outburst in verse 19 raises, it is worth noticing that there may be other kinds of trouble lurking in the background of Psalm 139. For 'it is possible that the psalmist had been accused of idolatry and that the appeal in verses 23–24 serves as the psalmist's affirmation of innocence'.[5] This suggestion is based on the possibility that the phrase 'any wicked way' in verse 24 alludes to 'the way of idolatry … or of apostasy'.[6] The stakes are raised when it is explained that the 'punishment for this would be death' (cf. Deut. 13.13–16; 17.2–7).[7]

With that in mind it is feasible to interpret the psalm as a prayer of thanksgiving, rising from the lips of someone who had been falsely accused but acquitted by God. Faced with such serious allegations, this believer had taken his appeal to the highest court imaginable, presenting his case to the God who knows his every thought (verses 1–6). This is the Lord who is present in every experience, good and bad, that life brings (verses 7–12). The psalmist is content to place his case in the hands of the one whose care has been constant since before his birth (verses 13–18).

Interpreting this psalm in the context of the psalmist's troubling experience of being falsely accused might make the angry words of verse 19 more comprehensible but it does not resolve all the difficulties associated with them.

Stephen Dawes suggests that the ways people respond to the problems raised by such angry language about enemies fall broadly into 'two different but often intertwining and mutually reinforcing approaches'.[8]

What he describes as 'Psychological' approaches to these problem passages:

> begin by accepting that the feelings these verses express are real, and that real people have them, including people of faith today. When people are threatened, hurt, humiliated or distressed, particularly in a situation of powerlessness, they can and do respond with anger.[9]

In other words, these verses allow us to glimpse the raw humanity of the psalmist, whose gut reaction to evil and hatred is strangely familiar. Many can identify with such powerful feelings, for it is not difficult to imagine responding to extreme pressure in similar ways. Among other things, this outburst of rage implies that God is big enough to absorb our pain and hurt, our cries and laments, as well as our songs of praise. The angry words in Psalm 139.19 fall short of the love embodied in Jesus, but the raw humanity of the psalmist does not diminish the grandeur of the God he worships.

… naïvely, almost childishly, 139, in the middle of its hymn of praise throws in (19) 'Wilt thou not slay the wicked, O God?' – as if it were surprising that such a simple remedy for human ills had not occurred to the Almighty.[10]

The second family of approaches Dawes describes are 'Justice' approaches, which give voice to the longing for the divine judge to intervene to 'deliver us from evil' once and for all. Far from being guilty of idolatry or apostasy, the psalmist here is pledging allegiance to God in the battle for justice, for:

> people who belong to God (vv. 1–18) and who try to live as God intends (vv. 23–24) will always be opposed by those who oppose God … While vv. 19–20 inevitably sound like a request for personal revenge, their import is much broader and deeper; they request that God set things right in the world; in other words 'thy will be done'.[11]

In other words, in this fallen world where many oppose God's will, the psalmist is declaring loudly and clearly that he is firmly on the side of the divine justice and righteousness.

The psalm ends not on a note of vengeance but with a prayer of surrender and trust (verses 23–24). Kenneth Slack suggests that these final verses leave the reader to ask some searching personal questions. He wonders:

> Does the psalmist suddenly realize that wickedness is not as simple as that? What about *his* thoughts? What is it that God really does know about him? … If God searches me, wondered the psalmist, digs deep into me – in the very way I have been praising – what will he find? What motives will be uncovered, what dark layers of failure and resentment and the rest? If God were really to deal as abruptly with the wicked as I long, can I be sure of my own fate?[12]

Wrestling with the psalm in this way provides further evidence of the value of taking the three 'worlds' of the text seriously. The understandable questions people today ask about the angry words of verses 19–21 arise from the *world in front of the text*. Thinking about the possible personal scenario that may lie *behind the text* can deepen our understanding of this passage. Paying close attention to *the world within the text* also has a part to play because the specific words used in verse 24 offer clues to the nature of the accusation levelled against the psalmist.

Working homiletically with the trouble in Psalm 139

There are many different ways of developing a sermon based on this passage that takes the whole of the psalm into account. The following outline is just one way.

Introduction	One way of introducing the sermon might be to ask members of the congregation to think about their favourite passages in the Bible. For some people, Psalm 139 is a favourite passage that inspires and comforts.
1 A vision of God	It is not difficult to see the attraction of this psalm, which paints an uplifting picture of: • the God who knows us (vv. 1–6); • the God who is with us in all times and places (vv. 7–12); • the God whose care for us stretches back to the time when we were in our mother's womb (vv. 13–16). Faced with such a vision of God it is not surprising that the psalmist cries out: 'How weighty to me are your thoughts O God' (v. 17).
2 A cry of pain	But then having been lifted up to the heavens, we're brought back to earth with a jolt! For there's a dramatic change of mood in v. 19, where we hear the psalmist's angry cry of pain: 'O that you would kill the wicked, O God.' So what are we to make of this cry of pain? When we look more closely at this text, which seems to reflect the experience of someone who'd been falsely accused of worshipping other gods, maybe we can begin to understand what lies behind such angry sentiments. These sentiments are not included in the psalms to encourage us to react in this way, but they reveal the raw and flawed humanity of the person who had caught an inspiring vision of God.

3 A prayer of surrender	A church member once described her experience of growing up in a church where a picture of a large eye had been painted on the wall, symbolizing the idea of God watching over his people. As a child this picture did not have a reassuring effect, rather a chilling and fearful one. For the psalmist, however, knowing that God is the one 'from whom no secret is hidden' is a source of joy. For he trusts that the God who knows the whole story still loves and cares for him. And so he gladly surrenders his life to God, praying 'Search me, O God …'.
Conclusion	The coming of Jesus Christ convinces us that the God who knows all there is to know about us is the one who offers his love unconditionally to us. Knowing that the Son of God loved us and gave himself for us encourages us to place our lives in God's hands, praying 'Search me, O God …'.

Looking for trouble in the text

In Chapter 2 we explored how paying attention to the three worlds of the text provides a basis for engaging in a 'close reading' of a text such as Matthew 5.38–48. Thinking about that passage, it is not difficult to see that there is plenty of trouble in the text. For example, there is a whole lot of trouble in verse 43, where Jesus directs his followers to love their enemies.

There is no trouble in translating this passage from the Greek original, but there certainly is plenty in putting this into practice. Is it realistic to expect us to love our enemies, and is it humanly possible? Look what happened to the person who told us to love our enemies!

The following exercise invites you to read another extract from the Gospels in which a number of different kinds of trouble can be found.

PAUSE FOR THOUGHT

- Read Luke 9.18–27.
- What trouble can you see in this particular text?
- How might that trouble provide a starting point for preaching?

Finding the trouble in John 13

Over the years it has been a privilege to preach at a number of ordination services. On one recent occasion the person being ordained invited me to preach a sermon based on John 13. Previously I had preached on parts of this chapter at Communion Services on Maundy Thursday. Wanting to look at this passage in a fresh way, I asked a group of students to spend some time looking at the text with me.

Talking about the three worlds of the text helped us unearth some useful raw materials for preaching.

Appreciating the cultural *world behind the text* alerted us to the shocking nature of Jesus' behaviour. For in first-century Middle-Eastern culture, foot washing was a 'task reserved for Gentile slaves and for wives and children'.[13]

Paying close attention to the *world within the text* reveals more than enough materials for many sermons. For example, at the start of John 13 it is explained that 'Jesus knew that his hour had come.' This comment needs to be read in the context of the repeated mentioning of the 'hour' of Jesus throughout John's Gospel (see John 2.4; 7.30; 8.20; 12.23, 27; 13.1; 17.1). This stress on the hour that has come is a reminder that the events soon to follow are not some tragic accident but the outworking of a divine plan.

Acknowledging our place in the *world in front of the text*, we brought our questions into conversation with the text. A number of these concerned the role of Judas. Early in the chapter it states that 'The devil had already put it into the heart of Judas son of Simon Iscariot to betray him' (John 13.2). As the narrative unfolds, Jesus warns his friends that one of them will betray him and that when this happens, Scripture will be fulfilled (John 13.18). So did Judas make this disastrous decision of his own free will, or did God override his personal freedom so that Scripture might be fulfilled? There is certainly plenty here to wrestle with in a sermon.

Alongside those complex questions about the relationship between divine sovereignty and human freedom, someone asked the straightforward and profound question: 'Did Jesus wash Judas' feet?'

Even such a cursory glance at John 13 unearths plenty of *trouble* in, around, with and about this text. In designing the sermon for the ordination, I deliberately made use of some of the *trouble in the text*.

Using the trouble in John 13 in a sermon

In the sermon at the ordination, I used the experience of getting a shock from a light fitting to suggest that my friend had chosen a rather shocking passage of Scripture for her ordination service. That idea of something 'shocking' or 'troubling' provided a useful refrain, which helped hold the sermon together.

To begin with, I explained that John 13 contained a *shocking action* because it described how Jesus took the role of the servant and washed the disciples' feet (John 13.2–5). Foot washing is a bit of a shock to the system for people today living in a society where so many are competing and fighting to get to the top. In the days of Jesus, it was even more shocking.

> For 'in the world of Jesus' day servants might wash the feet of their master on his return from a journey, a wife might wash her husband's feet or students the feet of their master, but not the other way round.'[14]
>
> Another writer makes the same point when he explains that 'the menial nature of foot washing in Jewish eyes is seen in its inclusion among works which Jewish slaves should not be required to do ... the task was reserved for Gentile slaves and for wives and children.'[15]
>
> And Jesus the teacher, Jesus the master, shocks everyone in the room by stooping down to do the work of a servant and washing his disciples' feet.
>
> Within such a patriarchal culture the actions of Jesus, as a man, were shocking and disturbing. For a Jewish man to assume the role of a slave in this way was a prophetic sign, calling into question gender stereotypes and challenging men – and women – in every age to follow his example (John 13.14–15).
>
> The action of Jesus is shocking for it turns the usual pattern of things upside

down – it goes in the opposite way to the normal run of things, where people all scramble to get to the top.

Watching this shocking action of Jesus, we're left asking: 'What's he up to?' 'What will happen if the status quo isn't observed?' 'What will happen if servants don't obey masters?' I mean, 'What is the world coming to?'

This shocking action of Jesus provoked a *shocked response* from Simon Peter (John 13.6–10). The Gospels make clear that Peter has a real ability to misunderstand, to get things wrong. Perhaps the most shocking thing about Peter is that he had shared life with Jesus for three years and still did not fully understand what Jesus is all about.

At this point in the sermon I publicly acknowledged the help my seminar group had given me in preparing it and referred to their question: 'Did Jesus wash Judas' feet?'

And if we're shocked that Peter doesn't fully understand Jesus even after three years in Jesus' school of discipleship and theology – we're even more shocked to see that one of Jesus' friends could betray him like this.

One preacher puts it like this, that among the disciples: 'there is one who remains in the service of the power of this age. There is treason at the very heart of the Church, and Jesus knows it and has known it from the beginning. His disciples must know it too, and be forewarned against the collapse of faith.'[16]

And we know that still today the truth is that '*There is treason at the very heart of the Church*' because there are people like me and people like us who continue to deny Jesus as Peter went on to do, and who betray Jesus like Judas, by the wrong we do and the good we fail to do.

But lest we all end up feeling totally demoralized, let me point you to some good news amid the denials and betrayals.

Did Jesus wash Judas' feet?

I believe the answer is 'Yes' – he washed Judas' feet and those of all the disciples. And by washing their feet he was showing the full extent of his love for them all – and that included Judas.

If we read on in this chapter we find an important detail that it's maybe easy to overlook, which is how Jesus dipped a piece of bread in the dish of herbs and gave it to Judas (John 13.23–30).

For when we look into *the world behind the text*, we discover that in that culture, for the host to dip the bread in the dish of herbs and pass it to someone was a sign of love and friendship. So right to the end, through the washing of his feet and by making this gesture of love and friendship, Jesus was offering his love to Judas.

It's summed up well by the preacher who explains that: 'At this point Jesus, who had already honoured Judas by placing him at his side, silently makes a further gesture of love and friendship – dipping a morsel in a dish and giving it to him.'[17]

And that encourages me for it points to the reassuring truth that the risen, living Jesus continues to offer us his love even though we stumble and fall so often, even though we deny him by the wrong we do and the good we fail to do.

So what's more shocking?

- That Judas betrays Jesus?
- Or that Jesus goes on loving Judas?
- That we betray Jesus?
- Or that Jesus goes on loving us?

The sermon moved on to refer to arguments between politicians wanting to win our votes at elections. This prompted me to suggest that Jesus probably would not be successful in an election because he makes the *shocking suggestion* that we are supposed to follow his example in serving others in costly sacrificial ways (John 13.12–17).

In the final stage of the sermon, I drew attention to a small detail from the *world within the text*, for I referred to John 13.4, which states that Jesus 'took off' or 'laid down' his outer robe. Interestingly, the word used here is the same one used earlier in John's Gospel, where Jesus talks about the Good Shepherd who *lays down* his life for the sheep (John 10.11, 15, 17, 18). A close reading of the text reminds us that this shocking action of Jesus is a sign, a prophetic sign pointing forward towards the cross where he will lay down his life in the supreme act of love to set people free.

So this story is indeed a shocking and troubling story, not only because the shadow of the cross falls across it but also because the costly shadow of the cross falls across the path of Christian ministry we were thinking about in the context of an ordination service.

> For in Christian ministry people are called to embark on a way of living that involves:
>
> - Laying down our lives for others.
> - Taking up the cross daily.
> - Enabling fellow believers to take up the cross daily.
> - Inviting everyone to take up the cross daily.
> - Following this Jesus in serving God and others in costly, sacrificial ways.

The importance of looking for trouble

Working with the trouble in the text is not a clever homiletical trick used by preachers desperate to find a way of arousing sleeping congregations. Any preacher who takes the Bible seriously stumbles over plenty of trouble before long. When that happens, theologically and pastorally it is essential that the preacher does not 'pass by on the other side' and go looking for a more cheerful text for next Sunday's sermon.

In the messy, real world, people listening to sermons know from experience that there is no guarantee 'Things can only get better'.[18] Failure to address the troubling dimensions of the text – and of everyday life – in our preaching can make it more difficult to communicate an authentic, grown-up faith that is robust enough to face life's challenges.

PAUSE FOR THOUGHT

> Read the following extract from an article by Matthew Boulton, who argues theologically for the retrieval and rehabilitation of the use of laments within Christian worship.

There is, I believe, more than one argument to be made for this sort of rehabilitation, not the least of which pertain directly to the emotional and psychological needs of suffering congregations like mine: these arguments involve the charge that to the extent that Christian churches implicitly or explicitly exclude modes of indignation and anguish from their liturgies, they effectively abandon indignant and anguished people, leaving them to suffer these agonies in isolation from the worshiping assembly and thus also, it may well seem to them, in isolation from God.

This is a problem of pastoral theology and practice, and it is pressing ... I contend that forms of lament do indispensable work in Christian liturgical life, not only by ministering to people consumed by anger or desperation, but also by properly reworking our efforts to worship God at all – that is, our efforts to thank, adore, ask, and, most particularly, praise God. Lament, in short, makes genuine praise possible – or better, it is the complex relation between praise and lament that makes possible the true worship of God, and so if we neglect Christian liturgies of lament, we risk the propriety not only of our praise, but of our whole movement together toward God in worship.[19]

- What thoughts and feelings do his comments raise?
- To what extent do you think his comments also apply to preaching?

Making sense of trouble in the text

As an Old Testament scholar, Walter Brueggemann encourages us to pay much greater attention to troubling passages, such as the Lament Psalms.

In a groundbreaking article, he opened up fresh perspectives by suggesting that 'the sequence of *orientation-disorientation-reorientation* is a helpful way to understand the use and function of the Psalms'.[20] Recognizing this dynamic helps explain the role the Psalms played within the life and worship of God's people in the past, and also offers resources for nourishing faith today. Working on this basis, he divides the Psalms into three groups reflecting contrasting dimensions of people's experience of God.[21]

Psalms of Orientation, such as **Psalm 145**, exude faith, trust and confidence in the God whose loving power ensures that all is well and all manner of things will be well. Under this heading, **Brueggemann** includes 'some of the Psalms of Ascent (e.g., 127; 128; 131; 133) which reflect domestic life which is in good order. They are the voice of genuine gratitude and piety for such rich blessings.'[22]

In *Psalms of Disorientation*,[23] believers protest loudly to God about the suffering and injustice they are enduring. Such laments arise from painful and tragic experiences that call into question their inherited beliefs. That questioning of cherished beliefs is evident in the lament that stretches over Psalms 42 and 43, and in the anguished cry of Psalm 22.1, 'My God, my God, why have you forsaken me?' Brueggemann argues that Lament Psalms of dislocation:

> are the voices of those who find their circumstance dangerously and not just inconveniently changed. And they do not like it. These are the speeches of caged men and women getting familiar with their new place, feeling the wall for a break, hunting in the dark for hidden weapons, testing the nerve and patience of those who have perpetrated the wrong ... The speakers of these Psalms are in a vulnerable, regressed situation in which the voice of the desperate, fear-filled, hate-filled reality is unleashed and no longer covered by the niceties of conventional sapiental teaching.[24]

Brueggemann points also to *Psalms of Reorientation*,[25] which celebrate the God who comes and who meets people in their distress so that a new, deeper and unexpected brand of faith is brought to birth. These hymns of celebration reflect 'the unarguable experience of persons who have discovered that the world has come to an end but a new creation is given. Life has disintegrated but has been formed miraculously again.'[26] As a result, the worshipper invites others to celebrate this new reality; 'O sing to the LORD a new song, for he has done marvellous things' (Psalm 98.1).

Homiletics and orientation – disorientation – reorientation

This way of reading the Bible appears to have influenced Barbara Brown Taylor's approach to preaching, for she explains that when it comes to designing sermons, her default approach is to think 'in terms of orientation, disorientation and reorientation'.

I actually write the letters one under the other on a page – O, D, R – and try to fill in the blanks. Orientation has to do with what we all know, or think we know, about this text. That is my first goal: to start with some shared perspective on the passage at hand. That will give people a chance to settle down with me as I try to establish my trustworthiness with them.

If I can do that, the chances are better that they will stay with me when I introduce a little bit of disorientation into the conversation. The disorienting point, form, is whatever shifts my perspective on the text. It often corresponds to the spot where I became most interested in my own study of it ... What upsets the balance?

But I don't want to leave people disoriented, so the third stage is reorientation. Once the passage has been tipped off balance, how does it settle down again? What I hope for here is some shift in perspective – even if it's only five degrees – so that the passage gains a new hearing. None of this is manufactured for the congregation, by the way. If I don't experience a shift in the way I see things, then neither will they. If there is no sense of discovery for me, then there won't be one for them either. So it is important that I hold out for some kind of revelation and then report it as best I can.

While I officially believe that preachers should experiment with all kinds of sermonic structures, this is my old reliable.[27]

Psalm 139 and orientation – disorientation – reorientation

Revisiting the sermon outline on Psalm 139 developed earlier in this chapter, there is a sense in which a kind of *orientation – disorientation – reorientation* process was being worked through.

Orientation Starting with some shared perspectives on the passage at hand.	The preacher builds rapport and trust with the congregation by affirming the key elements of the psalm's vision of God. Together we want to affirm our faith and trust in the God whose care for us stretches back before our birth.
Disorientation Introducing a little bit of disorientation into the conversation.	The impassioned cry 'O that you would kill the wicked, O God' strikes a harsh, discordant note, introducing more than a little bit of disorientation into the conversation. We don't expect to hear such bloodthirsty language in church – so what are we to make of it?
Reorientation Once the passage has been tipped off balance, how does it settle down again?	As a community theologian, the preacher's task is to help the congregation think biblically, and Christianly, about the issues raised by this angry outburst. In this context, perhaps, reorientation might mean helping people catch a new vision of a God who is more than able to cope with our troubling emotions. Knowing such a God offers the basis for a faith that is robust enough to face the painful and disturbing dimensions of life.

Resources for thinking about trouble

Another writer who puts trouble to good use in the service of preaching is Paul Scott Wilson, whose *Four Pages of the Sermon* approach[28] works through the following stages:

1 Trouble in the Bible.
2 Trouble in the World.
3 God's action in the Bible.
4 God's action in the World.

'This is the problem ... this is the response of the gospel ... these are the implications.'

One of the templates for designing sermons that Thomas Long identifies connects with this discussion about handling trouble in sermons.

'Sometimes called a "law-gospel" or "problem-solution" form, this form begins by exploring the human dilemma and announces the claim of the sermon in response to that. It is most effective when the hearers have some shared sense of need or crisis.'[29]

The trouble is that no one will listen

Zedekiah son of Josiah, whom King Nebuchadnezzar of Babylon made king in the land of Judah, succeeded Coniah son of Jehoiakim. But neither he nor his servants nor the people of the land listened to the words of the Lord that he spoke through the prophet Jeremiah.

Jeremiah 37.1–2

In Jeremiah 37 we find a king, Zedekiah, who was up to his neck in trouble. He was a powerless puppet ruler who had been set up as king by the victorious King of Babylon, Nebuchadnezzar. Caught in the crossfire between the superpowers of Egypt to the south and Babylon to the north, Zedekiah wonders which way to turn. In the light of recent troop movements, his advisors are recommending an alliance with Egypt. 'The king, pitiful political creature that he is, is at risk in the midst of this raging context of great powers.'[30]

The theological perspective explicit in the *world within the text* suggests that the major reason for the king being so deeply in trouble is his failure to listen to God. In stark contrast to Jeremiah, who responded with obedience to the 'word of the LORD' that came to him (e.g. Jeremiah 1.4, 11; 2.1; 3.6; 11.1; 13.1; 15.16), for Zedekiah, 'the central issue is that the king did not "listen"'.

> **37.1–2**: Zedekiah is a creature of Babylon (cf. 2 Kgs. 24.17). He rules only at the whim of despised Nebuchadnezzar. The fact that he is an imperial puppet must have evoked resistance from 'true patriots'. This is the first fact of Zedekiah's rule. For the text, however, that Babylonian fact is only a framing piece of data. The central issue is that the king did not 'listen' (*shema'*). No one listened – not the king, not his royal entourage, not the city nor its citizens. 'Listening' becomes the key motif for this part of the text. In the use of that single word, the text makes present not only the urgent advocacy of Jeremiah but the entire torah tradition of obedience and fidelity. 'Listening' is to acknowledge that Yahweh and the torah tradition provide the dominant clues to life and to power. Zedekiah's refusal to listen is a decision to ignore the tradition, to reject the prophet, to scuttle a theological identity, and to disregard a transcendent purpose in power politics. A refusal to listen is to imagine that the king is autonomous and therefore destined for self-sufficiency. In his refusal to listen, so the text suggests, the king has sealed his own fate and that of his people. His future depends not upon his ingenuity nor his power, but upon his readiness to accept the theological reality of his life and his rule, that is the reality of Yahweh's rule.[31]

Listening to the text

Individually we may not be facing the sorts of personal and political pressures that made it hard for King Zedekiah to 'listen' to the word of the Lord. However, in the era of 24-hour news, with text messages continually announcing their arrival on our phones and the steady supply of emails, there are plenty of other distractions that can make it difficult for us to slow down sufficiently to read the biblical text and listen for God.

Thus far this chapter has suggested a fairly active process of wrestling with the trouble in the text, as a useful first step in the sermon preparation process. Now the time has come to change gear and slow the process down by using a classic way of reading the text known as *Lectio Divina*.

A ... practice of biblical spirituality, or transformative engagement with the Word, that is ancient but is enjoying a renaissance in our own time is lectio divina. The practice is described in the episode in Acts 8.26–39 in which the Ethiopian court official of Queen Candace is reading and meditating on the Servant Song of Isaiah (cf. 53. 7–8), which he does not understand. He appeals to Philip for enlightenment. Philip's teaching results in the official's conversion and subsequent baptism.

The origin of the practice of lectio divina among Christians can be traced back to the desert fathers and mothers whose spirituality consisted primarily of prayerful rumination on biblical texts. Later, in the Benedictine monasteries organized around the Rule of St. Benedict (c. 540), the practice was both legislated and to some extent formalized. The Carthusian Guigo II (d. ca. 1188) finally supplied a carefully articulated 'method' for the practice of lectio divina in his spiritual classic, *Ladder of Monks*, which has been adapted by contemporary spiritual teachers for our own times.

Lectio divina is a four-step process that begins with the slow, leisurely, attentive *reading* (lectio) and re-reading of a biblical text. Often the text is committed to memory in the process. By internalizing the text in its verbal form, one passes on to a rumination or *meditation* on its meaning (meditatio). The medieval commentaries on scripture bear witness to both the spiritual depth and the imaginative breadth to which this process could lead.

Today this second step might involve study of the text through consultation of commentaries, or reading of the text in the context of the liturgy and thus of other biblical texts from both testaments that the church sees as related, or other forms of study that open the mind to the meaning of the passage. The purpose of meditatio is deepened understanding of the text's meaning in the context of the person's own life and experience.

Because the text is engaged in experiential terms, the meditation gives rise to *prayer* (oratio) or response to God, who speaks in and through the text. Prayer of thanksgiving, adoration, praise, sorrow, repentance, resolve, petition, indeed all the kinds of prayer one experiences in the Psalms, are elicited as response to the Word.

> Finally, fervent prayer may reach that degree of interiority and union with God that the great masters of the spiritual life have called *contemplation* (contemplatio). Contemplation has acquired many meanings in the history of Christian spirituality, but in this context it indicates the full flowering of prayer in imageless and wordless union with God in the Spirit.[32]

An online search quickly indicates that there are plenty of resources and guidelines for anyone wishing to practise *Lectio Divina*. For example, both the Bible Society in the UK and the American Bible Society provide guidelines for using this method of reading the Bible. Their resources include materials for individuals or groups to encounter Bible readings from the lectionary using the *Lectio Divina* approach (see Appendix 2). Comparing different sets of guidelines for this approach demonstrates that while the labels being used may vary, the basic fourfold process remains the same.

In *Imaginative Preaching*,[33] Geoff New reflects on the experience of eight ministers and pastors who committed themselves, for a four-month period, to employ both *Lectio Divina* and Ignatian Gospel Contemplation as part of their weekly sermon preparation process. A useful appendix in his book provides practical guidelines for preachers wishing to employ these spiritual disciplines as aids to a prayerful engagement with the biblical text.

There is nothing complicated about this way of engaging with Scripture, and the following simple guidelines, drawn from a range of sources, provide just one way into this process. If you are already familiar with this practice, you may prefer to move straight on to the 'Listening for preaching' exercise below.

Getting started with *Lectio Divina* – Divine Reading

> The Bible is the Word of God, always alive and active, always new. *Lectio Divina* means 'divine reading' (or 'spiritual reading') and describes a way of reading and praying the Scriptures whereby we open ourselves to what God wants to say to us.

1 **Reading / Listening** – Lectio divina begins with developing the ability to listen deeply as we read, to hear 'with the ear of our heart' God's word for us personally. This is very different from the way we would read newspapers, books or even the Bible for study. Read and re-read the passage until a part of it begins to hold our attention.

2 **Meditation** – Once we have found a word or a passage in the Scriptures which speaks to us in a personal way, we make the time to take it in and 'ruminate' on it,... allowing it to interact with our thoughts, our hopes, our memories, our desires. We allow God's word to become personal, a word that touches us and affects us at our deepest levels.

3 **Response: Prayer** – This form of prayer is what we want to say specifically arising out of our meditation. It is a dialogue with God, a loving conversation with the One who has invited us into His embrace; an offering to God of our lives. In this prayer we allow the word that we have taken in, and on which we are pondering, to touch and change us at a deep level.

4 **Rest: Contemplation** – Finally we simply rest in the presence of the One, who through His Word, has invited us to accept His transforming embrace. No one who has ever been in love needs to be reminded that there are moments when words are unnecessary. It is the same in our relationship with God. Wordless, quiet rest in the presence of the One who loves us has a name in the Christian tradition – contemplation.[34]

PAUSE FOR THOUGHT

Listening for preaching

- Select the passage of Scripture you expect to be preaching about. This may be one of the readings set for a particular Sunday in the Revised Common Lectionary or a Bible passage from a preaching series.
- Slowly read and re-read this passage using the process of *Lectio Divina*.
- As you listen to the passage in this way, what do you hear?
- In what ways might the things you are hearing contribute to a sermon?

Called to listen

> Then King Zedekiah sent for [Jeremiah], and received him. The king questioned him secretly in his house, and said, 'Is there any word from the LORD?'
>
> Jeremiah 37.17

This encounter between the prophet and the 'fearful, eager, desperate last king in ancient Judah'[35] prompts Brueggemann to reflect on the mixed motives that preachers and listeners bring to worship. He detects a shared longing to hear a hopeful word from the Lord that might shed a new light on the whole of life and not just the 'spiritual' needs of an individual.

The wonder of preaching is that people show up. Of course there are all kinds of reasons for that, all sorts of mixed motives and no doubt ignoble motivations among them. The mixed motives that propel the congregation to show up match the mixed motives the preachers have for living out their vocational impulse. In the midst of all that, however, there is no doubt an unvoiced wonderment in which the gathered listening congregation is not unlike the fearful, eager, desperate last king in ancient Judah, Zedekiah ...

We show up like Zedekiah: Is there a word from the Lord? The king showed up to ask 'secretly' ... not unlike Nicodemus who came 'by night' to Jesus (John 3:2). The king came because his city was besieged by the Babylonians, before whom he could not stand. The king came because his conventional 'support system' and his 'intelligence community' had exhausted their resources and had no clue. The king came because he hoped that his present dire circumstance did not need to be his final truth. The king came because he had heard whispered around him old memories of times past when YHWH had done saving miracles, and he hoped for yet one more saving miracle (see Jer. 21:2). In the midst of his dire circumstance and his devouring anxiety, he came in timid, desperate hope. That hope is fearful, partly grounded in a faith tradition, partly grounded in deep ambiguities of lived circumstance. Such hope is partly a theological particularity and partly a generic human impulse. Either way, the king showed up. He was ready to listen, even if he found the listening nearly unbearable, so unbearable that he took pains to establish 'deniability' about having come to listen at all (Jer. 37:24–28). In the same way, I imagine, we show up for preaching, not unlike Zedekiah, half hoping, half fearful, embarrassed to be there, but half believing that our present circumstance of 'weal or woe' is not the last truth of our life.[36]

Notes

1 Eugene Lowry, 'Surviving the Sermon Preparation Process', *Journal for Preachers* 24:3 (2001), pp. 28–32.

2 Lowry, 'Surviving the Sermon Preparation Process', p. 28.

3 Lowry, 'Surviving the Sermon Preparation Process', p. 29; emphasis in original.

4 Lowry, 'Surviving the Sermon Preparation Process', p. 29; emphasis in original.

5 J. Clinton McCann, Jr., 'The Book of Psalms', in Leander E. Keck et al., *The New Interpreter's Bible, Vol. 4* (Nashville, TN: Abingdon Press, 1996), p. 1235.

6 A. A. Anderson, *The Book of Psalms, Volume 2: Psalms 73—150*. New Century Bible Commentary (Grand Rapids, MI: Eerdmans, 1972), p. 912.

7 Anderson, *Book of Psalms*, p. 912.

8 Stephen Dawes, *SCM Studyguide to The Psalms* (London: SCM Press, 2010), pp. 84–6.

9 Dawes, *SCM Studyguide to The Psalms*, p. 85.

10 C. S. Lewis, *Reflections on the Psalms* (London: Fontana, 1961), p. 24.

11 McCann, 'Book of Psalms', p. 1237.

12 Kenneth Slack, *New Light on Old Songs* (London: SCM Press, 1975), p. 40; emphasis in original.

13 G. R. Beasley-Murray, *John*. Word Biblical Commentary, Vol. 36, 2nd edn (Dallas, TX: Word, 2002), p. 233.

14 J. Ramsey Michaels, *John*. New International Biblical Commentary (Peabody: Hendrickson, 1989), p. 238.

15 Beasley-Murray, *John*, p. 233.

16 Lesslie Newbigin, *The Light Has Come: An Exposition of the Fourth Gospel* (Edinburgh: Handsel Press, 1982), p. 169.

17 Newbigin, *Light Has Come*, p. 173.

18 D:Ream, 'Things Can Only Get Better', from *D:Ream On Vol. 1*, Magnet Records, 1993.

19 Matthew Boulton, 'Forsaking God: A Theological Argument for Christian Lamentation', *Scottish Journal of Theology* 55:1 (2002), pp. 58–78.

20 Walter Brueggemann, 'Psalms and the Life of Faith: A Suggested Typology of Function', *Journal for the Study of the Old Testament* 17 (1980), pp. 3–32 (6); emphasis in original.

21 Walter Brueggemann, *The Message of the Psalms: A Theological Commentary* (Minneapolis, MN: Augsburg Publishing House, 1984).

22 Brueggemann, 'Psalms and the Life of Faith', p. 7.

23 Brueggemann also describes these as *Psalms of Dislocation*.

24 Brueggemann, 'Psalms and the Life of Faith', p. 12.

25 Or *Psalms of New Orientation*.

26 Brueggemann, 'Psalms and the Life of Faith', p. 10.

27 Barbara Brown Taylor, 'Bothering God', in Jana Childers (ed.), *Birthing the Sermon: Women Preachers on the Creative Process* (St. Louis, MO: Chalice Press, 2001), pp. 153–68 (156–7).

28 Paul Scott Wilson, *The Four Pages of the Sermon: A Guide to Biblical Preaching* (Nashville, TN: Abingdon Press, 1999).

29 Thomas G. Long, *The Witness of Preaching*, 3rd edn (Louisville, KY: Westminster John Knox Press, 2016), p. 163.

30 Walter Brueggemann, *A Commentary on Jeremiah: Exile and Homecoming* (Grand Rapids, MI: Eerdmans, 1998), p. 354.

31 Brueggemann, *Commentary on Jeremiah*, p. 355.

32 Sandra M. Schneiders, 'Biblical Spirituality', *Interpretation* 56:2 (2002), pp. 133–42 (139–40).

33 Geoff New, *Imaginative Preaching: Praying the Scriptures so God Can Speak Through You* (Carlisle: Langham Global Library, 2015); see Appendix C, 'Preacher's Manual: *Lectio Divina* and Ignatian Contemplation in Preaching', pp. 129–55.

34 Guidelines for *Lectio Divina* prepared by the Revd Dr Chris Ellis for a Quiet Day for the South Wales Baptist College, September 2013.

35 Walter Brueggemann, *The Word Militant: Preaching a Decentering Word* (Minneapolis, MN: Fortress Press, 2007), p. 3.

36 Brueggemann, *Word Militant*, pp. 3–4.

4

Preaching in Context

For a video introduction to Chapter 4 visit studyguidepreaching.
hymnsam.co.uk

An email arrives inviting me to come and preach in a church I have not been to before. If I am available on the requested date, I contact the church and ask a few questions. What kind of service are they expecting? Are they following a preaching series or is the visiting preacher expected to preach from the lectionary readings for the day? Will children be involved in the service; and what kinds of hymns and songs are the congregation familiar with? If there is a church website, I may visit their virtual shopfront to get some impression of the situation that awaits me. Perhaps I shall have a chat with a friend who has preached there already, to fill in a bit more of the background. As best as I can, I want to build up a picture of the congregation that I can hold in my mind as I prepare the sermon for them.

I had been doing this for a while before discovering that some writers describe this instinctive process by using the strange-sounding language of 'exegeting the congregation'.[1] Indeed, as Haddon Robinson claims: 'we must know the people as well as the message, and to acquire that knowledge, we exegete both the Scripture and the congregation.'[2]

Effective preaching not only requires us to exegete (that is, to interpret) biblical texts. It also requires us to exegete congregations and their contexts ...

Exegeting congregations is important both pastorally and theologically. Pastorally, if we are going to preach effectively to a congregation, we need not only to come to know parishioners individually. We also need to know them collectively: who they are and who they have been as a faith community, their history, their culture(s), their hopes and dreams for the future, as well as their disappointments and struggles …

Exegeting the congregation helps us become more aware of the cultural worlds our congregations inhabit so that we can speak a meaningful and relevant word in their midst.[3]

After a few years' apprenticeship working alongside an experienced minister, I moved 80 miles north to a church in the West Midlands. There I quickly discovered that sermons that had gone down reasonably well in one context sometimes went down like a lead balloon in another. What I was beginning to learn was that effective preaching needs to be local and contextual, for if preaching involves discovering a message from God from the Bible *'for this group of people, at this particular time'*, that means the preparation process needs to interpret the congregation and the times in which we live, as well as the Bible. So what sorts of things might we want to pay attention to that might help us preach effectively in context?

Good preaching is now much more local

Tom Long once observed that 'the best preachers may never become known beyond their own congregations'. Rather than lamenting this he argued that it was 'evidence that good preaching is now much more local'.[4] This should come as no surprise, because as a preacher puts down roots in a particular congregation, he or she gradually gets to know the stories that shape the ways that group of people tick. The hope is that the process of building up these insights into the culture of a local congregation will provide a basis for preaching that can speak to their condition.

As a visiting preacher, the process of finding out information may be limited, but Leonora Tubbs Tisdale suggests a strategy for exploring the culture of congregations that focuses on:

some of the key signs and symbols of congregational life in order to see what they can tell us about congregational worldview, values and ethos. By so doing we also become more deeply aware of the 'local theologies' people in faith communities hold dear. While not all of the symbols will be equally helpful in every context, investigating more than a few of them will give the preacher a more holistic and multi-faceted understanding of congregational life.[5]

The following list mentions just a few of the questions that she suggests could help preachers get beneath the surface of the culture of a local church.

Seven symbols for congregational exegesis

1 Congregational narratives and stories
Who emerge as heroes in congregational stories, and what are the qualities that have made them so? Who emerge as villains, and what are the characteristics that have made them so?

2 Rituals of congregational life
What is distinctive about the congregation's worship practices?... Are there any common theological themes you discern in hymns, prayers, sermons or anthems that give you clues about congregational identity?

3 Art and architecture
What do you learn by the art, architecture, furnishings, and spatial arrangements of the church sanctuary?

4 People
Who are the people who seem to be living 'on the margins' of congregational life and why?

5 Events
What types of events or activities receive the most attention, time, energy, and investment of resources (people and money) in congregational life?
What activities /events have stirred up the greatest controversy, and why?

6 Website information, history, and archive materials
What do you learn about the church from browsing its website and reading any histories that have been written about the life of its congregation?

7 Demographics
What is the current demographic makeup of the congregation in regard to age, gender, race, ethnicity, social class, and so on? How would you describe a 'typical' member? Who is noticeably absent?[6]

PAUSE FOR THOUGHT

Think of the congregation you belong to. What would be revealed about the culture of the congregation by asking questions about these topics?

- Congregational narratives and stories
- Rituals of congregational life
- Art and architecture
- People
- Events
- Website information, history and archive materials
- Demographics.

Or to put it another way – what do you think visiting preachers need to know if they are to preach effectively in your home church?

Preachers and their audiences

In addition to exploring congregational culture, the process of interpreting the congregation also involves taking into account the many different kinds of people likely to be listening to the sermon.

One approach to this process of 'interpreting the congregation' is advocated by Leslie Francis, who argues for the value of drawing on insights emerging from the Myers-Briggs Personality Type Indicator. He argues that:

> personality differences may ... have important implications for teachers and for preachers. It has, for example, long been recognized that introverts and extraverts prefer to learn in different ways, and as a consequence of their own learning preferences may prefer to teach others in the way that they themselves would prefer to be taught.[7]

Francis suggests that *Sensing Types, Intuitive Types, Feeling Types* and *Thinking Types* engage with the Bible, and with sermons, in very different ways. With this in mind it is important for preachers to be self-aware. That will involve being aware of the ways their own personality preferences influence both the way they engage with the Bible and the way they preach. Being self-aware, and choosing to be aware of others who are different, can help preachers design sermons that have a greater potential to communicate with people who think and feel in different ways.[8]

Whether or not you are adept at using the language of personality type indicators, the general principle remains that it is helpful to think deliberately and sensitively about the different groups of people in the congregation you will be speaking to. In Chapter 9, one exercise will encourage you to think of people who are different from you and consciously try to write a sermon introduction that might appeal to that group of people.

From a different perspective, Alice Mathews explores some of the issues involved in helping preachers connect more effectively with women. She offers six questions to help preachers think about the impact of preaching on women:

- Do we typecast men and women in traditional stereotyped roles?
- Do we represent both men and women as whole human beings?
- Do we accord men and women the same level of respect?
- Do we recognize both men and women for their own achievements?
- Does our language exclude women when we talk about humanity as a whole?
- Do we use language that designates and describes men and women on equal terms?[9]

PAUSE FOR THOUGHT

Think of the last sermon you preached or listened to.

- Did it typecast men and women in traditional stereotyped roles?
- Did it represent both men and women as whole human beings?
- Did it accord men and women the same level of respect?
- Did it recognize both men and women for their own achievements?
- Did it use language that excluded women when talking about humanity as a whole?
- Did it use language that described men and women on equal terms?

Preaching in a media-shaped world

If preaching involves discovering a relevant message '*for this group of people, at this particular time*', it is also worth thinking about the time and the culture in which both preacher and hearers live and move and have their being.

Although there is not space to explore this in any depth here, there is clearly value in engaging in a form of cultural exegesis that seeks to understand some of the deeper social and political currents shaping people's lives.[10] At a much simpler level, one practical way of listening to culture is to be aware of what people are regularly watching on television. In his parables, Jesus chose everyday happenings to illustrate and communicate his message. For those with eyes to see, the cultural context in which we live offers many insights into how people think, and rich resources for preaching.

One response to a media-savvy society is to incorporate PowerPoint presentations or video clips into the preaching event. Some guidelines for the use of PowerPoint in preaching can be found in Chapter 10; but at this point it is worth asking to what extent the use of PowerPoint enhances or weakens preaching. On some occasions listening to some preachers using PowerPoint can feel a bit like watching a tennis match. Should I be looking left at the screen or to the right where the preacher is standing? If preaching is a person-to-person form of communication, then is there a real danger that the screen competing for my attention will succeed in distracting me from listening carefully to what the preacher wants to say? There would appear to be reasonable grounds for noting Richard Lischer's warning that 'when the brain is asked to multi-task by listening and watching at the same time, it always quits listening'.[11]

The issues become even more problematic when it comes to including video clips within a sermon, for as Kate Bruce explains:

> The theological entailments of a film clip may be at odds with the theological focus of the sermon; preachers need to take care to exegete the film carefully. Images operate as 'eye candy', and as long as an image is on the screen people will look to the image rather than the preacher.[12]

David Heywood similarly suggests that:

> The contrast between the written and the spoken word means that we have to be careful when using electronic media as a supplement to the spoken word

in preaching. It is common in some circles for the preacher to use PowerPoint to emphasize the main headings of an address. As soon as this happens, the written word changes the congregation from a united audience to a collection of individuals and the emphasis is shifted from the intention of the sermon to its information content.

However, Heywood goes on to suggest that:

> If ... PowerPoint is used to project images rather than words, the warm relational aspect of the sermon is preserved and even enhanced. Images speak to the affective and intuitive aspects of our minds, the 'right side of the brain', in contrast to the written word, which tends to make us analytical and individual.[13]

Projecting images that complement the sermon is one useful way of using PowerPoint. In one sermon on John 3, for example, I put on the screen a picture of Nicodemus visiting Jesus, painted by the African-American artist Henry Ossawa Tanner in 1899. Leaving the picture on the screen for one part of the sermon, I suggested that it was probably deliberately a bit dark because the narrative says of Nicodemus that 'he came to Jesus by night'.

And it is significant that he came to see Jesus **at night** – under cover of darkness.

- Why might that be?
- Could it be that the evening was the only chance to have a long uninterrupted conversation with Jesus?
- Or was it that Nicodemus was frightened that his standing in society would be damaged if people knew he was talking to this Jesus?
- Maybe ...?

Now within John's Gospel the language used is often highly symbolic, and when in John's Gospel we're told that it's '**night**', that word sometimes represents the darkness that's at war with the light and love of God. It represents those who're cut off from the presence of God.

There's a very clear example of this in John's account of the Last Supper. For in chapter 13, which describes Judas leaving the Last Supper to go and betray Jesus, we're told that 'After [Judas] received the piece of bread, Satan entered into him. Jesus said to him, 'Do quickly what you are going to do.' ... So, after receiving the piece of bread, [Judas] immediately went out. And it was night.' (John 13.27–30)

And it was night.

When Judas set out to betray Jesus he turned his back on the light of Jesus and stepped into outer darkness. When Judas turned his back on God's light he ended up in the darkness of evil in rebellion against God. He was turning his back on the light and cutting himself off from the presence of God – and that's why **it was night**.

So it's no accident we're told that **it was night** when Nicodemus came to see Jesus. It's a way of saying that Nicodemus was totally in the dark – he's been blinded by the powers of darkness and he can't understand what God is doing.

PAUSE FOR THOUGHT

The gospel of technology

'The real benefits of projecting a clip from *Friends* or a series of bullet points on a screen are negligible. In themselves, these techniques only reproduce what we already have in our family rooms and offices. And that's the point! The very presence of such media serves to associate the sermon (and church and preacher) with the glamour, power and authority of the same technology that rules the world. The medium really *is* the message. Technology is the new symbol of power. If the old symbol was the high pulpit and canopy, the new power-symbol is the remote in the shepherd's hand.'[14]

* To what extent do you agree with Richard Lischer's claim?
* What steps do preachers need to take to ensure that technology supports the spoken word rather than undermining it?

Preaching at special occasions

In addition to preaching as part of the church's regular worship, there are many other occasions when opportunities for preaching can arise. This chapter is not seeking to provide guidance for all of those occasions. At this point the desire is simply to underline the idea that the key in every situation, be it wedding, funeral, radio broadcast or civic service, is to preach in ways appropriate to that specific context. In the following example these reflections on preaching at funerals offer one attempt to illustrate some of the factors that may need to be taken into account.

Preaching in context at funerals

Chapter 3 considered some of the ways 'looking for trouble' in and around the text can be a helpful step in the process of discovering and designing a sermon. On those occasions when I have been entrusted with the privilege of preaching at a funeral, however, there is no need to go looking for trouble, for there are plenty of troubling emotions close to the surface as both mourners and preachers are brought face to face with their own mortality. So in preaching at funerals there is no need to upset our hearers' equilibrium[15] any further, rather the preacher's calling is to offer gospel words of comfort and hope. In an age when many people have little knowledge of the Christian story, preaching in the context of people's grief involves pointing them gently to the heart of the Christian faith, which affirms that Jesus Christ 'was crucified, died, and was buried' and that on 'the third day he rose again'.

Funerals take many forms, and preaching in such a context may involve speaking at a simple ceremony in the family home or delivering a brief sermon at a short service at the local crematorium. Preaching at a thanksgiving service celebrating the life of a faithful church member may give the preacher a bit more space and time. However, the general rule for preaching at funerals is for sermons to be shorter rather than longer.

When time is limited and when emotions are understandably raw, it is vital to choose your words carefully. That being the case, there is great value in writing an oral script[16] for the sermon, for the process of preparing such a sermon script is a helpful way of weighing your words with care and with sensitivity to the people experiencing grief. Funerals are emotional occasions, not only for the mourners but also for the preacher. Having a script to work with, and if necessary to return to, can help the preacher navigate safely through the strong and unpredictable emotional currents that are never far from the surface.

The scripts of two sermons preached at funerals are included in Appendix 3. They do not call for an immediate response from the congregation but seek to point towards the God who is a source of comfort and hope. The first sermon is held together by the image of a jigsaw that has been shattered, which serves as a picture of lives disrupted by a family bereavement. The second sermon, based on Luke 24, draws parallels between the painful emotions of the women who went to Jesus' tomb to pay their last respects and the feelings we carry as we come at a funeral to pay our last respects to someone we love who has died.

A valuable resource for thinking about the nature and practice of Christian funerals is Thomas G. Long, *Accompany Them with Singing: The Christian Funeral* (Louisville, KY: Westminster John Knox Press, 2009). He suggests two things that help to describe a Christian funeral sermon.

> First, like all Christian sermons, it is both biblical and contextual. Funeral preachers go to Scripture to hear the word of life and hope, but they do not go as blank tablets. They take with them the circumstances of the funeral – *this* death, *these* people, *this* loss, *these* needs. Second, funeral sermons are preached 'on the road', so to speak. Because the funeral is essentially a processional, funeral sermons are preached figuratively as the church walks to the grave. They are proclamations of what the gospel has to say about *these* people walking along *this* path carrying the body of *this* brother or sister to sorrow over *this* loss and in joyful hope of the resurrection.[17]

PAUSE FOR THOUGHT

- Think of a funeral sermon you found helpful. What were the things that made it helpful?
- If you have experienced a funeral sermon that left you feeling uncomfortable, what was it about it that seemed out of place or inappropriate to that context?

The sermon in context

Fred Craddock suggests that 'a sermon, to be properly understood and to have its purpose fulfilled, has to be experienced in its context, or rather in its several contexts'. He goes on to consider the historical, pastoral, liturgical and theological contexts within which the preaching event needs to be understood. The following exercise invites you to reflect on the contexts within which you preach.

PAUSE FOR THOUGHT

The sermon in context

The historical context One aspect of the historical context that Craddock describes consists of those preachers in our own history who have subliminally shaped our ideas and expectations about what good preaching sounds like.	• Who are the significant people in your history you are trying to please, or unconsciously trying to imitate, when you preach?
The pastoral context 'Preaching occurs in a pastoral context and is in many significant ways influenced by that context … Study and preparation involve careful listening to the congregation as well as to the text. The interpretation of the parishioners in their personal, domestic, political, and economic contexts does not replace but joins the interpretation of Scripture in its context to create the message.'[18]	• What are the particular pastoral contexts you need to bear in mind when preparing to preach? • What part do you think the congregation plays in the preaching event?

The liturgical context 'Having considered the service of worship as the context for the sermon, it remains to be said that preaching is not simply in a setting of worship, but is itself an act of worship.'[19]	• Think about the last service you attended. To what extent did the sermon work within the context of the overall service of worship? • To what extent did the hymns, songs and prayers complement the sermon?
The theological context 'theology prompts preaching to treat subjects of importance and avoid trivia ... Theology urges upon the pulpit a much larger agenda: creation, evil, grace, covenant, forgiveness, judgment, suffering, care of the earth and all God's creatures, justice, love, and the reconciliation of the world to God. It is not out of order for theology of preaching to ask of preaching, What ultimate vision is held before us?'[20]	• Think of the sermons you have preached – or listened to – in the last six months. To what extent have the big issues listed by Craddock been addressed in those sermons?

Having focused in these opening chapters on some of what is involved in *discovering the word of the Lord from the Bible, for this group of people, at this particular time,* the next four chapters consider some of the strategies that can be used in the process of designing effective sermons.

Further reading

Fred B. Craddock, *Preaching* (Nashville, TN: Abingdon Press, 1985); see ch. 5, 'Interpretation: The Listeners'.

Leslie J. Francis, 'Psychological Type and Biblical Hermeneutics: SIFT Method of Preaching', in David Day, Jeff Astley and Leslie J. Francis (eds), *A Reader on Preaching: Making Connections* (Aldershot: Ashgate, 2005), pp. 75–82.

Leslie J. Francis and Andrew Village, *Preaching with All our Souls: A Study in Hermeneutics and Psychological Type* (London: Continuum, 2008).

Thomas G. Long, *Accompany Them with Singing: The Christian Funeral* (Louisville, KY: Westminster John Knox Press, 2009).

Haddon W. Robinson, *Expository Preaching: Principles and Practice* (Nottingham: InterVarsity Press, 2001).

Thomas H. Troeger and Leonora Tubbs Tisdale, *A Sermon Workbook: Exercises in the Art and Craft of Preaching* (Nashville, TN: Abingdon Press, 2013); see ch. 8, 'Exegeting the Congregation for Preaching'.

Notes

1 Thomas H. Troeger and Leonora Tubbs Tisdale, *A Sermon Workbook: Exercises in the Art and Craft of Preaching* (Nashville, TN: Abingdon Press, 2013); see ch. 8, 'Exegeting the Congregation for Preaching'.

2 Haddon W. Robinson, *Expository Preaching: Principles and Practice* (Nottingham: InterVarsity Press, 2001), p. 28.

3 Troeger and Tubbs Tisdale, *Sermon Workbook*, p. 56.

4 Thomas G. Long, 'Preaching with Ordered Passion', *Leadership* 12:2 (Spring 1991), pp. 137–8.

5 Troeger and Tubbs Tisdale, *Sermon Workbook*, p. 57.

6 Leonora Tubbs Tisdale develops this more fully in Troeger and Tubbs Tisdale, *Sermon Workbook*, pp. 58–60.

7 Leslie J. Francis, 'Psychological Type and Biblical Hermeneutics: SIFT Method of Preaching', in David Day, Jeff Astley and Leslie J. Francis (eds), *A Reader on Preaching: Making Connections* (Aldershot: Ashgate, 2005), p. 75.

8 See also Leslie J. Francis and Andrew Village, *Preaching with All our Souls: A Study in Hermeneutics and Psychological Type* (London: Continuum, 2008).

9 Alice P. Mathews, *Preaching that Speaks to Women* (Grand Rapids, MI: Baker Books; Leicester: InterVarsity Press, 2003), pp. 158–62.

10 In the British context, for example, the sociologist Grace Davie, in *Religion in Britain: A Persistent Paradox*, 2nd edn (Chichester: Wiley-Blackwell, 2015), provides valuable insights into some of the deeper currents shaping people's attitudes.

11 Richard Lischer, *The End of Words: The Language of Reconciliation in a Culture of Violence* (Grand Rapids, MI/Cambridge: Eerdmans, 2005), p. 25.

12 Kate Bruce, *Igniting the Heart: Preaching and the Imagination* (London: SCM Press, 2015), p. 111.

13 David Heywood, *Transforming Preaching: The Sermon as a Channel for God's Word* (London: SPCK, 2013), p. 24.

14 Lischer, *End of Words*, p. 27.

15 See Chapter 7, 'Telling a Story', which considers Eugene Lowry's ideas about 'the homiletical plot'.

16 For ideas about preparing an oral script, see Chapter 9, 'First Steps on the Preaching Journey'.

17 Thomas G. Long, *Accompany Them with Singing: The Christian Funeral* (Louisville, KY: Westminster John Knox Press, 2009), p. 187.

18 Fred B. Craddock, *Preaching* (Nashville, TN: Abingdon Press, 1985), p. 39.

19 Craddock, *Preaching*, p. 43.

20 Craddock, *Preaching*, p. 49.

Part 3

Designing Sermons

5

A Recipe for Preaching

For a video introduction to Chapter 5 visit studyguidepreaching.
hymnsam.co.uk

For me preaching is like ... cooking and serving a good meal. You start with raw ingredients, prepare them, put them in the oven, leave it for a while and then serve it to people.[1]

The basic bread recipe

Recently I was given a handbook about baking bread as a birthday present. The colourful pictures of focaccia, ciabatta and sourdough looked so appealing that I wanted to tackle those recipes straight away. But then I noticed the author's warning to novice bakers like me, that 'if you skipped bread making step by step ... you really need to go back and un-skip it'.[2] Before experimenting with more complex forms of baking, it is important to master 'the basic bread recipe'.

Break Thou the bread of Life,
Dear Lord to me,
As Thou didst break the loaves
Beside the sea;
Beyond the sacred page
I seek Thee, Lord;
My spirit pants for Thee,
O living Word![3]

Preparing and offering up the bread of life is one way of describing the task of preaching. The following chapters of this Studyguide identify a number of recipes that can be used as we prepare to preach and feed God's people.

This chapter focuses on one approach that can be seen as a basic preaching recipe. Indeed, some might claim that this kind of basic recipe is one with which every preacher needs to get acquainted.

The developmental sermon

A few years ago I read a dissertation in which a student reflected on her experience of listening to a number of different preachers. Some of the sermons evaluated in that study lacked any discernible structure, and the author eventually decided to classify them as 'expository rambles'. You may have been subjected to similar 'expository rambles'; I am left wondering how many of my sermons have merited such an assessment.

One of the ways of preventing sermons from becoming untidy collections of holy thoughts is to identify an argument or idea that can provide the connecting thread to hold it all together; or, to use the terminology suggested by John Killinger, there is value in designing and delivering a 'developmental sermon'. Such a sermon is 'one that has a central idea or controlling purpose that is worked out through a series of two or more progressive stages in which the idea or purpose grows to its climax'.

There are grounds for claiming that this approach provides a basic preaching recipe all preachers can benefit from if, as Killinger argues, it 'is the workhorse form of the Christian pulpit, the one most frequently taught in seminaries and used on Sunday morning'.[4]

It is not difficult to see why such an approach has enjoyed widespread use, for sermons or lectures that have a clear argument or theme have proved over the years to be effective means of communication. On the other hand, if the preacher is not clear about the central argument of the sermon, it will not be surprising if some in the congregation are left feeling in the dark about what the preacher was trying to put across this morning.

Finding the 'big idea'

This developmental view of preaching bears some resemblance to the approach popularized by Haddon Robinson. In his vigorous advocacy of one form of *expository preaching*, he argues that preachers should seek to find the 'big idea' in the biblical text so that that can supply the 'big idea' holding the sermon together.

Robinson unpacks his concept of the big idea by suggesting that the 'idea' contains a *subject* and also an *object*, which complements the *subject*. Pointing, for example, to Psalm 117, he explains that the *subject* in this passage is not just about praising God in general, because 'the precise subject is why everyone should praise the Lord'. The psalmist, in Robinson's language, offers two 'complements to his subject', for this passage gives two main reasons why the Lord should be praised: 'first because His love is strong and second, because His faithfulness is eternal'.[5]

> Expository preaching is the communication of a biblical concept, derived from and transmitted through a historical, grammatical, and literary study of a passage in its context, which the Holy Spirit first applies to the personality and experience of the preacher, then through the preacher applies to the hearers.[6]

This stress on finding the big idea in a biblical text is part of a more detailed process of wrestling with the text and designing sermons that Robinson explores. Identifying the big idea from the biblical text and then allowing it to shape the form of the sermon is a way of clarifying the aim of the sermon that many preachers find helpful. It scores highly in terms of clarity, and when done well there is a good chance listeners will have a clear message to take away with them.

Robinson's stress on the communication of biblical concepts and ideas is open to question at some points. An approach that emphasizes concepts and ideas fits comfortably with passages such as 1 Corinthians 1.18–25, in which Paul is carefully developing a theological argument about the theology of the cross. If, however, the preacher tries to distil narrative passages, such as the book of Ruth, down to one controlling idea, then perhaps there is a danger of preaching *against* rather than *with* the grain of Scripture. Respecting the literary genre or form of biblical narrative may result in sermons that are shaped more by considerations of plot and character than by propositions and ideas.

Form-sensitive preaching

That desire to take the literary form of biblical texts seriously has been powerfully advocated by Thomas Long. In his seminal book *Preaching and the Literary Forms of the Bible*, he commends 'the simple idea that the literary form and dynamics of a biblical text can and should be important factors in the preacher's navigation of the distance between text and sermon'.[7]

PAUSE FOR THOUGHT

'Preachers who have sought to be open and attentive to biblical texts in their preaching have long sensed that a sermon based upon a psalm, for example, ought somehow to be different from one that grows out of a miracle story, not only because of *what* the two texts say but also because of *how* the texts say what they say. A psalm is poetry, a miracle story is narrative; and because they are two distinct literary and rhetorical forms, they 'come at' the reader in different ways and create contrasting effects. What is needed, then, is a process of sermon development sufficiently nuanced to recognize and employ those differences in the creation of the sermon itself.'[8]

- Read Psalm 8.
- Read Mark 4.35–41.
- How would you describe the differences between those two passages?
- How might those differences affect the way you designed sermons on those two texts?

Thinking about these passages might focus on the differences between Psalm 8, which expresses a sense of awe and wonder before the vastness of creation and God's greatness, and Mark 4.35–41, which narrates the drama of Jesus stilling the storm.

- How might a sermon on Psalm 8 respect its poetic character?
- What does the narrative in Mark 4 reveal about the characters involved in this episode?
- What ideas for the sermon might emerge by identifying with some of the characters in the narrative in Mark 4?

Stating the claim of the text

Bearing in mind the need to pay attention to the literary form of the text, Thomas Long suggests that a useful first step in moving from the text to the sermon is to discern and name the specific 'claim of the text'.

The process of wrestling with a biblical passage will throw up all sorts of interesting ideas and resources. At this point it is important to stress that not all these valuable insights need be included in every sermon. Having discovered many interesting things about the text during the preparation process, preachers can be tempted to squeeze all of that material into the sermon. This is a temptation that needs to be avoided, and not just because it is likely to lead to information overload.

The preacher's calling is not to give an exhaustive and exhausting lecture about the set passage but to discern, for this occasion, the particular message God wants to communicate to the congregation. For as Long explains:

> the claim of the text is quite occasion specific; it is what we hear on *this day*, from *this text*, for *these people*, in *these circumstances*, at *this juncture* in their lives. Is there a word from the Lord *today*?[9]

With this aim in view, Long argues that at the end of the exegetical process of wrestling with the text, the preacher should try to complete the following sentence:

> In relation to those who will hear the sermon, what this text wants to say and do is ...[10]

His desire is to help preachers see that the biblical text is not an inert, ancient object but something that performs a function and has an impact on its readers. In other words, it *does* things to them. Inspiring, encouraging, challenging and rebuking are some of the things the text *does* to its hearers. In a similar way, sermons arising from the biblical text will also seek to have an impact on their hearers.

Long suggests that:

> what the sermon aims to say can be called its 'focus', and what the sermon aims to do can be called its 'function'. Since the whole sermon will be gathered

around these two aims, the preacher needs to become clear about the sermon's focus and function as an initial step in the process of actually building the sermon.[11]

Long offers an example of what this looks like in practice by considering Paul's celebration of the love of Christ in Romans 8.28–39. He suggests that:

the preacher who listens to this text on behalf of a troubled and perplexed congregation may well state the claim of the text this way:

Claim of the text	The God we have come to know in Jesus Christ will not forsake us in distress, but will instead love and care for us even in the face of experiences that seem to deny this.

Moving toward the sermon this preacher may turn this claim into the following *focus* and *function* statements:

Focus	Because we have seen in Jesus Christ that God is for us, we can be confident that God loves and cares for us even when our experience seems to deny it.
Function	To reassure and give hope to troubled hearers in the midst of their distress.[12]

Focus and Function	A *focus statement* is a concise description of the central, controlling and unifying theme of the sermon. In short, this is what the sermon will be "about".
	A *function statement* is a description of what the preacher hopes the sermon will create or cause to happen for the hearers. Sermons make demands upon their hearers, which is another way of saying that they provoke change in the hearers (even if the change is a deepening of something already present). The function statement names the hoped-for change.[13]

It is worth spending some time working with Long's ideas of *focus* and *function*. The following examples are not model answers but give some idea of the process of writing *focus* and *function* statements.

The parable of the Sower

Luke 8.4–8

Having read this passage, if we then ask what it is actually *saying*, there are many possible answers. The following suggestions are not an exhaustive list, but these *focus* statements arise from a careful reading of the passage.

Reading this passage may prompt us to suggest that it is *saying*:

- God's word is like the seed;
- God is planting his word in people's hearts;
- God's word meets with many different responses;
- God's final harvest is certain.

If we then move on to consider the impact of this parable on Jesus' hearers, we can begin to get a feel for what the passage is *doing*. The following *function* statements alert us to some of the ways this parable disturbed and encouraged people in the past. They may also offer clues to the parable's message for contemporary listeners.

When we try to tune in to what this passage is *doing*, it appears that it is:

- challenging people to respond to God's word;
- warning people about the dangers of half-hearted discipleship;
- warning believers that mission will be difficult;
- encouraging demoralized believers that God's bumper harvest is guaranteed.

The gospel of the resurrection

1 Corinthians 15.1–11

Reading this extract from Paul's first letter to the Christians in Corinth, we find him seeking to correct serious misunderstandings of the Christian faith. In the opening section of this chapter the apostle reminds people of the message that had previously been handed on to him.

In a preliminary way, we can argue that this passage is *saying*:

- Christ died for our sins and rose again from the dead;
- many credible witnesses encountered Christ after his resurrection;
- Paul himself had encountered the risen Christ;
- there is a solid foundation for a Christian doctrine of resurrection;
- the death and resurrection of Jesus are central to Christian faith.

In this epistle it seems likely that we are overhearing a conversation between Paul and the people in Corinth. As in earlier stages in this letter (1 Corinthians 7.1, 25; 8.1; 12.1), here Paul is responding to questions believers in Corinth have raised in a letter to him. At some points he has been asked to respond to practical and doctrinal problems within the life of the church. It may have been the case that some teachers were arguing that there was no future resurrection to look forward to. So as well as affirming that Christ has risen from the dead, this chapter goes on to challenge some false ideas about resurrection.

An enquiry into what this passage is *doing* might then lead us to state that it is:

- reminding believers of the message they had received and responded to;
- challenging doubts about the resurrection by explaining that a large number of people met with Christ after his resurrection from the dead;
- defending the truth of resurrection by showing that Christ appeared to more than 500 people after his resurrection;
- witnessing to Paul's experience of the risen Christ;
- reassuring believers that death is not the end.

The process of identifying what a biblical passage is *saying* and *doing* prepares the way for the next stage of preparation, which involves developing *focus* and *function* statements for the sermon. These statements then indicate what the sermon arising from this passage will seek to *say* and *do*.

The cloud of witnesses

Hebrews 12.1–3

The letter to the Hebrews appears to be directed at believers being tempted to give up on the race of faith. Having referred in Hebrews 11 to the inspiring examples of those who have lived by faith in the past, what might these verses in chapter 12 be *saying*?

Among other things, they appear to be *saying*:

- that we are surrounded by a cloud of witnesses;
- that the life of faith is like a race;
- that the race of faith needs perseverance;
- that Jesus Christ is the pioneer and perfecter of our faith;
- that Jesus Christ endured suffering because of the joy set before him.

If part of the function of Hebrews was to encourage believers to remain faithful to Jesus Christ at a time when many were being tempted to give up, that may offer some hints as to what the passage is *doing*. It seems reasonable to suggest that it is:

- encouraging disheartened believers, who are being strongly tempted to give up, by pointing them to the inspirational example of Jesus;
- seeking to inspire people to run the race of faith with perseverance;
- warning believers that the race of faith will involve difficulties.

Viewing this passage through the twin lenses of *focus* and *function* encourages the preacher both to point to the Jesus who fully shared our humanity and to encourage those who today are being tempted to give up on the race of faith.

PAUSE FOR THOUGHT

Working with Luke 15.1–7

Part 1

This exercise moves through two stages. First, it invites you to read Luke 15.1–7, and then to write in your own words a list of *focus* and *function* statements. These statements will explore what you perceive the biblical text to be *saying* and *doing*.

Focus What is this text *saying*?	This text is *saying* that:
Function What is this text *doing*?	This text is:

Part 2

Having identified a list of possible *focus* and *function* statements, you will now need to concentrate the main ideas for the sermon in one single *focus* statement and in one *function* statement. This will help you then begin to clarify the aim of the sermon as you state the 'claim of the text' by answering the question: 'In relation to those who will hear the sermon, what this text wants to say and do is …'

	Luke 15.1–7
Claim of the text	In relation to those who will hear the sermon, what this text wants to say and do is …
Focus What is this text *saying*?	
Function What is this text *doing*?	

PAUSE FOR THOUGHT

Preparing for your next sermon

Part 1

Now you can repeat the exercise by working with the set text for your next sermon. It may be the biblical passage you have been invited to preach about or it may be one of the set readings contained in the lectionary for the Sunday when you are preaching.

After reading the set passage, in your own words write a list of *focus* and *function* statements. These statements will explore what you perceive the biblical text to be *saying* and *doing*.

Focus What is this text *saying*?	This text is *saying* that:
Function What is this text *doing*?	This text is:

Part 2

Having identified a list of possible *focus* and *function* statements, you will now need to concentrate the main ideas for the sermon in one single *focus* statement and in one *function* statement. This will help you then begin to clarify the aim of the sermon as you state the 'claim of the text' by answering the question: 'In relation to those who will hear the sermon, what this text wants to say and do is ...'

Claim of the text	In relation to those who will hear the sermon, what this text wants to say and do is ...
Focus What is this text *saying*?	
Function What is this text *doing*?	

A basic recipe …

Thomas Long acknowledges that 'most experienced preachers do not actually write down the focus and function of a sermon; they have an intuitive grasp of what they hope the sermon will say and do'. Echoing the theme of this chapter about mastering 'the basic bread recipe', he suggests that there is value in distilling the essence of a passage in this way, for 'beginning preachers are helped greatly by the discipline of writing out formal focus and function statements'.[14]

Designing a developmental sermon

> I have a conviction that no sermon is ready for preaching, not ready for writing out, until we can express its theme in a short pregnant sentence as clear as a crystal. I find the getting of that sentence is the hardest, the most exacting, and the most fruitful labour in my study.[15]

Perhaps a simpler way of thinking about the process of designing a developmental sermon is to try to write a sentence that summarizes the heart of the sermon you hope to preach. As the preacher from an earlier generation quoted above hints, the process will involve effort and imagination.

One way of doing that may be to take time to clarify the heart of the sermon by completing the following sentence:

> This sermon proclaims the good news that …

So what might that look like in practice?

Designing a developmental sermon on Mark 14.32–42

We shall return to Mark's account of Jesus' struggle in Gethsemane in Chapter 6 to illustrate another approach to designing sermons. Thinking about the task of designing a developmental sermon on this passage, one way of summarizing the heart of the sermon would be to say:

> This sermon proclaims the good news that the Son of God who struggled in the Garden of Gethsemane can help us as we struggle to obey God today.

With this summary in mind, the next stage would be to develop a sermon exploring this theme. One of the ways it might unfold would be like this:

Outline for a developmental sermon on Mark 14.32–42

Introduction	
1 Sonship	This section of the sermon could explore the intimate relationship with God that Jesus experienced, which is visible in the address 'Abba, Father'.
2 Struggle	Alongside the Father–Son relationship visible in this episode (as in other parts of the Gospels), we sense that obedience to death on a cross was a real struggle for Jesus.
3 Surrender	The struggle to be obedient to the Father was a real one, but the climax of the story was not the struggle but the way Jesus willingly surrendered to carrying out God's saving plan.
Conclusion	This passage demonstrates that obedience for Jesus was difficult, and this encourages us to believe that the living Jesus can strengthen people like us who often struggle to be faithful to God.

Designing a developmental sermon on Romans 8.28ff.

'We know that in all things God works for the good of those who love him ...'

This sermon proclaims the good news that the God who raised Jesus from the dead is able to bring good out of painful situations.

Introduction	
1 Bad things happen to good people	We live with the painful reality that faithfulness to God does not guarantee a smooth journey through life. Experience of life leads us to acknowledge that bad things do happen to good people. This appears to challenge what Paul was saying in this passage.
2 Evil appeared to be victorious at the cross	In order to respond to questions raised by pain and suffering, it is necessary to draw on theological resources both from within this passage and from the faith of the Church. On the first Good Friday it must have seemed to the disciples that God and good had been defeated.
3 The resurrection demonstrates God's power to bring good out of evil	The empty tomb and the appearances of the risen Christ convinced the disciples and convinces Christians today that God is able to bring good out of evil; that in all circumstances God is able to work for the good of those who love him.
4 Conclusion	

Designing a developmental sermon on Isaiah 64.1–12 and Mark 1.1–13

The Old Testament reading for the First Sunday in Advent in Year B of the Revised Common Lectionary is Isaiah 64.1–9, with its evocative plea to God: 'O that you would tear open the heavens and come down.'

Consideration of the world behind this text from Isaiah 64 points to the people of Israel enduring painful times. After the devastating experience of exile in distant Babylon, the returning exiles arrived to find a desolate land and their beloved Temple lying in ruins. Not surprisingly, the Israelites felt defeated and abandoned, and wondered 'Where is our God?' For a people who felt forsaken by God, the only appropriate response was the cry of lament: 'O that you would tear open the heavens and come down.'

As their lament ascends to heaven, they begin to confess that they have brought this chaos and disaster down on their own heads (see verses 5b–7). In the midst of their despair, hope begins to dawn as they remember that God their Father is the divine potter who can reshape their broken lives (see verses 8–9).

The process of preparing this particular Advent sermon came to life when Isaiah 64 was brought into dialogue with reflections on the baptism of Jesus in a theological commentary on Mark's Gospel written by William Placher.

Placher notes that when Mark describes the heavens opening when Jesus emerges from the River Jordan:

> the verb describing what happens to the heavens is an extremely forceful one, meaning 'ripped apart' or 'torn open'. Both Matthew and Luke tone it down to something like 'opened'. But as Donald Juel noted, 'What is opened may be closed; what is torn apart cannot easily return to its former state.'[16]

This leads Placher to claim that in Mark's version of the story, 'the relation of heaven and earth has been permanently changed'.[17]

> The tearing of the heavens, like the quotation from the prophets, is more ambiguous. When Second Isaiah prayed 'O that you would tear open the heavens and come down ...' (Isa. 64:1), he was hoping for the vindication of Israel against its enemies. In contrast, Donald Juel used to tell about the seminary student whose first reaction to this passage was, 'It's scary. God is loose in the world.' That reaction does not seem entirely wrong. Can any of us be confident enough of ourselves to welcome God's presence among us without hesitation?[18]

Reading the Isaiah passage in dialogue with Mark's account of Jesus' baptism suggested new perspectives on both passages: that the baptism of Jesus represents the dawning of a new era as God comes in person to begin the process of redeeming a broken world.

With all of that in mind, it took a couple of attempts to sum up the heart of the sermon:

- **Sermon summary – draft 1**

  This sermon proclaims the good news for people in pain that God has opened the heavens and stepped into our world in the person of Jesus to remake our broken lives and use us in making his love real to people today.

- **Sermon summary – draft 2**

  This sermon proclaims the good news for people in pain that God has stepped into our world in the Jesus who remakes our broken lives, and can use us to make his love real to people today.

With this second summary in mind, a sermon along the following lines began to emerge.

Introduction	As we hear about economic crisis ... a voice within cries out to God: 'O that you would tear open the heavens and come down.'
	As we hear about violence on our streets ... a voice within cries out to God: 'O that you would tear open the heavens and come down.'

	As we face pain and heartache within our own families ... a voice within cries out to God: 'O that you would tear open the heavens and come down.'
	And when we cry out like that, we're standing in a long tradition, because over and over again God's people have cried out: 'O that you would tear open the heavens and come down.'
1 Lament	At a particularly painful time in the life of the people of God, when returning exiles struggled to rebuild a ruined land, the people pour out their pain in a lament, crying out to God: 'O that you would tear open the heavens and come down' (Isaiah 64.1–5a).
2 Confession	Suddenly the mood changes and we begin to move from that cry of lament into a prayer of confession (Isaiah 64.5b–7), as they admit and confess that they've brought this chaos down on their own heads.
	And the first step towards healing and hope is for them to come to their senses and turn back to God, seeking his forgiveness.
3 Hope	In addition to those notes of lament and confession, we begin to hear words of hope and comfort emerging from this passage. For here the prophet remembers that God is the Father who refuses to abandon them, and also the divine potter who can take the shattered pieces and rebuild broken lives (Isaiah 64.8–9).
	Christians have confidence in God because of the way God has opened the heavens and come down to earth in the coming of Jesus.

	Jesus was baptized in the Jordan river, and as he was coming up out of the water, *he saw the heavens torn apart* and the Spirit descending like a dove on him.
	The language used here can be translated as 'ripped apart' or 'torn open'. This is significant, for as one scholar comments: 'What is opened may be closed; what is torn apart cannot easily return to its former state' (Donald Juel).
	The words here resonate with the plea in Isaiah 64 for God to tear up the heavens and come down to earth. Those echoes reinforce the sense that the dramatic events associated with Jesus' baptism indicate, for those with eyes to see, that 'the relation of heaven and earth has been permanently changed'.
	On the First Sunday of Advent, Christians celebrate that with the coming of Jesus, 'the relation of heaven and earth has been permanently changed'. Advent begins a special journey towards Christmas – remembering not only the Christ who came but also the Christ who will come again. Hope is found in knowing that the future is in God's hands.
4 Conclusion	In a world in which people in pain do cry out: 'O that you would tear open the heavens and come down', the good news is that God has stepped into our world in the Jesus who remakes our broken lives.
	Still today God uses ordinary people like us to embody and express his love to other people.

PAUSE FOR THOUGHT

Designing your developmental sermon

So it is your turn to consider designing and developing your own developmental sermon that 'has a central idea or controlling purpose that is worked out through a series of two or more progressive stages in which the idea or purpose grows to its climax':[19]

Designing a developmental sermon on …
This sermon proclaims the good news that …

1 Introduction	
2	
3	
4	
5 Conclusion	

Building on the basic bread recipe

Having practised the basic bread recipe for some months, my baking repertoire has started to expand. So far the experiments with focaccia, baguettes and *Pan Rustico* have been edible and successful enough to encourage me to continue trying out new mixtures and recipes.

This chapter has focused on one basic and useful approach to the task of preparing to preach. Mastering the homiletical skills it describes provides a healthy basis for adding other ways of designing sermons to the preaching repertoire. In the next three chapters we shall consider some of those other ways.

Notes

1 Image expressed by a student during a preaching class at Spurgeon's College, London.

2 Daniel Stevens, *The River Cottage Bread Handbook* (London: Bloomsbury, 2009), p. 86.

3 Hymn: 'Break Thou the Bread of Life', Mary Lathbury, 1841–1913.

4 John Killinger, *Fundamentals of Preaching* (London: SCM Press, 1985), p. 52.

5 Haddon W. Robinson, *Expository Preaching* (Nottingham: InterVarsity Press, 1980 and 2001), pp. 41–3.

6 Robinson, *Expository Preaching*, p. 21.

7 Thomas G. Long, *Preaching and the Literary Forms of the Bible* (Philadelphia, PA: Fortress Press, 1989), p. 11.

8 Long, *Preaching and the Literary Forms of the Bible*, p. 11.

9 Thomas G. Long, *The Witness of Preaching*, 3rd edn (Louisville, KY: Westminster John Knox Press, 2016), p. 98.

10 Long, *Witness of Preaching*, p. 108.

11 Long, *Witness of Preaching*, pp. 108–9.

12 Long, *Witness of Preaching*, pp. 110–11; emphasis added.

13 Long, *Witness of Preaching*, pp. 108–9.

14 Long, *Witness of Preaching*, p. 109.

15 J. H. Jowett, *The Preacher: His Life and Work* (New York: George H. Doran, 1912), p. 133; cited in Robinson, *Expository Preaching*.

16 William C. Placher, *Mark*. Belief: A Theological Commentary on the Bible (Louisville, KY: Westminster John Knox Press, 2010), p. 22, quoting Donald Juel, *Mark*. Augsburg Commentary on the New Testament (Minneapolis, MN: Augsburg, 1990), p. 33.

17 Placher, *Mark*, p. 22.

18 Placher, *Mark*, pp. 22–3.

19 Killinger, *Fundamentals of Preaching*, p. 52.

6

Creating a Sequence

For a video introduction to Chapter 6 visit studyguidepreaching. hymnsam.co.uk

Creating a sequence

At one stage while working as a local church minister, I presented a live Sunday-morning radio programme on an independent local station. The show kicked off at 7.00 a.m. and lasted for 90 minutes. It was an exciting but tiring start to what was always a busy day, with a couple of church services to contend with later on.

A lot of time each week was spent gathering and shaping all the materials. Our ecumenical radio group gathered news from around the county and there was usually lots of material to choose from. Sometimes there were pre-recorded interviews; sometimes a guest in the studio or maybe an interview 'on the line' with a bishop. In addition, there was music from the station's playlist, adverts, tracks from Christian artists, competitions, plus bits of local and national news. Having gathered all this material, the challenge was to find a way of moulding it into a coherent sequence. I hope we managed to get it right, at least some of the time.

Similar skills are involved in putting together a PowerPoint presentation for a lecture at college. On the one hand there is a need to gather suitable materials. Some slides include quotations illustrating the topic, others have diagrams or pictures, while others include lists of bullet-point headings. Occasionally there may be audio or video clips embedded in one of the slides. On the other hand, in seeking to avoid causing 'death by PowerPoint', it is important to make sure that the slides are chosen carefully and then arranged to create a logical sequence.

Now it may seem perverse to liken sermon preparation to the process of preparing a radio programme or a PowerPoint presentation, especially when some concerns about preachers using technology inappropriately have been expressed in Chapter 4. However, what all these activities have in common is the need to select and organize materials to create a meaningful sequence that viewers and listeners will be able to follow. One strategy for designing sermons that takes seriously the need to create a sequence can be described as 'episodic preaching'.

So what is episodic preaching?

Mike Graves provides a clear picture of this approach to preaching. He suggests that:

> episodic preaching entails viewing the sermon as a series of vignettes, stitched together in quilt-like fashion. Think of it as putting together a slide show. You can imagine a PowerPoint presentation if you want, although an old-fashioned carousel of slides will do just fine. Instead of conceiving of the sermon as so many major points – three, or a creative variation of two or four – the sermon consists of a series of slides.[1]

In Chapter 7 we shall consider some aspects of narrative preaching, an approach that is itself not without critics: some argue that narrative sermons, which stitch stories together, may prove effective in a culture in which people are already familiar with the biblical story, but much less so in a post-Christendom context in which biblical literacy is low. In the context facing most preachers in the West today, the argument goes that the preacher needs to be a teacher and not just a storyteller.

An episodic approach to preaching offers a way of embracing the best of both inductive and deductive approaches. If we use Graves' image of an 'old-fashioned carousel of slides', there is scope to insert slides or frames containing explicit Christian teaching, as well as some employing stories or images.

Foundations of episodic preaching

Current thinking about episodic preaching is supported by the homiletical work of David Buttrick. In his book *Homiletic*, he explores at length how to build sermons containing a series of 'moves'.

Instead of conceiving sermons as being made up of 'an introduction, 3 points and a poem', Buttrick envisages sermons that consist of a sequence of 'moves'. Within this framework a 'move' is a series of frames or slides that combine to communicate an idea or evoke a response in the consciousness of the listener.

> Sermons involve an ordered sequence – they are not glossolalia. Sermons are a movement of language from one idea to another, each idea being shaped in a bundle of words. Thus, when we preach we speak in formed modules of language arranged in some patterned sequence. These modules of language we will call 'moves'.[2]

One way of picturing this may be to imagine an instalment of a soap opera like *EastEnders*. From one perspective, each half-hour instalment contains a number of 'moves' connected into a sequence. To begin with, one move focuses on staff and customers in the café. Another move concentrates on whatever drama is taking place at the *Queen Vic* public house, while another drops us in the middle of whatever is going on in the market. Thus step by step we are drawn into the drama of the complicated lives of people living in Albert Square.

At another level, each of these moves contains several frames as the camera invites us to glimpse things from different angles. We see different people, we overhear snatches of dialogue and we see sinister things about to happen. We are not given an explanation as to why the sequence progresses from the café to the pub or to the local car lot; but there is a sequence of images and our minds instinctively fill in some of the gaps as we follow the developing storylines.

If we follow this analogy through, it suggests that the process of planning a sermon is less like writing a lecture and more like designing the episodes that combine to make a good film. Thomas Long sums this up helpfully by saying that:

> put together simply, Buttrick presents good sermon form as a sort of well-crafted filmstrip, moving sequentially and logically from frame to frame, each

frame casting light on a key insight, all of the frames working together to achieve the total communicational impact of the sermon.[3]

Preparing for episodic preaching

The process of preparing this kind of sermon involves working through all the stages outlined in the earlier chapters of this book. It begins with a prayerful listening to God speaking through the Bible. It demands the hard work of interpreting the biblical text and considering the varied needs and interests of our hearers. It is at the design stage that a different strategy is called for.

Acknowledging our differing personality profiles and our varied learning styles means there is unlikely to be only one way of preparing an 'episodic' sermon. What follows here is just one way of embarking on the process.

As a student at theological college I had to write lots of essays. So on first moving into local church ministry my tendency was to prepare sermons in a similar way to preparing essays. I would place a blank sheet of A4 paper on the desk in the vertical 'portrait' position, and then moving from top to bottom, I created a list of things I wanted to say, moving in a linear fashion through points 1, 2 and 3.

At some point my sermon preparation process began to change. I turned the A4 sheet horizontal, placing it on my desk in the 'landscape' format, and started sketching a series of speech bubbles or 'boxes', working from left to right across the page. Connecting these speech bubbles resulted in a storyboard or flow chart, identifying the different phases the sermon was going to work through. Figure 6.1 is an example from a recent sermon on Mark's account of Jesus' struggle in the Garden of Gethsemane, and is untidy and fuzzy at the edges. Reading from left to right, it should convey something of the way this sermon is intended to flow and develop.

This chart was not designed for anyone else to read, but it helped me discern the shape of this evolving sermon. It is not a rigid framework, because all sorts of additional ideas emerged during the sermon-writing process. However, once I am happy with the shape of the storyboard, I can press ahead with writing the sermon.

At some point I showed one of these storyboard charts to a colleague, who suggested that 'It's an example of Buttrick's "moves"'. Without realizing it, I had

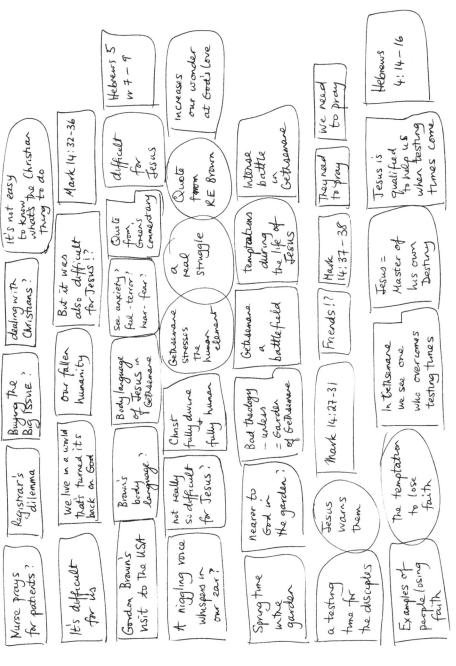

Figure 6.1 Creating a storyboard of the different phases of a sermon

stumbled into episodic preaching: designing sermons made up of episodes or 'moves'.

David Buttrick suggests that 'within about twenty minutes of speaking to a congregation, we can only discuss five, and certainly no more than six, different subject matters in sequence'.[4] Looking back, this sermon contains seven 'moves', and the intention was that each move represented another step in the process of inviting listeners to enter more deeply into the familiar story of Jesus praying in the Garden of Gethsemane. Reflecting on the sermon now it is possible to summarize each of the moves much more clearly than I would have been able to at the time.

PAUSE FOR THOUGHT

You may find it helpful to see how the following descriptions of the moves in the Gethsemane sermon connect with the storyboard chart above.

Charting the 'moves' in the Gethsemane sermon[5]

1 It's not always easy for us to know what is the Christian thing to do in different situations.

2 It's not surprising we find it difficult, but it may surprise us to think that it was difficult for Jesus too.

3 Did Jesus really find it difficult? Tuning in to the story of Gethsemane makes it clear that a real struggle to do God's will was going on.

4 But a voice whispers that it wasn't really so difficult for Jesus. What's at stake here is the true and full humanity of Jesus.

5 People have romantic views about gardens, but the Garden of Gethsemane was a battlefield. Jesus was tested throughout his life and that struggle is intense in Gethsemane.

6 There are testing times for all disciples, and we need to pray for strength to endure.

7 People's faith in God will pass through testing times, and Gethsemane tells the story of one who is able to help us in our struggles.

The building blocks for an episodic sermon – choosing the slides

Mike Graves argues that there are three kinds of 'slides' we can choose to use to create a sermon. He suggests that 'some of them are exegetical in nature, others are illustrative, still others, some kind of application'.[6] In the storyboard for the Gethsemane sermon we can see examples of each of these kinds of slides.

The sermon begins with four illustrative slides: brief scenarios picturing the difficulties Christians face in different contexts as they seek to discern what is the 'Christian' way to act or behave.

In terms of 'exegetical' materials, one slide includes a quotation from a commentary on Mark's Gospel by the New Testament scholar Joel Green. Alongside that there are several slides that involve simply reading the relevant extract from a biblical book without seeking to explain it.

In the final movement of the sermon there are several slides that provide 'some kind of application', arguing that all Christians will face times when their faith undergoes testing, but that when those times come, Christ is fully qualified to give us the help we need.

Mike Graves' list of three kinds of slides provides a useful overview, but each of his categories needs to be explained and expanded if the full range of resources is to be appreciated. Perhaps it is an interest in systematic theology that leads me to suggest that it would be helpful to expand his 'exegetical' category into two, under the headings 'biblical' and 'theological'.

The biblical category is important because a strong rooting in Scripture is essential for Christian preaching. The theological category is also necessary because the preacher needs to be able to stand back and reflect theologically on issues raised by experience, and is expected to explain core Christian beliefs. At times preachers will be required to argue against some of the caricatures of Christian belief that enjoy widespread circulation.

The following table illustrates that slides drawn from these four main categories come in different shapes and sizes. It also suggests that preachers seeking to design 'episodic' sermons have plenty of resources to work with. You may have other examples to add to the grid.

		Examples					
Types of 'slides'	*Biblical*	Reading biblical extracts	Explaining biblical texts and themes				
	Theological	Theological reflection on issues	Teaching core Christian doctrines	Theological discussion and debate			
	Illustrative	News stories	Stories of faith	Personal examples	Examples from films and novels	Images	Historical examples
	Application	Relevance of faith to everyday life	Invitation to confession and commitment	Challenge to personal discipleship	Challenge to church life		

Responding to some of the questions that have been raised about narrative preaching, Thomas Long suggests that preaching the good news involves more than simply telling evocative stories. He argues that:

> preaching today is going to need to learn to speak in multiple voices, some of them more direct, commanding, and urgent than narrative. The power in Christian preaching comes not only from narration but also from declaration ('Christ has been raised from the dead!'), explanation ('If for this life only we have hoped in Christ, we are of all people most to be pitied'), invitation ('Be steadfast, immovable, always excelling in the work of the Lord'), confession ('By the grace of God, I am what I am'), and even accusation ('O death, where is your victory?').[7]

Long's terminology may be different from that used by Graves, but he similarly helps us see that there is a vast range of resources that can and should be included in sermons. As David Buttrick makes clear, it is the combined effect of these images, stories and arguments that creates effective communication.

> A sermon, like a poem, is a structure of words and images. One 'perfect' flashing image will not make a poem. Instead it is an interaction of images within a structure that adds up to a fine poem. What makes a good sermon is not one single illustration, but a gridwork of interacting images, examples and illustrations.[8]

Storyboard for an 'episodic' sermon

The full version of a sermon on Isaiah 6.1–8 and Colossians 3.12–17 can be found in Appendix 4. The sermon was preached at an ordination service in August 2009. One of its aims was to challenge listeners to see that God not only calls some to ordained ministry but calls all believers to serve him in the down-to-earth reality of their ordinary lives.

The storyboard has been tidied up for public consumption, and aims to provide an overview of the 'frames' or 'slides' used in this 'episodic' sermon. After reading through the storyboard, you may like to have a look at the full text of the sermon.

The exercise that follows then invites you to experiment with dismantling the sermon into its constituent parts, as shown in Figure 6.2.

Figure 6.2 The dismantling of the sermon into its constituent parts

Storyboard – frame-by-frame overview of sermon on Isaiah 6.1–8 and Colossians 3.12–17

1 Violence on London's streets We wonder ... where will it end?	Global financial crisis We wonder ... where will it end?	Rising death toll in Afghanistan We wonder ... where will it end?	A time of uncertainty Now	A time of uncertainty – In OT times 'in the year that King Uzziah died ...'	Isaiah 6.1–3	In Isaiah's vision we 'see' the God we worship and serve
2 In a time of uncertainty this passage points to **The Lord who reigns**	Vision of the Lord seated on the throne. A vision that declares that God is king God reigns	We live in a world where it seems that: Evil reigns ... Sin reigns ... Death reigns	Christ's death and resurrection lead us to believe that **The Lord reigns**	In an age of uncertainty there is hope in knowing **The Lord who reigns**		
3 In a time of uncertainty this passage points to **The Lord whose glory fills the whole earth**	BBC Advert for Radio 3 – stepping into a circle – **Step into our world ...** of classical music	Some think there's only a small part of the world where you can hear the music of God's love	Some think that outside the 'spiritual life circle', all is 'secular' and God is absent. Are there godforsaken places?	Isaiah 6 declares nowhere is godforsaken for God's glory fills the whole earth **Isaiah 6.3**	God's glory fills the earth Psalm 139.7–12 John 1.14	Incarnation – God takes the stuff of ordinary life and reveals himself there; e.g. Communion
4 In a time of uncertainty this passage points to **The Lord who calls people to serve him**	Traditionally think of God calling people to be ministers or mission partners	Also means God calls all to take the ordinary stuff of life and use it to serve God.	A teacher seeing her work as a God-given vocation.	Whatever your context you are called to use the ordinary stuff of life to serve God and others.	Is this diluting the idea of vocation? No – see Colossians 3.12–14 and 3.17.	You are called to use the ordinary stuff of life to serve God
5 Questions about the further privatization of the Royal Mail generate heated discussion.	Privatization of faith is a serious and widespread problem	Faith is personal, but not a private matter. It affects all areas of life	You are called to take the everyday bits of your life and use them to serve God.	Your mission if you will accept it ... **Whatever you do ... do it all in the name of the Lord Jesus**		The God who uses ordinary everyday things, can use our ordinary everyday lives.

PAUSE FOR THOUGHT

Identifying some homiletical 'slides'

Read the following extract from a sermon on Isaiah 6.1–3 and Colossians 3.12–17. It represents the section of the sermon marked as 'move' number 3 on the storyboard.

First read through the extract and then, referring to the storyboard, identify where each new 'episode' or 'slide' begins. Be warned: some slides are shorter than others. You should find eight slides', and you may like to put an asterisk at the start of each.

The next task is to identify the kind of slides being used here. Using the categories **biblical**, **theological**, **illustrative** and **application**, please label each of the eight slides.

When you have finished, you may like to have a look at the annotated version of the extract that appears as Appendix 5.

Sermon extract

And there's another thing this vision reveals, for as we look carefully at this passage, we see *The Lord whose glory fills the whole earth.*

Holy, holy, holy is the LORD Almighty;
the whole earth is full of his glory.

I wonder if you noticed an advert that was on BBC not so long ago. A man and a woman were walking through a shopping centre carrying some bags of shopping. When the woman stepped into a little red circle on the floor, classical music started playing. And when she stepped out of that red circle, the classical music stopped.

The advert invited us to *Step into our world* – which was the world of Radio 3 – the world of classical music.

Now, some people think there's just a small part of the world where you can hear the music of God's love.

Some people feel there's this little circle called '*the spiritual life*' where you can find God, but that outside that little spiritual circle, the rest is what's called 'secular'. Some people feel that every place outside the spiritual circle is a place from which God is absent.

And sometimes we betray this way of looking at the world when we say: 'Oh such and such a place is a godforsaken place.' That district, that part of the city is just too hard for God and for the gospel.

Now the message of the Bible is very clear. The Bible says there's no god-forsaken place anywhere on this planet, because as this passage tells us, '*the whole earth is full of his glory*'. God's glory fills the whole of this earth.

And that message crops up in other parts of the Bible too. Listen to how the psalmist puts it in Psalm 139.7–13.

> Where can I go from your Spirit?
> Where can I flee from your presence?
> If I go up to the heavens, you are there;
> if I make my bed in the depths, you are there.
> If I rise on the wings of the dawn,
> if I settle on the far side of the sea,
> even there your hand will guide me,
> your right hand will hold me fast.
> If I say, 'Surely the darkness will hide me
> and the light become night around me,'
> even the darkness will not be dark to you;
> the night will shine like the day,
> for darkness is as light to you.
> For you created my inmost being;
> you knit me together in my mother's womb.

And in the New Testament the same message comes through in John 1.14, which tells us that '*The Word became flesh and made his dwelling among us.*'

> God came in the person of Jesus Christ – the divine Word became flesh.
> And when we say that the divine Word became flesh we're saying that:

> God took an ordinary human life;
> God took ordinary human flesh and blood;
> God took the stuff of ordinary everyday life and used that ordinary stuff to reveal his love and to carry out his saving work.

And that's what we see happening over and over again when we share in Holy Communion. We see the living God taking ordinary things like bread and wine and using them to communicate his presence and his love.

You see, incarnation means that God stepped into the little circle that is the life of this world, and he made it his circle. And that means that all of life belongs to him, and because the whole earth is full of his glory, it means he can meet us in every part of life. And it means he can take the ordinary, every-day bits of this world, and the ordinary stuff of our lives, and use them to bless us and to bless others.

PAUSE FOR THOUGHT

Designing your own episodic sermon

- If you are planning to preach a sermon on a particular biblical passage, you may like to experiment with using a storyboard chart to help you design your sermon.
- Alternatively, you may like to look up the next Sunday's readings in your church's lectionary and experiment with designing a 'move' that might introduce a sermon on one of the set texts.

The aim of this Studyguide is not to impose one rigid format for preaching sermons in the context of Christian worship. It aims to consider a range of strategies that can be used for designing sermons. If we always design sermons in the same way, our hearers will know what to expect and this may make it harder for us to hold their attention. If, however, we have a repertoire of preaching styles, then it is possible to design and deliver a more varied fare to our listeners.

This chapter has explored a strategy for sermon design known as 'episodic preaching'. It has considered how various 'slides' can be used to build a coherent sequence of 'moves'. In the next chapter we move on to explore some of the connections between preaching and narrative.

Notes

1   Mike Graves, *The Fully Alive Preacher: Recovering from Homiletical Burnout* (Louisville, KY: Westminster John Knox Press, 2006), p. 115.

2   David Buttrick, *Homiletic: Moves and Structures* (Philadelphia, PA: Fortress Press, 1987), p. 23.

3   Thomas G. Long, 'Form', in W. Willimon and R. Lischer (eds), *Concise Encyclopedia of Preaching* (Louisville, KY: Westminster John Knox Press, 1995), p. 151.

4   Buttrick, *Homiletic*, p. 26.

5   The full text of this sermon, and further comments about it, can be found in Peter K. Stevenson and Stephen I. Wright, *Preaching the Incarnation* (Louisville, KY: Westminster John Knox Press, 2010), ch. 6.

6   Graves, *Fully Alive Preacher*, p. 115.

7   Thomas G. Long, *Preaching from Memory to Hope* (Louisville, KY: Westminster John Knox Press, 2009), p. 18.

8   Buttrick, *Homiletic*, p. 153.

7

Telling a Story

For a video introduction to Chapter 7 visit studyguidepreaching.
hymnsam.co.uk

One of my enduring childhood memories is of my father reading me bedtime stories when he came home from work. That, plus the experience of growing up in a house full of books, helped establish a lifelong love affair with reading stories. That passion for stories came in handy during a spell in hospital while I was at secondary school, for I'm sure the experience of being able to disappear into the world of fiction played a helpful part in my recovery. Not surprisingly, over the years my taste in novels has developed, but getting lost in a good story remains one of my favourite ways of relaxing.

PAUSE FOR THOUGHT

- Think of a novel or film you have enjoyed recently.
- What was it about it that caught your imagination and held your attention?
- What kinds of stories do you most enjoy?
- What is it that makes them enjoyable?
- What is it about them that catches and keeps your attention?
- What is it about them that makes them *good* stories?

How stories work

Reflecting on a few of the stories I enjoy suggests some of the factors that help to catch and hold my attention

Master and Commander

In recent years I have enjoyed the novels by Patrick O'Brien that explore the fortunes of a sea captain, Jack Aubrey. The historical *setting* in which these naval adventures unfold is the era of the Napoleonic Wars, and the novels give a flavour of what it might have been like to serve on board a fighting ship in those troubled times. At times the language is deliberately a touch archaic, which is all part of the author's desire to create an atmosphere and paint a vivid picture of the *setting* within which the stories unfold. The *plots* often involve overcoming enemies in sea battles and surviving the storms that threaten to overwhelm Aubrey's ship.

As the sagas develop, the *character* of Captain Jack Aubrey begins to unfold in all its complexity. Alongside him there is a more mysterious *character*, the ship's Irish surgeon, Dr Stephen Maturin. This multitalented medic not only performs amazing operations on wounded sailors but his fluency in several languages enables him to engage in undercover work behind enemy lines.

Inspector Rebus

From a different historical era, the *setting* for Ian Rankin's popular detective novels is the modern-day city of Edinburgh. The bustling capital city and its environs supply the social *setting* within which Inspector John Rebus' investigations into villainous crimes are played out. The reader quickly gains insights into the policeman's *character*, for Rebus turns out to be a rough diamond who finds it difficult to sustain long-term relationships and is a bit too fond of the drink for his own good.

Rankin's stories hold my attention not just because he creates vivid *characters* but because his *plots* keep me guessing. On several occasions I have tried to guess the solution to the crime when I am about a third of the way through the book. Having been gripped by the *plot*, I can't then put the book down until the end, when I discover that, as usual, I'd prematurely jumped to the wrong conclusion.

Fiona Griffiths

Fiona Griffiths, a detective with the South Wales Police, is a more recent arrival in the world of crime fiction. The central *character* at the heart of these stories, within the *setting* of Cardiff, is unusual because she lives with Cotard's Disease, which shapes her way of working and her relationships. Some of the *characters* who pop up in the stories, including her father, have 'interesting' and shady back stories.

Living in the Welsh capital it is easy for me to picture the offices where she and her colleagues are based, and to recognize the Welsh *setting* that provides the background to the stories. At times perhaps the *plots* push the boundaries of plausibility, but their unexpected twists and turns certainly succeed in holding my attention.

Stories that work

These brief examples illustrate that in stories that work there is a rich interplay between *plot*, *character* and the *setting* or *scene*. This chapter seeks to demonstrate some of the ways thinking about *plot*, *character* and *setting* can be helpful to preachers as they think about shaping and designing sermons.

1 FINDING THE PLOT

> Each story has a beginning, a middle, and an end; that is, stories are structured. Each story has a plot of some kind. We are presented with a problem that is to be solved; quite likely there are difficulties to be overcome on the way or consequences when the main events are over.[1]

One person who has actively promoted the value of keeping *plot* at the heart of preaching is Eugene Lowry.[2] Back in 1980 he sparked fresh thinking about preaching in his book *The Homiletical Plot* by arguing that a 'sermon is not a doctrinal lecture. It is an *event-in-time*, a narrative art form more akin to a play or novel in shape than to a book.' This led him to suggest that it is much better to envisage the 'sermon as a homiletical plot, a narrative art form, a sacred story'.[3]

Understanding a sermon as a *plot*, rather than a lecture, means that the sermon has as its key ingredient what Lowry calls:

> a sensed discrepancy, a homiletical bind. Something is 'up in the air' – an issue not resolved. Like any good storyteller, the preacher's task is to bring the folks home – that is, resolve matters in the light of the gospel and in the presence of the people.[4]

With this in mind Lowry suggests that instead of every sermon having an introduction, three points and a conclusion, it is helpful for the preacher to move through five stages during the course of a sermon, as shown in Figure 7.1.

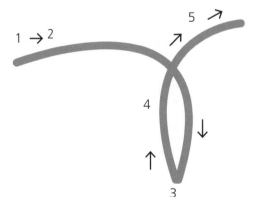

1 Upsetting the equilibrium
2 Analysing the discrepancy
3 Disclosing the clue to resolution
4 Experiencing the gospel
5 Anticipating the consequences[5]

Figure 7.1 The five-point Lowry loop

Plots and detectives

On a first reading these unfamiliar labels may appear confusing. However, on closer inspection we can see how each episode of popular detective programmes, such as *Inspector Morse*, regularly employs a similar *plot* structure.

1   To begin with, the programme upsets the viewer's equilibrium by leading us to a murder scene in or around the dreaming spires of Oxford. At the outset it may or may not be clear who has committed this heinous crime.
2   The next stage of the *plot* finds the grumpy, veteran detective being asked to track down the killer, and he and his loyal colleague, Lewis, then embark on their quest to analyse the evidence and capture the criminal. But for a time, as the story unfolds, it seems less and less likely that Morse will be successful, because one line of enquiry after another turns out to be just a dead end. Things go from bad to worse, and because progress is so slow he is regularly summoned back to headquarters to explain why the investigation is going nowhere fast.
3   For a time all appears lost until the penny drops and Morse has a hunch about who carried out the murder and how they did it. Finding the clue to the resolution marks the turning point in the story.
4   From then on the plot speeds up, and we enjoy watching the police race from one place to another in their bid to capture the crooks before the end of the programme.
5   The final stage of the drama is when the crime is solved and the killers are captured. From then on everyone lives happily ever after, or at least until the next episode (with the exception of those who were killed at the beginning of the programme).

Plots and preachers

As viewers, we know that the story is likely to take this kind of shape, but we happily watch week by week to see how that basic plot will unfold this time. There is plenty of scope for variations on a theme to keep us interested, because the twists in the story can happen in many different ways.

In a parallel way Lowry suggests that preachers can arouse interest by *upsetting the equilibrium* of their hearers by identifying a problem at the start of a sermon. This could, for example, be a troubling situation in the news that calls God's goodness into question. Or in line with our thinking back in Chapter 3, it might involve drawing attention to some kind of *'trouble in the text'*.

Moving into the stage of *analysing the discrepancy* might involve probing more deeply into that trouble, and at times the more closely we look, the more tangled and difficult it can appear.

In our preaching, however, the desire is not to lead the congregation into the Slough of Despond but to *disclose the clue to resolution*. This is achieved in the sermon by bringing the good news of Jesus Christ to bear on this situation. From a human point of view, certain situations may indeed appear hopeless; but in the light of the cross and the empty tomb, we dare to believe that there are grounds for a living hope.

Having shed the light of the Christian gospel on to the problem leads the preacher on to offer examples and illustrations that flesh out what such a living hope looks like in practice. In this stage of the sermon, both preacher and congregation begin to *experience the gospel*.

In the final stage of this sermon journey we seek to *anticipate the consequences* for Christian life and witness today. Such sermons might conclude by encouraging each and every listener to work out for themselves the sermon's relevance for their own situations.

Such an approach to preaching can claim a biblical basis in the example of Jesus who taught in parables. In common with many gospel parables this form of narrative preaching is an indirect method of communication in that the sermon concludes by inviting and encouraging the hearers to work out the ending for themselves. This emphasis has been welcomed by many because it provides a plausible alternative to a more traditional 'three-point' approach to preaching. Whereas some forms of propositional preaching may be in danger of appealing only to the intellect of the hearers, this approach operates in a more holistic way in that it seeks to engage the imagination and the emotions of the hearers as well.

Such an approach is not without its own set of difficulties. Indeed, there would appear to be the real possibility that the preacher who always adopts a narrative approach is just as much in danger of downplaying the variety within scripture, as the one who constantly resorts to a more didactic style of preaching. While it is true that Jesus taught in parables which often provoked his hearers to work out the application of the story for themselves, it would be misleading to say that this is the only way in which Jesus taught and preached. The Sermon on the Mount shows that there were occasions where Jesus was happy to operate in a more didactic manner.

A detailed critique of this style of narrative preaching has been advanced recently by Charles Campbell[6] who feels that the emphasis upon formal matters of *plot* tends towards a neglect of more significant issues about the *character* of the one who is at the heart of Christian preaching. The important thing is not that we can be like Jesus in the way we preach in parables but that the character of Jesus should be at the heart of all preaching. As several forms of narrative preaching adopt an inductive method, beginning from human experience and leading individuals on towards an experience of transformation, Campbell feels that the end result is that human experience dictates the terms of the discussion carried out in the sermon. This need not be the case as within Lowry's schema it would also be possible to begin with a problem within the biblical text, or between two apparently contradictory passages, and to move on to seek a biblical resolution to that particular problem.

The homiletical plot may not solve all the problems facing the contemporary preacher, but it suggests another viable way of structuring sermons which merits further exploration and experimentation.[7]

Acknowledging that Lowry's *homiletical plot* is not the final word in terms of designing sermons, it will be helpful now to look at examples from both the Old and New Testaments of the kinds of sermons that could plausibly emerge using this sort of approach.

Working through the stages of the homiletical plot – 1

Sermon outline based on James 1.1–8

Preachers turning to James 1.1–8 quickly stumble over some 'trouble in the text', because the opening verses say: 'My brothers and sisters, whenever you face trials of any kind, consider it nothing but joy' (James 1.2). In a risk-averse society that seeks to minimize problems as far as possible, this does not sound like the best recipe for human flourishing.

Rather than ignoring this kind of trouble in the text, the preacher may find it more helpful to grasp the nettle, and by highlighting the problem inject some interest and energy into the sermon.

Clearly this New Testament epistle is not a story with a *plot* of its own, but I want to suggest that it is possible to develop a sermon on James 1 that is held together by a simple *plot*.

So with James 1.2 in mind, what might be involved in working through the stages of the *homiletical plot*?

Perhaps it could look like something like this:

Upsetting the equilibrium This sermon might begin by posing some questions.	*Consider it nothing but joy …* • when your favourite team is relegated? • when you're made redundant? • when the doctor diagnoses a serious illness? • when someone you love dies? You **cannot** be serious. Surely this is pastoral insensitivity of the highest order? For all of us know that it just doesn't make sense to *'consider it nothing but joy'* when such challenging situations cast their shadow over our lives.
Analysing the discrepancy Moving on to the next stage of the sermon involves looking more deeply into this problem. To begin with, the closer we look, the more tangled the situation may appear to be.	And the more we think about it, the more we are convinced that it doesn't make sense to *consider it nothing but joy* when those things happen, because we live in a society that treasures health, wealth and happiness. Often people say: 'When you've got your health you've got everything.' So how can we possibly *consider it nothing but joy* if we're no longer enjoying good health? We live in a society in which the media give the impression that happiness involves having good looks and keeping young and beautiful. In a society like ours that highlights glamour and celebrity it's absolute nonsense to say to our brothers and sisters that whenever they face trials of any kind, they should *consider it nothing but joy*. But is that the only way to look at things?

Disclosing the clue to resolution At this point the sermon seeks to resolve some of that tension by reminding the congregation that the Church exists on the basis of another story that sheds a very different light on the **challenges that life brings**.	There is another way of looking at the trials and challenges life brings, for the Church proclaims a story that helps us see things in a new light. It's the story of God's Son, who shared in the rough and tumble of life on earth. It's the story of God's Son, who shared in the pain and the suffering that causes people to cry out: 'My God, my God, why have you forsaken me?' And as we stand at the foot of the cross we discover a God who is with us in our sufferings. As we stand at the threshold of the empty tomb we begin to see a God whose love is stronger than death. As we encounter the risen Christ we dare to believe that in all things God is able to work for the good of those who love him. (Romans 8.28)
Experiencing the gospel Having allowed the Christian gospel to shed light on these problems, the next phase of the sermon involves sharing some stories of people whose faith has helped them through testing times.	So let me introduce you to some of the people I know who've experienced this God as a very present help in their times of trouble. For example, I think of a couple who had to come to terms with … and looking back on that difficult time in their lives, they say it was painful but 'God was with us'. And I think of another person I know who had to face … Different people in different situations; who discovered a God who was able to work for their good in the midst of their suffering and their trials.

Anticipating the consequences In this final section of the sermon, which may be quite brief, the aim is not to teach people a lesson but to invite them to consider the implications of this sermon for their own lives.	Now I don't know exactly what you're facing today. But whoever you are, I know that if you're not facing difficulties today, the time is sure to come when you will! But whatever you're facing today and whatever life may throw at you in the future, it is possible even in difficult situations to *consider it nothing but joy* in the sense that you know that whatever may happen, the good news is that God is with you. He will always be with you and he promises never to leave you or forsake you. And it's only because we know that kind of God that we can dare to say with James, '*My brothers and sisters, whenever you face trials of any kind, consider it nothing but joy.*'

Working through the stages of the homiletical plot – *2*

Sermon outline based on Genesis 12.1–9

Genesis 12 is a set reading for the Second Sunday in Lent in Year A of the Revised Common Lectionary. Unlike the passage from James 1, the Genesis account of Abram's response to God's call clearly is a narrative passage, and sermons can benefit from working with the grain of the narrative.[8]

There are many good sermons that could be preached from this passage, but perhaps one using the stages of the *homiletical plot* might develop along the following lines.

Upsetting the equilibrium This sermon begins by referring to feelings of homesickness, and wondering if Abram would have felt disturbed by God's call.	Leaving school and going off to university was exciting, but it was also rather disturbing. For it meant moving away from all my family and friends. Feeling so very homesick that first term living away from home meant that the term seemed to go on for ever … And here in Genesis 12 we see Abram leaving behind family, friends and familiar surroundings, not to go off to college but to obey the call of God.
Analysing the discrepancy On this occasion the next phase of the sermon is not analysing a problem but simply raising a number of questions. It's not necessary to know the answers to all those questions we bring to the text. But asking those questions helps us and, we hope, our listeners to sink deeply into the narrative.	I can't help wondering … … How must Abram have felt being uprooted from all that was familiar? … Did it feel risky and irresponsible to leave everything behind? … Was it irresponsible of God to ask Abram to leave everything behind? Reading this passage from Genesis 12 prompts us to ask: 'Why does God uproot Abram?' Was it because Abram and his family served other gods (Joshua 24.2) and had to leave all of that behind before God could use him? So when God called Abram, he was calling someone who hadn't sorted out all his theological ideas. Fancy God calling a pagan to such an important job! Leaving everything behind must have been an enormous leap of faith for Abram. So why was Abram willing to take the step of faith?

Disclosing the clue to resolution

Although we are drawn naturally to the human characters, the main actor in this drama is God. The desire of divine love to bestow blessings on the world through Abram casts an entirely different light on this story. It's not so much about a hero of faith for us to imitate but about a God who invites us to play a part in this plan to bless others.

So far we've been focusing on Abram, but the truth is that the key figure here isn't old Father Abraham but the living God who takes the initiative and promises to bless (Genesis 12.1–3):

> Go ... to the land ... that I will show you. I will make of you a great nation, and I will bless you, and make your name great, so that you will be a blessing. I will bless those who bless you ... and in you all the families of the earth shall be blessed.

As we listen to this list of divine promises we begin to see that this personal and family upheaval was part of God's plan to bring blessing to the whole world.

God was calling Abram to leave behind the comforts of home and family in order to set in motion a great plan of salvation, which would bring great blessing for the world.

And so as the story unfolds, we should begin to see how Abram relies and acts on God's promises.

Experiencing the gospel

In this section of the sermon there are opportunities to provide down-to-earth examples of people today who are being used by God to bless others.

And like Abram of old, so we today are being called to stake our lives on God's promises.

God's promise is to bless us and use us to make his blessing available to all the world.

That's what we see happening with the thousands of people across the land who give up their Friday and Saturday nights to bless others, by caring through people as they serve as Street Pastors ...

That's what we see happening in the case of ...

Anticipating the consequences	
In this final section of the sermon, which may be quite brief, the aim is not to teach people a lesson but to invite them to consider the implications of this sermon for their own lives.	And all of us, like them, are called to build our lives on the promises of God. In the light of Jesus and his resurrection, we have so much more reason for trusting God and his promises. So as we think about the ways God called Abram to step out in faith, it raises questions each one of us has to answer for ourselves: • What steps into the unknown is God calling me to take? • In what ways is the living God calling you and me to play a part in his mission to this needy world?

PAUSE FOR THOUGHT

Working through the stages of the homiletical plot

Choose one of the following passages and spend some time reading and reflecting on it. Then experiment with designing a sermon on that passage using the five-stage framework above.

- Matthew 20.1–16
- Luke 9.12–17
- Luke 24.13–35

Upsetting the equilibrium	
Analysing the discrepancy	
Disclosing the clue to resolution	
Experiencing the gospel	
Anticipating the consequences	

How to read Bible stories

The unifying structure which links the various happenings in the story and organizes them into a continuous account is called '*plot*'. The plot safeguards the unity of action and gives meaning to the multiple elements in the story. It is on this specific point that narrative is distinct from the chronicle, which simply enumerates facts ...

... it is the plot that makes the narrative. It is through the plot that the reader perceives, in the series of related actions, something more than an accumulation of facts lined up in no particular order. The plot is the unifying principle of the narrative, its scarlet thread: it makes it possible to organize the stages of the story into a coherent scenario.[9]

There are parallels between the way Lowry's *homiletical plot* is developed and the Quinary Scheme originally outlined by P. Larivaille, which has been described as 'the canonical model by which any plot can be measured'.[10] As the name implies, the Quinary Scheme suggests that a narrative *plot* typically consists of five stages.

Quinary Scheme: a structural model splitting up the plot of the narrative into five successive moments:

1 *Initial situation (or exposition)*: the circumstances of the action (setting, characters), if need be a shortage of something is indicated (sickness, difficulty, ignorance); the narrative will show an attempt to remove it.
2 *Complication*: an element that sets off the narrative, introducing narrative tension (a lack of equilibrium in the initial state or complication in the quest).
3 *Transforming action*: the outcome of the quest, reversing the initial situation: the transforming action is either at a pragmatic (action) or a cognitive (evaluation) level.
4 *Denouement (or resolution)*: removal of the tension by the application of the transforming action to the subject.
5 *Final situation*: statement of the new state attained by the subject following the transformation. Structurally this moment corresponds to the reversal of the initial situation by the elimination of the shortage.[11]

Reading from Genesis to Revelation we encounter many different kinds of materials, but there are good grounds for arguing that 'of all the biblical genres of literature, narrative may be described as the central, foundational, and all-encompassing genre of the Bible'.[12] This means that if we seek to preach with the grain of Scripture on a regular basis, we are likely to find ourselves working with quite a number of narrative passages. In some cases it is possible, within those narratives, to identify the stages through which the underlying *plot* develops. The next example suggests the value of viewing one Old Testament text through the lenses of the Quinary Scheme.

Exploring the plot in Nehemiah 4

The world behind the text

In 445 BC, when the book of Nehemiah commences, Nehemiah is *cupbearer to the king*, that is, to King Artaxerxes of Persia. As a courtier, he has an important position in the Persian Empire. However, in his conversation with *Hanani, one of my brethren*, Nehemiah has to face the contrast that his own comfort and prestige make with the serious difficulties that the people of God, Nehemiah's own people, are presently enduring. *The Jews that survived, who had escaped exile*, are in Judah, but they are poor and weak. They have survived and escaped, while Nehemiah has risen to the comfortable position of cupbearer. Nehemiah is flourishing at the court of Artaxerxes, whereas in Judah and Jerusalem *the survivors there in the province who escaped exile are in great trouble and shame; the wall of Jerusalem is broken down, and its gates are destroyed by fire.*[13]

It may not be possible to analyse every narrative passage in this way, but looking at Nehemiah 4 it is possible to identify five successive stages of the *plot* in this passage.

1 Initial situation (or exposition)	The 'world behind the text' points to a period of time decades after the initial return of Jewish exiles from their captivity in Babylon. The rebuilding of the Temple, initiated in the times of the prophets Haggai and Zechariah, was now a distant memory, and the city of Jerusalem had fallen on hard times.
	The walls of Jerusalem are incomplete and the city's defences are in disarray. Morale is at a low ebb, and the city and its people are vulnerable to attack.
2 Complication	To make matters worse, the local politicians Sanballat and Tobiah were aggrieved at the idea of the city being rebuilt and no longer under their control. These angry neighbours taunt the people who are rebuilding the wall. They begin to plot and scheme. They plan to attack the city, to ensure Nehemiah doesn't re-establish control of the city.
	Soon Jerusalem is surrounded by angry and aggressive neighbours on all sides. As insults begin to fly, tempers and tensions begin to rise.
	Back in Jerusalem the insults are having their effect because it appears to be the case that the people rebuilding the city walls have become demoralized. In Nehemiah 4.10–12 we can detect their laments about the slow progress of the rebuilding and their wonder if the job will ever be completed.
	Some of their compatriots from the suburbs and adjoining districts plead over and over again to be allowed to return to their homes. There is a real danger that the job will never be completed but left half-finished.

3 Transforming action	Humanly speaking, the situation is turned around through the intervention of Nehemiah:

1 He addresses the people's fears by taking practical steps to defend the city against attack. Even if the building work slows down a bit, it is able to proceed because the people feel safer.

2 He also reminds them of the past when God had delivered his people from many problems. As judges and kings had rallied the people under the slogan 'Our God will fight for us' (verse 20), now Nehemiah reminds them that the God who is with them will help and defend them. 'This phrase (v. 20) is used only once in the whole of the NIV Bible, but the idea of God fighting for his people was a common Old Testament theme – "the warrior God" Exodus 15.3, Isaiah 42.13, Jeremiah 20.11.'[14]

3 Here is someone who leads by example, for along with his personal bodyguard, Nehemiah worked around the clock (4.23). He shares in the work and shows he is willing to shoulder the same burdens as everyone else.

4 Here is a leader who prays and puts his trust in the God who is stronger than his enemies and bigger than his fears (4.4–5, 9).

However, the key actor in this drama is neither Nehemiah nor his enemies Sanballat and Tobiah but the God who frustrated the plot of the troublemakers and gave his people strength to continue their work.

Nehemiah's work is guided by the conviction that 'The God of heaven is the one who will give us success' (2.20); that 'the LORD, who is great and awesome' (4.14) is with them; and that 'Our God will fight for us' (4.20). It is knowing this God that helps Nehemiah and the people to see their plight in a new light. Knowing this God transforms their situation.

4 Denouement (or resolution)	So 'When our enemies heard that their plot was known to us, and that **God had frustrated it**, we all returned to the wall, each to his work' (4.15). The threats were still hanging over them, but God enabled the people to carry on with the work and to bring it to a successful conclusion (2.20).
5 Final situation	The hard work mentioned in chapter 4 bears fruit in due course, because 'the wall was finished on the twenty-fifth day of the month Elul, in fifty-two days' (6.15).

Using the plot in Nehemiah 4 in a sermon

As a visiting preacher, I was once asked to deliver a sermon on Nehemiah 4. This was one of a series based on Nehemiah. Understanding the way the *plot* functioned in this particular passage served as useful background for a sermon that moves through the five stages of the *homiletical plot*. An outline of that sermon can be found in Appendix 6.

PAUSE FOR THOUGHT

Finding the plot in Ruth 2

In preparation for this exercise you might like to read the four chapters that constitute the short Old Testament book of Ruth and ask yourself about the plot that holds this story together.

With some ideas in your mind about the overall plot that unfolds throughout the book, this exercise invites you to consider what kind of plot might be present in one episode of this Hebrew narrative:

• Read Ruth 2 with the five stages of the Quinary Scheme in mind.
• What do you think is the basic plot in Ruth 2?

- What stages does the plot move through in Ruth 2?
- To what extent do you think it is possible to interpret Ruth 2 in terms of the Quinary Scheme?
- What insights does this way of reading the text offer?
- So if you were asked to preach a sermon on Ruth 2, what would you like to emphasize?

Further reading

Some ideas about finding a plot in Ruth 2 can be found in Appendix 7.

John Goldingay, *Models for Interpretation of Scripture* (Carlisle: Paternoster Press, 1995); see ch. 5, 'How Stories Preach'.

Thomas G. Long, *Preaching and the Literary Forms of the Bible* (Philadelphia, PA: Fortress Press, 1989); see ch. 5, 'Preaching on Narratives'.

Daniel Marguerat and Yvan Bourquin, *How to Read Bible Stories: An Introduction to Narrative Criticism* (London: SCM Press, 1999); see ch. 4, 'The Plot'.

2 IDENTIFYING THE CHARACTERS

Plot and characters cannot be separated; they belong together so closely that if we develop the one we shift the others. The characters are the visible face of the plot: they get it moving, they feed it, they dress it up; without them the plot is reduced to a skeleton. Conversely a handful of characters does not make up a narrative until a plot connects them together.[15]

Having explored some aspects of the plots that hold biblical narratives together, it is also worth thinking briefly about the characters we bump into when we read stories in the Bible.

PAUSE FOR THOUGHT

- Read the parable of the Prodigal Son in Luke 15.11–32.
- As you read that famous parable, with which of the characters do you instinctively identify?
- How do you feel about the other characters?

Thomas Long suggests that in most cases, when we read stories:

> identification with character occurs willingly and spontaneously. The reader intuits that a character in a story is in important respects like himself or herself … Storytellers work at presenting a character in such a way that will enable the reader to say 'I'm like that'.[16]

Thinking about the parable of the Prodigal Son in Luke 15, our own life experience may lead us instinctively to identify with one of the three main characters in the parable.

So it may be, for example, that painful family experiences prompt some people to identify with the loving father whose heart has been broken by his younger son's departure.

On the other hand, could it be that we identify with that respected pillar of the community who throws the book of etiquette out of the window and runs, disgracefully and lovingly, down the street to welcome the prodigal home?

Or is it for the younger, selfish son, who demands his inheritance and goes off to blow the lot, that we have some fellow feelings?

Perhaps, although we may not want to admit it in public, our default position is to identify with the grumpy older brother, who stands on his dignity complaining about his father's generosity.

Protagonists, walk-ons and agents

> The degree to which a character is present is ... tricky to determine, for the narrative itself generates, more or less distinctly, a hierarchy of major roles, subordinate roles and walk-ons. Those with major roles are called *protagonists*. The protagonists play an active role in the plot and are in the foreground ... In complete contrast to the protagonists, the *walk-ons* remain in the background; they can be individuals or collectives: a crowd, an inhabitant, a passer-by. Between these two extremes are the subordinate roles, which can be called *agents*. Their function is limited to helping the plot along; they can have a symbolic dimension.[17]

Returning to Ruth 2, we might say that Ruth and Boaz are *protagonists* in the narrative because they both have major roles in the story. At the same time, the young women and the workmen employed by Boaz to harvest the crops function only as *walk-ons* in the sense that they remain in the background as part of the agricultural setting for the story. There may be a number of *agents* at work helping to move the plot along, for the 'servant who was in charge of the reapers' (2.6) explains to his boss who this new woman is, and is careful to make sure he is aware she is a Moabite. In a rather different way the widowed Naomi helps the plot along by saying 'Go, my daughter' (2.2), thus granting the younger woman permission to go out and search for food. From this action many unexpected and exciting things will develop as the story unfolds. Perhaps the phrase 'As it happened' in verse 3 hints at the presence and activity of God in the development of the story. To what extent is God an *agent* who makes things happen, or is the God of Israel the main *protagonist* who plays the most important role even if that is carried out quietly behind the scenes? Or maybe God plays both roles in the story?

Now in terms of preaching, paying attention to the characters in biblical stories may not necessarily dictate the shape of the sermon. However, asking questions about how the *characters* and *plot* function within the story can help us slow down and pay much closer attention to the biblical text.

3 INTERPRETING THE SETTING

In reading biblical narratives there is a temptation to think that every story must have a moral that indicates something we need to do. However, when we turn to narrative texts in the Bible, their focus tends to be much more on the presence and activity of God. It is important to acknowledge the *theocentric* nature of Hebrew narrative, because God is the prime character at work, even when he might appear to human eyes to be absent.

In a helpful section about *Preaching Hebrew Narrative*,[18] Greidanus notes 'the pervasive presence of God' within the narrative scene. Indeed 'even in scenes where God, in a particular frame, is not one of the "characters" or is not represented by one of the characters, the scene as a whole will undoubtedly reveal the presence of God, for the human characters act out the scene against the backdrop of God's promises, God's enabling power, God's demands, God's providence.'[19]

The pervasive presence of God is expressed in a memorable phrase by Ronald Thiemann who says, as he comments upon the Old Testament accounts of David's accession to kingship, that '*God is not so much absent from as hidden within the biblical narrative.*'[20] Other places within the biblical narrative where the pervasive, but hidden, presence of God can be identified, are the Joseph cycle and the Book of Esther. In the Joseph cycle God is not a prominent actor, but at the end of the day Joseph affirms his belief that God has been at work (Gen. 50:20). In Esther the name of God is not even mentioned, but the book was preserved because the people believed that the hidden God had been at work to protect and deliver his people.

Although the Biblical narratives are clearly *theocentric*, Greidanus notes that many preachers tend to drift into an *anthropocentric* use of narrative passages. If God is the prime character in Hebrew narrative, *even when he is not mentioned*, then this implies that biblical preaching must avoid the temptation to use these narratives simply as sources of good examples for believers to follow. Theocentric materials call for theocentric sermons which are far more concerned with what a passage reveals about who God is than exhortations about what I must do.[21] This suggests that sermons on the Joseph narratives should not be primarily concerned to portray him as a glowing example for

Christians to imitate but should point much more in the direction of the sovereign God who is constantly at work in the midst of the tangled family affairs involving Joseph and his brothers. To argue that appropriate use of narrative calls for more theocentric preaching is another way of pleading for putting the gospel back into preaching.[22]

How sermons work

Building on an understanding of the elements of *plot*, *character* and *setting* that help to make stories work, this chapter has considered some of the ways such narrative elements can help make sermons work. The following chapter moves on to consider how images can help to shape sermons.

Further reading

Thomas G. Long, *Preaching and the Literary Forms of the Bible* (Philadelphia, PA: Fortress Press, 1989).

Eugene L. Lowry, *How to Preach a Parable: Designs for Narrative Sermons* (Nashville, TN: Abingdon Press, 1989).

Eugene L. Lowry, *The Sermon: Dancing the Edge of Mystery* (Nashville, TN: Abingdon Press, 1997).

Eugene L. Lowry, *The Homiletical Plot: The Sermon as Narrative Art Form*, expanded edn (Louisville, KY: Westminster John Knox Press, 2001).

Eugene L. Lowry, *The Homiletical Beat: Why All Sermons are Narrative* (Nashville, TN: Abingdon Press, 2012).

Daniel Marguerat and Yvan Bourquin, *How to Read Bible Stories: An Introduction to Narrative Criticism* (London: SCM Press, 1999).

Peter K. Stevenson, 'Preaching and Narrative', in David Day, Jeff Astley and Leslie J. Francis (eds), *A Reader on Preaching: Making Connections* (Aldershot: Ashgate, 2005), p. 103.

Stephen I. Wright, *Preaching with the Grain of Scripture* (Cambridge: Grove Books, 2001).

Notes

1 John Goldingay, *Models for the Interpretation of Scripture* (Carlisle: Paternoster Press, 1995), p. 76.

2 See Eugene L. Lowry, *The Homiletical Plot: The Sermon as Narrative Art Form* (Atlanta, GA: John Knox Press, 1980).

3 Eugene L. Lowry, *The Homiletical Plot: The Sermon as Narrative Art Form*, expanded edn (Louisville, KY: Westminster John Knox Press, 2001), pp. xx–xxi.

4 Lowry, *Homiletical Plot*, expanded edn, p. 12.

5 Lowry, *Homiletical Plot*, expanded edn, p. 26.

6 Charles L. Campbell, *Preaching Jesus: New Directions for Homiletics in Hans Frei's Postliberal Theology* (Grand Rapids, MI/Cambridge: Eerdmans, 1997).

7 Peter K. Stevenson, 'Preaching and Narrative', in David Day, Jeff Astley and Leslie J. Francis (eds), *A Reader on Preaching: Making Connections* (Aldershot: Ashgate, 2005), p. 103.

8 Stephen I. Wright, *Preaching with the Grain of Scripture* (Cambridge: Grove Books, 2001).

9 Daniel Marguerat and Yvan Bourquin, *How to Read Bible Stories: An Introduction to Narrative Criticism* (London: SCM Press, 1999), pp. 40–1.

10 Marguerat and Bourquin, *How to Read Bible Stories*, pp. 43–4.

11 Marguerat and Bourquin, *How to Read Bible Stories*, p. 44.

12 Sidney Greidanus, *The Modern Preacher and the Ancient Text* (Leicester: InterVarsity Press, 1988).

13 Matthew Levering, *Ezra and Nehemiah*. Brazos Theological Commentary (London: SCM Press, 2008), p. 127; emphasis in original.

14 Dave Cave, *Ezra and Nehemiah. Free to Build*. Crossway Bible Guides (Nottingham: Crossway, 1993), p. 157.

15 Marguerat and Bourquin, *How to Read Bible Stories*, p. 58.

16 Thomas G. Long, *Preaching and the Literary Forms of the Bible* (Philadelphia, PA: Fortress Press, 1989), p. 75.

17 Marguerat and Bourquin, *How to Read Bible Stories*, p. 60.

18 Greidanus, *Modern Preacher and the Ancient Text*, pp. 188–227.

19 Greidanus, *Modern Preacher and the Ancient Text*, p. 199.

20 Ronald F. Thiemann, 'Radiance and Obscurity in Biblical Narrative', in Garret Green (ed.), *Scriptural Authority and Narrative Interpretation* (Philadelphia, PA: Fortress Press, 1987), pp. 21–41.

21 Greidanus, *Modern Preacher and the Ancient Text*, pp. 216–21; see also Goldingay, *Models for the Interpretation of Scripture*, chs 2—5.

22 Stevenson, 'Preaching and Narrative', p. 104.

8

Painting a Picture

For a video introduction to Chapter 8 visit studyguidepreaching.
hymnsam.co.uk

For me, art classes at senior school got off to a very shaky start. On one memorable occasion we were asked to draw pictures of bicycles, but my attempts were so poor that the art teacher frogmarched me out to the bike shed and asked, 'Do any of those bike wheels look like the ones in your picture?' Clearly a career in fine art was not on the horizon; but over the years as a preacher I have spent a lot of my time trying to paint pictures with words. With that in mind, this chapter will consider some of the ways images and pictures can be used to help hold sermons together.

Images, narratives and arguments

Thinking about the Bible, David Schlafer helpfully notices that:

> Whether a text is a hymn of praise, a terse teaching, a historical account, a parable, or a theological essay, it communicates using *images*, *narratives* and *arguments*. The Scriptures engage our senses and emotions directly by means of images. They also invite us to enter as participants in stories ... They further confront us with arguments – orderly presentations of evidence intended to lead us to certain conclusions.[1]

Schlafer is well aware that in many passages there is an interplay between images, stories and arguments; but there are plenty of biblical materials that illustrate the point he is making.

He refers, for example, to the image of God as shepherd that occurs in passages such as Psalm 23, Ezekiel 34 and John 10. Alongside that example it is also possible to point to the image of Christ as the true vine in John 15, or the image of the Church as the body of Christ in Romans 12 and 1 Corinthians 12.

In earlier chapters we reflected on the stories of Abram setting out on a journey of faith in Genesis 12, and the story of the foreigner Ruth returning with her mother-in-law Naomi to Bethlehem in search of food and hope. In the Gospels we find not only stories about Jesus but also the stories Jesus told to communicate the radical message of the kingdom of God.

It is also easy to see how some passages in Paul's letters are held together by carefully constructed arguments. In 1 Corinthians 1.18–31, for example, we find the apostle responding to pastoral issues in the church by developing a detailed argument about the significance of Christ's death on the cross.

> Images, stories and arguments, selectively employed are constant integrating strategies in the preaching and teaching of Jesus. The kingdom of God is not an empire like Caesar's. Picture instead a grain of mustard seed, a buried pearl, a coin that is lost and found. Challenged to debate the legitimate limits of neighbourly responsibility, Jesus tells a story about a man who fell among thieves on the road to Jericho. He explains forgiveness with a tale about a young man who demanded his rights, squandered them, came home in desperation, and found himself facing a very different kind of music than he could ever have imagined in his wildest dreams.
>
> Sometimes, instead of resorting to images or stories, Jesus faces down both followers and opponents in blunt, head-on exchanges. 'What good is it to gain the whole world, and lose your life in the process?' 'You give tithes of the smallest herbs and neglect the weightiest matters of the law?'[2]

In a similar way, when it comes to preaching, Schlafer suggests that:

> In sermons that 'work', in sermons that actually make the Good News come alive, one of these three – *image*, *story* or *argument* – is the orchestrating, integrating principle that shapes the whole sermon. One of the three is chosen as the means best suited for *this* preacher at *this* time with *this* text to *these* people.[3]

PAUSE FOR THOUGHT

- Think of the last sermon you listened to.
- What held that sermon together?
- Was it mainly held together by an *image*, a *story* or an *argument*?
- If there was a combination of *images*, *stories* and *arguments*, which played the most important role?

Poets, storytellers and essayists

With these ideas about images, stories and arguments in mind, Schlafer suggests that it is helpful for preachers to discover their own distinctive 'preaching voice' or style of preaching.[4] He suggests that a preacher whose default approach is to develop sermons that progress step by step through a detailed argument could be described as an *essayist*. Another who regularly designs sermons held together by a narrative or a plot could be seen, from this perspective, as a *storyteller*. Yet another whose sermons are held together by a dominant image or picture could be viewed as a *poet*. To portray the preacher as *poet* does not imply that preachers should try to deliver their sermons in iambic pentameter or rhyming verses, but points rather to preachers who proclaim good news by employing images and word pictures to arouse and sustain their listeners' interest.

In using these three categories, the idea is not to pigeon-hole preachers by implying that they are only able to preach in one particular style. It may suggest, however, that each person who preaches on a reasonably regular basis will probably have a default style that they instinctively employ.

PAUSE FOR THOUGHT

Essayist, storyteller or poet?

- Think of a preacher you have listened to on a number of occasions. Which of these three categories might provide the best fit for that preacher?
- What do you think is your own 'default' approach to preaching sermons?
- What kind of preacher are you, or would like to be?

The recipe for preaching in Chapter 5 talked about the developmental sermon, which develops a theme. Perhaps the preacher as *essayist* is one who regularly develops an argument based on a biblical text, and presents that argument using three clear 'points'. In Chapter 7 we focused on the preacher as *storyteller*, not just telling lots of stories but developing sermons held together by a plot, seeking to preach with the grain of the narrative parts of Scripture. In this chapter the focus is on the preacher as *poet*, one who paints vivid word pictures to capture and hold people's attention.

The preacher as poet

So what are some of the implications for the homiletical task of understanding the preacher as *poet*? In what ways can *images* be used as the glue to hold a sermon together?

The following examples aim to stimulate you into imagining some of the many ways you could use *images* in the sermons you prepare.

The building site

Living in the fastest-growing city in the country, I regularly walk past a number of construction sites on my way to work. This experience prompted me in one sermon[5] to use the image of a building site as a way of organizing a sermon on

Zechariah 4.1–10, which points to a time when the people of God were being challenged to rebuild the Temple in Jerusalem under the leadership of Zerubbabel and Joshua. The New Testament reading was from 1 Peter 2.4–10, which uses the language of 'living stones' who are being 'built into a spiritual house'.

Extract from sermon on Zechariah 4.1–10 and 1 Peter 2.4–10

I'm in the fortunate position that I can walk to work from home in about 25 minutes. On my way to work I have to walk around a big building site, where the billboards tell me that several large buildings are going up – office blocks, university buildings, shops etc.

Now over the last nine months as I've walked past, I can see that they've made some progress. And already the skeleton of a 12- or 15-floor building is in place.

But it's a big building site and there still seems to be a lot of wasteland – a lot of rubble lying around. They've got a big job on their hands, and if progress continues at this rate it's going to be many years before they're finished.

Our Old Testament reading takes us back just over 500 years before the birth of Christ, to a time when the city of Jerusalem lay in ruins and the great Temple built by King Solomon was nothing more than a great mountain of rubble.

Sixty to seventy years earlier the city had been overrun by the armies of the king of Babylon, and they'd ransacked the city, destroyed the Temple and taken all the leading citizens off as prisoners to languish in exile, hundreds of miles from home.

Kingdoms rise and kingdoms fall – and as the years passed, the Babylonian kingdom was overthrown by the king of Persia, and this new king allowed the Israelites to travel back home to the land of Judah to begin rebuilding their nation and rebuilding their Temple.

Two of the prominent community leaders were the high priest, Joshua, and a governor by the name of Zerubbabel, whose name sort of rhymes with rubble. And these two leaders had an enormous job of rebuilding on their hands.

For their job was not only to rebuild the shattered buildings but to rebuild a shattered nation. Their task was to restore the spiritual life of the nation so that it would become all that God wanted it to be – a light to the nations.

Their task was to restore the spiritual life of the nation in such a way that they would be a people who would radiate the light of God's love to a needy world.

That image of the building site remained in the background for much of that particular sermon, for it considered some of the obstacles standing in the way of the people of Israel, who wanted to rebuild the Temple, and also some of the obstacles standing in the way of God's people today as they seek to build for the kingdom of God.

In that sermon I also mentioned seeing some builders carefully dismantling an old public house in preparation for its removal to the St Fagans National History Museum, which is only a few miles outside Cardiff. That image of dismantling and rebuilding provided a way of asking questions about some of the challenges affecting churches today.

Over the last few weeks I've been watching as an old pub, *The Vulcan*, has been taken down tile by tile and brick by brick.

All the bricks have been carefully labelled and taken away – so that over the next four or five years, *The Vulcan* can be rebuilt at St Fagans.

As Christians in the UK we live in difficult and challenging times. And maybe one part of what's going on is that the Lord is dismantling some of the ways we've gone about the business of being church.

Bit by bit, maybe God is dismantling some of the aspects of church life that are no longer fit for purpose in the twenty-first century.

But God's intention in doing this is not to put us in storage. For his desire is to rebuild his ruined Church brick by brick, believer by believer, living stone by living stone, so that together we can declare the marvellous deeds of him who called us out of darkness into his marvellous light.

It's not about embarking on bigger campaigns and more and more activities, for renewing and rebuilding God's Church is not something we can do ourselves – we need to rely on the power of the Holy Spirit.

View from the roof

For in Christ Jesus you are all children of God through faith. As many of you as were baptized into Christ have clothed yourselves with Christ. There is no longer Jew or Greek, there is no longer slave or free, there is no longer male and female; for all of you are one in Christ Jesus.

Galatians 3.26–28

In a series of sermons based on Galatians, I was preparing to preach on Paul's famous words in chapter 3, which 'in many respects' serve 'as the climax of the entire epistle'.[6] Around that time we had a family outing during which we climbed to the top of the dome of St Paul's Cathedral and enjoyed the breathtaking panoramic views in every direction over London. The view is impressive, but there is far too much visual information to take in at one go, and the reality is that it would take a long time to make sense of it all.

In my sermon I used that image of getting to the top of the building and discovering that there was too much to absorb in one visit. I suggested that when we come to the high point of Paul's letter to the Galatians, it provides, on the one hand, a marvellous, awe-inspiring vision of the people of God, where human divisions are overcome in Christ. On the other hand, it has taken the Church centuries to grasp hold of this glorious vision and work through its practical implications.

> In the community of the new creation, our oneness in Christ overcomes and delegitimates the distinctions of race, social class and gender that divided us when we were prisoners under the power of Sin. Of course the practical outworking of this vision of the new creation remains the ongoing task of the church in history as we 'eagerly wait for the hope of righteousness' (5.5).[7]

River of life

Following a visit to a shanty town on the edge of the city of Kumasi in Ghana, one preacher[8] painted a poignant picture of a river polluted by human and industrial waste that ran through the heart of that very poor community. The image of that river, with its deadly impact on people in that neighbourhood, was contrasted with the image of the river of life that is the focal point of the prophet's vision in Ezekiel 47. The glittering image that holds that chapter together is the vibrant picture of the river of living water that flows from the presence of God in the Temple, transforming the barren wilderness and bringing life wherever it flows. That image of God's life-giving river provided the structure for a sermon declaring the good news of God's ability to transform even the bleakest of situations.

The spin doctor

Following local elections, I once preached a sermon on Genesis 3 and used the image of the political spin doctor to convey the attractive, tempting voice of the serpent, for the spin doctor is one who always seeks to put a positive spin on the policies of their own party and a negative one on those of others. The sermon said various other things about a familiar passage, but the image of a spin doctor, twisting and distorting God's words, was one I think helped hold the sermon together.

> The idea of spin – that subtle twisting of things – goes back a long, long way in history. Indeed, the book of Genesis explains that it goes all the way back to the beginning.
>
> For right at the beginning we see the first spin doctor at work;
> For we see the serpent twisting and distorting God's words;
> we see the serpent subtly calling God's trustworthiness into question.
> And I'm calling the serpent the first spin doctor because he says: 'Did God really say …?'

Jesus began to teach them many things in parables

In employing images to communicate a message, the preacher as *poet* is following in the footsteps of Jesus, who conveyed the good news of the kingdom of God in parables choc-a-bloc full of memorable images.

In a famous study, the New Testament scholar C. H. Dodd offered this classic definition of parables:

At its simplest the parable is a metaphor or simile drawn from nature or common life, arresting the hearer by its vividness or strangeness, and leaving the mind in sufficient doubt about its precise application to tease it into active thought.[9]

PAUSE FOR THOUGHT

- To what extent does my preaching arrest the hearer 'by its vividness or strangeness'?
- To what extent does my preaching 'tease' my hearers into 'active thought'?

Visually speaking

While preachers are not called to read out poems, there is much they can learn from poets about creating images and using pictorial language. The value of employing such language is underlined by Jolyon Mitchell, who refers to a religious broadcaster, Ronald Falconer. He argued that:

> In radio we make our own pictures; on television they are made for us by another … Whatever the radio programme, whether drama, documentary or act of worship, we are in a more active state, mentally, than when we watch its television equivalent.

This leads Mitchell to suggest that:

> Part of the power of pictorial language is its ability to engage the imagination, and so motivate the listener to collaborate 'as an active participant'. Preaching which employs this approach and allows listeners to make their own pictures, has the potential to involve listeners in a more dynamic mental activity. By contrast watching the television or a film demands less 'active' imaginative participation.[10]

'Careless Talk Costs Lives'

A famous series of World War Two posters[11] urged people to be security conscious with the slogan, 'Careless Talk Costs Lives'. When it comes to preaching, the stakes may not be quite as high, but in sermons it is nevertheless essential to use words wisely and sparingly. Here is an area where the preacher has much to learn from poets, because they are highly skilled artists who know how to compress the maximum amount of meaning into a limited number of words.

> Use absolutely no word that does not contribute to the presentation.
> The more concretely and vividly we express the interaction of things the better the poetry ... We cannot exhibit the wealth of nature by mere sum-mation, by piling of sentences ... Poetic thought works by suggestion, crowding maximum meaning into the single phrase, pregnant, charged and luminous from within ...
> There must be no clichés, set phrases, stereotyped 'journalese'.[12]

If every word is important and powerful, then it is well worth preparing and editing what we write and say with great care, for while preaching is different from poetry in many ways, and while many sermons may take longer to perform than poems, both preachers and poets need to measure every word and every phrase.

Words can be explosive, and on many occasions, using fewer words may be even more powerful. Fewer words create more spaces for people's imaginations to kick in, allowing them to fill in those blanks with meaning and faith. For example, at one point in a sermon on the cry of dereliction in Mark 15, I invited my hearers to ask themselves a question.

> I wonder what helps you when you're feeling down ... when you're feeling blue?
> Maybe different personality types find different things helpful?
> For me it's often a piece of music which
> Touches a nerve
>   Changes a mood,
>   Pours oil on troubled waters.[13]

Rather than describing in detail what 'feeling down' is like, I hoped that a few words would begin to paint pictures and create images that might tease my hearers' minds into active thought about what was going on at the cross, and encourage a greater participation in the preaching event.

If words are so important, then the preacher needs to become skilled in both shaping and delivering words he or she prays will convey God's message clearly. If words are so potent and powerful, then perhaps preachers would do well to take heed of Cicero's quip that 'Too much is more offensive than too little.'[14]

> Too many words can prevent us from hearing the Word. Indeed, words can be a symptom of our hiding from the Word. If we are to have a proper relationship with the Word, perhaps we should stop wallowing in language. Most of us, to put it rudely, need to shut up, to be silent for a while, to listen. And when we do use language, we need to use it respectfully. All too easily our religious language can regress, and become merely little puffs of breath, empty sounds.[15]

Painting life-like portraits

> One underappreciated aspect of Spurgeon's preaching is his use of the five senses to create an experience for his listeners … Spurgeon understood that preachers have it in their power to help the listener experience the presence of God through the way they use their words. God gives his ministers a brush, and shows them how to use it in painting life-like portraits, and thus the sinner hears the special call.[16]

C. H. Spurgeon operated in a very different historical era from the one we inhabit, but he clearly understood the value of using pictorial, sensory language to appeal to his listeners. That is what I was trying to do at one point in a sermon on Mark's account of Jesus struggling to obey God in the Garden of Gethsemane (Mark 14.32–42).

In that sermon I referred to Prime Minister Gordon Brown's visit to Washington to meet with President Barack Obama. The newspapers had enjoyed speculating about what the PM's body language indicated about how nervous he may have felt. This led me to suggest that if we paid attention to the body language of Jesus in the Garden of Gethsemane, a very clear message begins to emerge.

Jesus said to them, 'I am deeply grieved, even to death; remain here, and keep awake.' And going a little farther, he threw himself on the ground and prayed that, if it were possible, the hour might pass from him. He said, 'Abba, Father, for you all things are possible; remove this cup from me ...'

Mark 14.34–36

- Can you **see** the anxiety etched on Jesus' face?
- Can you **feel** the terror throbbing in his veins as he throws himself on the ground and pleads for another way?
- Can you **hear** the fear in his voice as he cries out '*Abba, Father, for you all things are possible; remove this cup from me*'?

There's a real life and death struggle going on here. As Jesus advances towards Jerusalem the reality of his suffering and death comes home to him in an overwhelming way. And it's not just the pain of dying a brutal death that every fibre of his being reacts against. There's also the sense that he's the suffering servant of God who's taking upon his own shoulders the sins and burdens of a broken world.[17]

By using the verbs, 'see', 'feel' and 'hear' I was hoping to appeal to people's senses in a way that would help them identify more deeply with the struggle the incarnate Son of God experienced in Gethsemane. The sermon developed a clear argument about the significance of that key episode in the Gospel drama, but it was also deliberately seeking to appeal to people's emotions and imaginations as well as to their intellects.

PAUSE FOR THOUGHT

God gives his ministers a brush, and shows them how to use it in painting life-like portraits, and thus the sinner hears the special call.

C. H. Spurgeon

The following exercises invite you to paint some word pictures that would appeal to people's emotions and imaginations.

Using sensory language, paint a portrait of what Jesus was experiencing during the temptations in the wilderness. (Luke 4.1–13)

Using sensory language, paint a picture of what Peter might have been feeling in the courtyard of the high priest's house when the servant girl stared at him and said, 'This man was also with him.' (Luke 22.54–62)

Using sensory language, paint a picture of what Mary may have been feeling when she said to Jesus: 'Lord if you had been here my brother would not have died.' (John 11.32)

Preaching in the lyrical voice

An interesting parallel to the idea of portraying the preacher as *poet* can be found in the recent work of Kate Bruce, who encourages 'preaching in the lyrical voice', an approach that involves the imaginative use of language.

Preaching in the lyrical voice is marked by a desire to grasp the disclosure of the gospel imaginatively and communicate that by drawing from the craft of poetic expression ... At the heart of lyrical preaching is the concern to construct sermons that enable people to 'see' through their ears. This is at the heart of all good radio speech and is essential to effective preaching ... Lyrical preaching is not a version of the sermon for high days and holidays. The preacher needs to employ poetic insight and learn from the craft of poetic expression in the everyday, so that sermons, while not poems in themselves, have features of the lyrical about them. Such preaching seeks to be dramatic, artistic, invitational, tensive, prophetic and poetic.[18]

A matter of life and death?

Clearly there are things preachers can helpfully learn from poets about the power of language. In addition, it is also relevant to note how many poets deal with life-and-death issues, for there is something in good poetry that opens the windows of our imagination in such a way that we can catch a glimpse of things that are of vital importance.

In a similar way there is a strong case for saying that the preacher as *poet* is someone who needs to address life-and-death issues in their sermons. This challenging truth was crisply expressed by R. E. C. Browne, who once argued that: 'Great preaching like great poetry, deals with love and death, with life and birth, with hate and treachery, in such a way that something significant is said about the tragic aspect of human life.'[19]

In one way or another, each and every one of us has to come to terms with this 'tragic aspect of human life', and if preaching does not openly and realistically deal with that 'tragic aspect', then people on the receiving end of our sermons will quickly begin to feel short-changed.

Seeing the connections

The contemporary Irish poet Micheal O'Siadhail relates how a fellow poet, Richard Murphy, once told him that 'The word "poet" in Sri Lanka means "the one who sees the connections between things" and that he has since been told that this is also true in Hindi.'[20]

The idea of 'the one who sees the connections between things' is a very suggestive image, not only for the work of the poet but also for the preacher's task. It ties up creatively with the claim referred to in Chapter 1 by the Sri Lankan theologian Vinoth Ramachandra that: 'Theology is the enterprise of relating all human knowledge, as well as all our everyday activities, to God's self-disclosure in Christ.'[21]

It is surely the case that preaching is intended to be a form of practical theology that seeks to explore the connections between all human knowledge, our everyday activities and God's self-disclosure in Christ. Perhaps it is appropriate to say that the preacher is called by God to help people 'see the connections between things', in the sense of helping people recognize the God who is intimately connected to every aspect of life.

PAUSE FOR THOUGHT

Think of the most recent sermon you preached or listened to.

- To what extent did that sermon shed the light of the gospel on the 'tragic aspect of human life'?
- To what extent did that sermon explore the connections between our everyday activities and God's self-disclosure in Christ?
- In what ways might your next sermon explore those connections more adequately?

In thinking about the preacher as poet, this chapter has sought to invite reflection on the value for preaching of using images and word pictures that can help spark people's interest and capture their imagination.

The day of the poorly conceived, ill-prepared, dull, disconnected, boring, irrelevant, authoritarian, yawn-inducing, patronizing, pontificating, pointless and badly delivered sermon is *most emphatically over*.

However, I want to go in to bat for the enduring power of the sermon. Imaginatively conceived and delivered, guided by the revelatory impulse of God, the sermon has the potential to move and inspire people; in short, it can ignite the heart.[22]

Further reading

Some of the ideas explored in this chapter build on my article, 'The Preacher as Poet', *Ministry Today* 41 (2007), pp. 29–38. The full article can be accessed from the *Ministry Today* website: www.ministrytoday.org.uk/magazine/issues/41/286.

R. E. C. Browne, *The Ministry of the Word* (London: SCM Press, 1958); see ch. 2, 'Preacher and Poet – An Analogy'.

Kate Bruce, *Igniting the Heart: Preaching and Imagination* (London: SCM Press, 2015); see esp. ch. 3, 'Preaching in the Lyrical Voice'.

Walter Brueggemann, *Finally Comes The Poet: Daring Speech for Proclamation* (Minneapolis, MN: Fortress Press, 1989).

David Day, *Embodying the Word: A Preacher's Guide* (London: SPCK, 2005); see esp. ch. 7, 'Telling it Slant'.

Jolyon P. Mitchell, *Visually Speaking: Radio and the Renaissance of Preaching* (Edinburgh: T. & T. Clark, 1999).

Bonny Thurston, 'Words and the Word: Reflections on Scripture, Prayer and Poetry', *The Way* 44:2 (April 2005), pp. 7–20.

Notes

1 David J. Schlafer, *Surviving the Sermon: A Guide to Preaching for Those Who Have to Listen* (Cambridge, MA: Cowley, 1992), p. 63.

2 Schlafer, *Surviving the Sermon*, p. 65.

3 Schlafer, *Surviving the Sermon*, p. 65.

4 David J. Schlafer, *Your Way with God's Word: Discovering Your Distinctive Preaching Voice* (Cambridge, MA: Cowley, 1995), pp. 57–74.

5 Sermon preached at Moriah Baptist Church, Risca on 16 September 2012.

6 Charles B. Cousar, *Galatians* (Atlanta, GA: John Knox Press, 1982), p. 83.

7 Richard B. Hays, 'The Letter to Galatians', in Leander E. Keck (ed.), *The New Interpreter's Bible, Vol. 11* (Nashville, TN: Abingdon Press, 2000), pp. 278–9.

8 Sermon preached by the Revd Susan A. Stevenson at Chatsworth Baptist Church, West Norwood.

9 C. H. Dodd, *The Parables of the Kingdom* (London: Nisbet, 1935), p. 16.

10 Jolyon P. Mitchell, *Visually Speaking: Radio and the Renaissance of Preaching* (Edinburgh: T. & T. Clark, 1999), p. 220.

11 Imperial War Museum images at www.iwmprints.org.uk/search/keywords/Careless%20Talk.

12 Ezra Pound, cited in R. E. C. Browne, *The Ministry of the Word* (London: SCM Press, 1958), p. 24.

13 Peter K. Stevenson and Stephen I. Wright, *Preaching the Atonement* (London: T. & T. Clark, 2005), p. 64.

14 Cicero, *Orator*, xx.70.

15 Bonny Thurston, 'Words and the Word: Reflections on Scripture, Prayer and Poetry', *The Way* 44:2 (April 2005), p. 19.

16 Kenton C. Anderson, *Choosing to Preach: A Comprehensive Introduction to Sermon Options and Structures* (Grand Rapids, MI: Zondervan, 2006), pp. 123–4.

17 Stevenson and Wright, *Preaching the Incarnation*, (Louisville, KY: Westminster John Knox Press, 2010), p. 97.

18 Kate Bruce, *Igniting the Heart: Preaching and the Imagination* (London: SCM Press, 2015), p. 57.

19 Browne, *Ministry of the Word*, pp. 77–8.

20 Micheal O'Siadhail, *Say but the Word: Poetry as Vision and Voice* (Dublin: Hinds Publishing, 2015), p. 131.

21 Howard Peskett and Vinoth Ramachandra, *The Message of Mission* (Leicester: InterVarsity Press, 2003), pp. 22–3.

22 Bruce, *Igniting the Heart*, p. xiii.

Part 4

Preaching and Performance

9

First Steps on the Preaching Journey

For a video introduction to Chapter 9 visit studyguidepreaching. hymnsam.co.uk

Sitting at the traffic lights I was feeling on edge. Responding to a couple of pastoral emergencies had meant that the usually quiet days between Christmas and New Year had suddenly become demanding and tiring. The first Sunday of the New Year was fast approaching and I wondered where I'd find the space and time to prepare a sermon. Waiting for the lights to turn green I decided that whatever happened, I needed to trust God and make time for the family over the next few days. It was at that point something unusual happened: God reminded me of a biblical text, and I was 'gifted' with a clear outline for a sermon on that passage. On that occasion the journey from text to sermon was unexpectedly easy and rapid, and I remember that experience so clearly because it was so unusual.

For me the process of discovering and designing a sermon is usually a much longer and more tortuous affair. The stage in the preaching journey I find most difficult is the point at which I need to start actually writing the sermon. As an avid reader I'd much prefer to go on reading and researching than forcing myself to sit down and concentrate on the hard work involved in converting all sorts of ideas into a coherent presentation.

Preaching a sermon is relatively easy. Preparing one worth preaching is what is difficult.[1]

The working definition of preaching that undergirds this Studyguide suggests it is a process that involves:

> Discovering the word of the Lord from the Bible, for this group of people, at this particular time, and then delivering that word in the power of the Spirit, in ways that people can understand, so that they can respond in worship and service.

On the assumption that we have prayerfully listened to the biblical text and have discovered a message from God that is worth preaching, the next stage of the preaching journey is to design the sermon. Chapters 5 to 8 have suggested some of the templates we might use, so having gained some sense of the content and shape of the sermon, what happens next? What are the next practical steps in this preaching journey?

Before thinking about some of those steps it is important to say that the process of preparing a sermon is not a mechanical one that must always follow a certain pattern. Yes, there are helpful stages to work through, but it is not like following the instructions for constructing flat-pack furniture, where it is absolutely vital things are done in the correct sequence. With our different personality types and various learning styles, there is no one-size-fits-all approach. So it is important to develop a method of preparing sermons that fits comfortably with the person God has created us to be. Bearing all of that in mind, this chapter suggests some of the practical steps worth building into our thinking about the preaching journey.

A choice to make

At the outset there are choices to be made about whether you will write a full script for your sermon or preach from a set of notes. In certain church circles, glamour attaches to preaching without notes, but in the early stages of your preaching journey it is much wiser to use a full script or detailed sermon notes.

One way of designing sermons, described in Chapter 6, uses a storyboard chart to help plan sermons made up of episodes or 'moves'. Using that kind of chart can be a helpful way of thinking through the various stages of your sermon's development. If the storyboard is laid out clearly on one sheet of paper, and you feel comfortable with the material it represents, it is possible to preach from that storyboard, using it to remind you of the things you want to say. Sometimes I have found this convenient and helpful.

However, on most occasions I find it more helpful to build on that storyboard by writing out the script of my sermon in full. For many years that meant putting pen to paper but nowadays I do virtually all my work for sermons on the computer.

Now I readily admit that the process of writing out a sermon script in full can be a time-consuming business. Surely, some will say, that is not a good use of our limited time. One of the reasons I find it helpful, however, is that the process of writing out a sermon in full helps me think things through and impose some sort of coherent order on the jumble of materials I have gathered. At the same time, my experience is that the task of writing the sermon script is often a very creative process, for as I write, I find new ideas and associations popping into my mind as the sermon grows and develops a life of its own.

Sometimes the challenge lies in knowing what material can safely be left out, so that the congregation don't suffer information overload. I find it helpful to remind myself that I am not trying to give a lecture covering every jot and tittle of what this particular Bible passage contains. Seeking to discern what may be *the word of the Lord from the Bible, for this group of people, at this particular time* gives me room to select what is needed and to leave the rest for other occasions.

Having produced a full script, you then need to decide whether to preach from that script, create a set of notes summing up the heart of the sermon or make use of a storyboard chart and rely on those prompts to guide you through.

PAUSE FOR THOUGHT

Using a full script or preaching from notes?

- Which of those approaches do you feel most comfortable with?
- What are the strengths and weaknesses of the approach you have chosen?
- How might those weaknesses be overcome?

Mind your language

Prior to ordination I had spent several years at theological college writing essays on a regular basis. For an academic audience there are clear expectations that essays will employ a careful, precise style of writing that adheres to clear grammatical rules and conventions.

With that in mind, at this point there is need for a very important disclaimer! Advocating the value of writing a full sermon script does not mean encouraging would-be preachers to prepare cool, calm and collected academic essays that are then dumped on unsuspecting congregations.

In the early years of ministry I had the opportunity, as I mentioned earlier, to dabble in religious broadcasting on a local radio station. The introductory training in broadcasting was helpful to my preaching because it alerted me to the need to use the visual, pictorial language explored in Chapter 8. In contrast to my college essays, it was clear that sermons required a much more conversational style of writing. In terms of preaching, what is needed is an *oral script*, something consciously written for the ear rather than designed for the eye, and which can be read slowly and carefully.

Such an oral script does not ignore the rules of grammar but it interprets them in a more conversational way. Whereas in an essay I would avoid using contractions such as 'wouldn't' and 'didn't', when it comes to everyday conversation and communication those words are entirely appropriate. In a similar way, study-skills guides advise students to avoid starting sentences with 'and' and 'but'. However, that is clearly the way we speak to one another, so that is the style of speaking and writing I employ when preparing my oral sermon scripts. The *oral script* I prepare tries to reflect my natural way of speaking rather than a formal style of writing.

For your eyes only

It is worth remembering that your sermon script is *for your eyes only*. So if you want to use abbreviations or symbols that only make sense to you, that is fine. For example, you may like to put in some arrows or signs, or highlight some sentences, as visual reminders to pause at certain points or stress particular phrases. You are not writing an article for public consumption in a magazine or an academic journal but preparing an *oral script* you alone will be reading.

Your completed *oral script* needs to be something you can see clearly and easily. Printer cartridges are expensive and it is tempting to compress things on to a small number of pages to save space and money. This is an understandable temptation that must be resisted!

If your sermon notes are printed on paper, it is essential to use a large enough font so that you can read them comfortably at a glance when you are standing at the lectern. Making it visible probably also means leaving enough space between chunks of material on the page. If you are preaching from a Tablet computer, then again it is important to make sure the type on the screen is easily visible.

Testing for sound

One way of checking if you are succeeding in writing an *oral script* is to speak it out as you are writing it. Speak aloud the phrases and sentences you have written to hear whether or not they fit together in a natural way. If you stumble over various phrases in your script, that is usually a sign that your sentences are overcomplicated. To avoid getting tongue-tied you will need to rewrite that bit of your *oral script* in a simpler way so that the message comes across more naturally.

PAUSE FOR THOUGHT

Review the script or notes you produced for a recent sermon.

- Is it genuinely an *oral script* or is it more like an academic essay?
- To what extent does it include Christian jargon?
- In what ways do you think parts of the sermon could be rewritten to reflect your normal style of speaking?

Getting started

Some years ago, researchers polled a list of 'top speakers'. One of the questions was: Which part of a speech was the most fixed – written out, and all but memorized? Answer: the introduction. The answer may surprise us because introductions sometimes seem quite improvisational, an informal sparring with an audience. Nevertheless, the answer makes sense. Introductions give focus to sermons. Introductions establish shared purpose between a speaker and an audience. Introductions command attention. So the introduction to a sermon must be designed with great care.[2]

There is no one perfect way to start a sermon. Bearing in mind the wide variety of personality types and learning styles found in the average congregation, it is not easy to devise sermon introductions that will instantly connect with everyone. The diversity within our congregations might suggest that it would be helpful to vary the styles of introductions we use from time to time. In that way, over a period of time we shall be better able to connect with a broader range of people.

It is certainly not necessary to start every sermon with a joke, in an attempt to break the ice and build up rapport. Unless you are destined to become a stand-up comic, producing funny stories every week is not the best use of your time. Whether it is the best way of introducing a sermon is debatable anyway, for the danger is that people will remember the story but forget what the sermon was meant to be about. The more serious reflection here is that preachers do not need to do ever more zany things week by week, just to catch the congregation's attention. At the start of a sermon, congregations generally are already paying attention, so the challenge is not to grab attention but hold on to it. For that to happen, the introduction, not surprisingly, must find some way of introducing people to what is coming.

For the sermons held together by *images*, which were mentioned in Chapter 8, the introduction simply consisted of painting the picture of the building site or of the river that was functioning as the *image* holding the sermon together.

In a sermon exploring some 'trouble in the text', the introduction may simply consist of disturbing our listeners' equilibrium by drawing attention to the problem in the text the sermon will go on to explore. For example, on the Seventh

Sunday in Epiphany in Year A of the Revised Common Lectionary, preachers are invited to work with a juicy extract from the Sermon on the Mount in which Jesus issues the command, 'Love your enemies' (Matthew 5.38–48).

There is plenty of trouble in this text, not so much in knowing what it means but in putting it into daily practice. Across the Christian centuries various attempts have been made to soften this 'utopian demand' and ask 'whether loving enemies is not asking too much of a person'.[3]

To love one's enemies is, then, to treat them as God treats those who have rebelled against him. Thus the children, the disciples, should imitate their heavenly Father ...

The final, climactic antithesis turns to the great love commandment of the OT. Jesus, interpreting the law in the light of the dawning kingdom, extends the application of that commandment so as to include even one's enemies. The love he describes, of course, is not an emotion ... but volitional acts for the benefit and well-being of others, even those we may dislike. In this love that knows no boundaries, the disciples are to reflect the generosity of God, who sends blessing upon both the righteous and the unrighteous and who has brought the kingdom to the unworthy.[4]

PAUSE FOR THOUGHT

- Read Matthew 5.38–48.
- Read the following four attempts at an introduction to a sermon that will wrestle with some of the questions confronting us in this passage.
- When you have read through all four, reflect on which 'works' best for you.
- Then spend time writing your own introduction to a sermon on this passage.

Introduction 1

Now I don't want to frighten you … but I've got to alert you to the fact that something explosive was smuggled into church this morning.

It was actually smuggled into church this morning – in between the pages of the Bible.

And you may've noticed that explosive idea as Daphne read those words from the Sermon on the Mount where Jesus says, 'Love your enemies' …

Introduction 2

'We'll be tough on crime and make sure that going to prison isn't like going to a holiday camp.'

In the run-up to every election it seems that politicians are queuing up to persuade us that they've got the best policies for dealing with crime.

Judged by what most people think, I don't think Jesus would win too many votes in an election, because in Jesus' manifesto for the kingdom of God, which we know as the Sermon on the Mount, he states that we must 'love our enemies' …

Introduction 3

What do you think is the most difficult part of Christianity?

- Is it the doctrine of the Trinity?
- Is it trying to work out how Jesus fed 5,000 people with a handful of bread rolls and a few fish?
- Or might the most difficult thing about Christianity be that Jesus actually commands us to love our enemies?

Introduction 4

> When I got the email, I can tell you it made me feel so angry. My blood began to boil because this man had plainly misunderstood what I was trying to do and was jumping to all sorts of wrong conclusions.
>
> I could feel my heart begin to beat faster and faster and I started to write a reply that would show him, in no uncertain terms, why he'd got things wrong.
>
> Now, strangely enough it was just at that point that the phone rang and a friend was on the line; so I told him about the email and about the reply I was about to send.
>
> And he said, 'Peter, don't send that message. Wait. Sleep on it, and see how you feel in the morning.'
>
> And of course he was right. For he'd learnt from Jesus that there's a better way to deal with problems, that the way forward involves loving our enemies.

Accumulating thought

In offering guidance about oral composition, or 'writing for the ear',[5] Paul Scott Wilson affirms the value of a process whereby preachers 'accumulate thought'. By this he means allowing:

> some material to be simply accumulated, rather than analysed, sorted and subordinated … Thus to establish that people today are afraid, one need not turn the sermon into a research paper; rather, one can accumulate a few quick simple situations from the news media or elsewhere to make it concrete.[6]

> A young mother comes home with her preschool child, closes the door, turns the lock, pushes the dead-bolt and sets the chain; secure at last. A man in mid-forties with a family and mortgage eases off on the gas pedal of his pickup as the factory comes into view, and he wonders, 'Will this be the day I get my notice?' A new resident in the home sees the sunlit newspaper in the lounge lying open at the obituaries page and picks it up fearfully. We all live in fear of one thing or another.[7]

The way this works is that it is the combined impact of the series of short pen pictures that communicates the message. Now Paul Scott Wilson is not necessarily suggesting that this is a strategy for sermon introductions, but my experience suggests that effective introductions can also employ this kind of approach.

In Chapter 4, I referred to a sermon on John 3 about Jesus and Nicodemus. On that occasion I introduced the sermon with a series of short scenarios, drawn from recent news stories, that brought to mind some of the difficulties we see in the world today. At the end of each of those scenarios I added the phrase, '*it's not always easy to see signs of the kingdom of God*'.

And then when we take the time to look in the mirror and reflect on our own lives – with all of their ups and downs – and when we think of the people we are and the people we'd like to be – *it's not always easy to see signs of the kingdom of God*.

- We live in a world where it seems that might is right.
- We live in a world where bad things happen to good people.
- We live in a world where the rich get richer and the poor get poorer.

And in this broken, hurting, unjust world – *it's not always easy to see signs of the kingdom of God*.

Having highlighted this problem, I then went on to suggest that if we had the aid of a top notch theologian, someone like Nicodemus perhaps, maybe then we might be able to 'see' the kingdom of God and discern where God is at work in the world. However, as mentioned in Chapter 4, the comment about Nicodemus visiting Jesus in the dark of night (John 3.2) seems to imply that even the noble and distinguished Nicodemus is still very much in the dark when it comes to 'seeing' the kingdom of God.

PAUSE FOR THOUGHT

Accumulating thought exercise

Write a series of three or four short snapshots or situations that communicate one of the following topics:

- The kinds of people Jesus calls us to love.
- People today have forgotten God.
- People today are looking for love.
- People today are without hope.
- The world is not as God planned.

Accumulating thought and introductions

Write a series of three or four short snapshots or situations that could serve as an introduction to your next sermon.

Writing introductions

Introductions can be as varied as the sermons they introduce and the preachers who devise them ...

- *First*, the best introductions are usually brief ...
- *Second*, good introductions are usually arresting ... They say in effect 'Here is something you want to listen to, something you will be glad you heard ...'
- *Third*, good introductions are often memorable ... they leave us with an image or an idea that will later help us to recall the entire sermon ...
- *Finally ... a good introduction is conductive ...* It leads people into the sermon. It does not pose an image or an idea for its own sake, then leave it dangling at the start of the sermon ...[8]

PAUSE FOR THOUGHT

- Think of the congregation you belong to.
- How would you describe the make-up of the congregation?
- How many different categories, or labels, would you need to describe the different kinds of people in the congregation?
- Which of those groups of people are you most like?
- With whom in the congregation do you most naturally identify?
- Think of one group of people in your congregation who are different from you, and write an introduction for your next sermon that you think might appeal to them.
- You might also go on to try to write a couple of other kinds of introduction that might appeal to different groups in your congregation.

Setting up signposts

Before moving on to think about ways we can bring sermons to a positive conclusion, it is worth pausing to notice the importance of constructing some verbal signposts along the way. These 'transitions' or 'connectors' can help hearers have an idea of where they are in the developing flow of the sermon.

At a very basic level this might involve briefly summing up the previous stages of the sermon, thus alerting people that a new phase is about to begin. So a sermon on the prophet's vision in Isaiah 6 might simply introduce the third and final stage of the sermon journey by saying: 'In this passage we're given a vision first of the *God who reigns*, and also of the *God who forgives*, and here we can also catch a glimpse of the *God who calls and sends*.'

Thinking back to the idea, explored in Chapter 6, of episodic sermons that progress through a series of 'moves', the 'connector' might simply involve pausing and saying nothing for a few moments. In that quiet space the preacher is giving the congregation time to catch their breath mentally and emotionally, in order to get ready for the next sequence of 'slides' that will constitute the next of the sermon's 'moves'.

> Traditionally these small in-between pieces of sermon have been called 'transitions', since they mark the points of transfer from one section to the next. Many preachers mistakenly do not consider them to be very important, and it is common for transitions to be dull and mechanical insertions into the sermon flow ... When we view this transitional material from a communicational point of view, however, it becomes clear that these connectors (as we will call them) between the segments of the sermon are absolutely vital to the sermon's clarity, vitality and movement.[9]

One of the values of developing an *oral script* for sermons is that it gives us a chance to think seriously about those connecting sections. If I choose to preach from notes instead of a script, these transitional passages are well worth including in my notes, so that if in preaching I feel prompted to depart from the script in some way, then a glance at some of those connecting passages can help me see the points at which I can comfortably re-join the flow of the sermon.

I've started so I'll finish ...

> There's an old joke about how preachers end a sermon. A child asked her father, 'Daddy, what does it mean when the preacher says, "And finally ..."?'
> And the father says, 'It doesn't mean a thing.'[10]

For the first few years of Christian ministry I benefitted greatly from working alongside a very gifted pastor and preacher.[11] I am sure that in many ways my approach to preaching was shaped very positively by that early experience of such a good preaching mentor.

In those early months of ministry, the transition from preaching occasionally to producing sermons on a regular basis took some getting used to. I remember clearly the evening when my senior minister turned to me and said: 'One day I must teach you how to end a sermon'!

Over the years since then I have been doing my best to try to learn various ways of ending my sermons. The following examples are not the only ways to conclude sermons but they are some I have often found helpful.

Ending where it started

Sometimes it is helpful to finish the sermon by returning to the text or the theme outlined at the beginning. For example, the sermon outline in Chapter 7, based on James 1.1–8, draws attention at the outset to the text itself: 'My brothers and sisters, whenever you face trials of any kind, consider it nothing but joy.' Having explored some possible problems associated with that text if it is taken out of its biblical context, the sermon concludes by revisiting and affirming the text. In this kind of sermon, it is the text itself that acts as a set of bookends, standing at both ends and helping to hold it together.

> It is possible even in difficult situations to *consider it nothing but joy* in the sense that you know that whatever may happen, the good news is that God is with you. He will always be with you and he promises never to leave you or forsake you. And it's only because we know that kind of God that we can dare to say with James, *'My brothers and sisters, whenever you face trials of any kind, consider it nothing but joy.'*

Ending with a summary of the message

Preaching on Isaiah 6 on one occasion, I brought the sermon to a simple conclusion by offering a brief summary of the message.

> At a time of national uncertainty Isaiah was given this amazing vision of the God who reigns; who forgives; and who calls and sends.
>
> We have seen the glory of God shining the face of Jesus Christ, and because of him we have even more reason to believe that:
>
> - God reigns – now and for ever;
> - God forgives – we can be forgiven;
> - God calls and sends people like us to make Christ known.

Concluding with an invitation to faith and commitment

The theme for a broadcast service was 'Faith in God's plan'.[12] On that occasion the sermon was broken up into several bite-sized chunks. The final section concluded with a simple invitation to have faith in the Christ who calls people to follow him. My final sentence conveyed that invitation by simply quoting the first line of the hymn that followed immediately afterwards.

Faith means cooperating with the Holy Spirit, and that process takes place as we run the race of faith with our eyes fixed on Jesus, the pioneer and perfecter of faith (Hebrews 12.1–3).

And today this living Jesus invites us to have faith in God's good purposes and he says to you and to me, '*Will you come and follow me?*'

Ending by inviting people to ask themselves some questions

Chapter 7 also includes a sermon outline based on Genesis 12.1–9. It suggests ending the sermon by leaving a couple of questions for people to answer for themselves.

So as we think about the ways God called Abram to step out in faith, it raises questions each one of us has to answer for ourselves:

- What steps into the unknown is God calling me to take?
- In what ways is the living God calling you and me to play a part in his mission to this needy world?

If the sermon ends on that kind of note, it is appropriate and helpful to create some space in the service for a time of silent, prayerful response, rather than hastily rushing on to invite people to stay for coffee after the service.

Concluding by inviting people to share in Communion

One of my favourite passages in the Bible is the episode in Luke 24.13–35, which tells of the risen Christ meeting with those two disheartened disciples on the road to Emmaus. After this encounter the couple declare in wonder, 'Were not our hearts burning within us while he was talking to us on the road, while he was opening the scriptures to us?' Later they tried to explain to their puzzled companions how Jesus 'had been made known to them in the breaking of the bread'.

It is a great privilege to preach on such a passage, which affirms how the living Christ reveals himself to people, both through the Scriptures and through the breaking of the bread. Building on that narrative, there are good grounds for affirming that still today the risen Christ meets with his worshipping people both as God's word is proclaimed, and as we share in bread and wine together.

With that in mind I really enjoy preaching in the context of a service of worship that includes a celebration of the Lord's Supper. For it seems to me that often one of the most helpful ways of concluding a sermon is to invite people to respond to God in faith by sharing in the Communion meal that follows.

For example, in the sermon considered in Chapter 8, which focused on Zechariah 4 and considered some of the challenges facing God's people as they build for God's kingdom today, I concluded by inviting people to share in the bread of life around the Lord's Table.

I'm glad that we're sharing in Communion this morning. For as we gather around the Lord's Table we have an opportunity to encounter the living Christ who is the one who can fill us with his Holy Spirit. For as one writer puts it, at Communion: *'The bread and the wine, taken in small amounts reveal the presence of a love greater than our hearts can contain and our minds can understand.'*[13]

- At Communion we come to encounter someone who is greater than our hearts can contain – greater than our minds can understand;
- At Communion we come to encounter the living Christ, through whom all things were made;
- At Communion we come to encounter the living Christ who fills us afresh with his Spirit.

As we prepare for this new phase of life and work here in this church, we're well aware that there are many challenges facing this fellowship and facing every church in Wales at this time. But we face the future with hope and confidence because we know that it is 'not by might nor by power but by God's Spirit' that we shall be empowered to tackle the mission tasks we're called to do.

And as we prepare for this new phase of life and work here in this congregation, we come to this Table – to take bread and wine – and to encounter the living Christ who desires to renew us and restore us, so that together we can live a new life following the commandments of God.

PAUSE FOR THOUGHT

Reflect on a recent sermon you have heard or that you have preached.

- In what way did that sermon conclude?
- How effective was that way of ending the sermon?
- In what ways do you think the ending of that sermon could be improved?
- Experiment with writing other possible conclusions for that sermon.

Editing your oral script

This chapter has suggested that one of the early steps on the preaching journey is to prepare an *oral script* for the sermon. In creating such a script, it is important to pay attention to beginnings, connections and endings. As Jolyon Mitchell helpfully explains, having created that oral script, it is vital also to make time for checking and editing it.

One way of communicating effectively is to edit the sermon script or outline so that it allows variations in pace, pitch, tone, images and the texture of the presentation. The editing process can be time-consuming and painful, but it invariably leads to a vastly more effective result. Editing should not be so severe, however, that the apparently spontaneous and oral quality of the sermon is lost. Think of it not as a piece of writing, but as a piece of oral communication.[14]

Further reading

Fred B. Craddock, *Craddock on the Craft of Preaching* (St. Louis, MO: Chalice Press, 2011); see ch. 16, 'Thirteen Ways to End a Sermon'.

Thomas G. Long, *The Witness of Preaching*, 3rd edn (Louisville, KY: Westminster John Knox Press, 2016); see ch. 7, 'Beginnings, Connections, and Endings', as well as Appendices C and D, where Long analyses two sermons and draws attention to beginnings, connectors and endings.

Jolyon P. Mitchell, *Visually Speaking: Radio and the Renaissance of Preaching* (Edinburgh: T. & T. Clark, 1999); see esp. chs 8—10.

Thomas H. Troeger and Leonora Tubbs Tisdale, *A Sermon Workbook: Exercises in the Art and Craft of Preaching* (Nashville, TN: Abingdon Press, 2013); see esp. 'Part 2: Writing Like a Preacher'.

Paul Scott Wilson, *The Practice of Preaching*, rev. edn (Nashville, TN: Abingdon Press, 2007); see esp. ch. 10, 'Speaking for the Ear' .

Notes

1 Eugene Lowry, 'Surviving the Sermon Preparation Process', *Journal for Preachers* 24:3 (2001), p. 28.

2 David Buttrick, *Homiletic: Moves and Structures* (Philadelphia, PA: Fortress Press, 1987), p. 83.

3 Ulrich Luz, *Matthew 1—7*. Hermeneia: A Critical and Historical Commentary on the Bible, rev. edn (Minneapolis, MN, Fortress Press, 2007), p. 291.

4 Donald A. Hagner, *Matthew 1—13*. Word Biblical Commentary, Vol. 33a (Dallas, TX: Word, 1998), p. 136.

5 Paul Scott Wilson, *The Practice of Preaching*, rev. edn (Nashville, TN: Abingdon Press, 2007), pp. 187–207.

6 Wilson, *Practice of Preaching*, p. 198.

7 Wilson, *Practice of Preaching*, p. 198.

8 John Killinger, *Fundamentals of Preaching* (London: SCM Press, 1985), pp. 81–4.

9 Thomas G. Long, *The Witness of Preaching*, 3rd edn (Louisville, KY: Westminster John Knox Press, 2016), p. 183.

10 Fred B. Craddock, *Craddock on the Craft of Preaching* (St. Louis, MO: Chalice Press, 2011), p. 157.

11 Revd Peter Ledger in Bedford.

12 *Sunday Worship*, BBC Radio 4, Sunday 6 September 2015.

13 Henri Nouwen, 'Foreword', in *Rule for a New Brother* (London: Darton, Longman & Todd, 1989), p. xi.

14 Jolyon P. Mitchell, *Visually Speaking: Radio and the Renaissance of Preaching* (Edinburgh: T. & T. Clark, 1999), pp. 232–3.

10

Performing the Sermon

For a video introduction to Chapter 10 visit studyguidepreaching. hymnsam.co.uk

Listening to children practising scales on a violin can, at times, be a less than enjoyable experience. As time progresses the benefits of regular practice start to become apparent. The regular rhythm of practice enables key skills to be developed and internalized, with the result that young musicians become able to play more interesting pieces of music. Given time and further practice, that can lead to the enriching experience of playing with an orchestra and provide a healthy basis for musical spontaneity and improvisation.

To some extent the previous chapters in this Studyguide function as some of the 'scales' would-be preachers need to practise and master. With regular use, these hermeneutical and homiletical habits of the preaching life will become more and more instinctive, and an individual preaching style will begin to emerge.

For me preaching a sermon is like … composing a symphony. You are inspired to put black dots on staves on a page – join them together, set into movements, label parts for instruments and voices, add a key signature, indicate levels of speed and expression. A finished manuscript is copied and arranged on the music stands, but you only have an inkling in your mind's eye of how it might sound.

You step on to the rostrum, the audience quietens in anticipation, the orchestra sits poised and attentive, you raise the baton and with that first beat out of the silence those black dots come to life; from the page a glorious sound rises, filling space and time; heard by the ear, touching the heart and stirring the soul. Those black dots have become God's Symphony.[1]

The previous chapter suggested that one of the habits of the preaching life worth cultivating is the skill of writing an *oral script*. In addition to concerns about the time involved in producing such a script, some may also wonder if there is a danger of producing preachers who are so tied to reading their scripts that their preaching becomes a lifeless affair devoid of spontaneity.

It is tempting to wonder to what extent our image of spontaneous speech is derived from watching skilful TV presenters, who look us straight in the eye and speak *apparently* without notes. The reality is, of course, that this is a well-rehearsed and practised form of structured spontaneity, for presenters are often reading a prepared and carefully timed script from the autocue or teleprompt machine fixed to the camera they are looking at. There is a high degree of skill involved as they use their hearts and hands and voices to perform their script in such a way that it comes across in a natural and spontaneous manner. So it is a false antithesis to see script and structure as the opposite of spontaneity and clear communication.

In thinking about different ways of understanding the work of preaching, Kate Bruce examines the metaphor of 'the preacher as jazz musician'.[2] One of the attractions of this image of the preaching task is the way it highlights the value of both preparation and improvisation:

> jazz teaches us that improvisation has nothing to do with poor preparation … The preacher who has prepared well, who is familiar with the move-ment and intent of the sermon score, has the freedom to improvise in the moment, responsive to the other players in the group: the Spirit, the hearers, the Scripture and the sermon script. In this metaphor the sermon script, be it an outline or full notes, might best be seen as a musical score, reminding the preacher of the melodic line should their improvisation need disciplining by the drive and the intent of the whole piece.[3]

In a parallel way, when it comes to preaching it is important to underline that having produced an *oral script* for a sermon, the next step is not to read it to people but to bring it to life by *performing* it.

And whenever you pray, do not be like the hypocrites; for they love to stand and pray in the synagogues and at the street corners, so that they may be seen by others.

Matthew 6.5

'The word ὑποκριτής in Hellenistic Greek commonly meant 'actor', i.e., one who performs in front of others, pretending to be something he or she is not. In the NT it is used consistently in a negative sense.'[4]

To encourage preachers to *perform* a sermon does not imply that he or she is being asked to put on an act or speak with an artificial accent. Partly it is simply recognizing that preaching, as a form of public speaking, is not the same thing as having a quiet conversation with someone over a cup of coffee. While preaching clearly needs to have a personal dimension, it is also a public act that proclaims something vitally important. If effective communication is to take place, I shall need not only to project my voice but also to put my whole personality into the process of *performing* the sermon.[5]

Finding and using your voice

The key elements of using your voice in preaching are not complicated, but it is worth highlighting some strategies that can help us make our voices heard. The following exercise invites you to experiment with using your voice in performing extracts from the Bible.

PAUSE FOR THOUGHT

- Choose one of the biblical passages listed below.
- Find a place where you can read it aloud without being interrupted. This might be a room in your home or it may be in a hall or empty church.
- Read the passage aloud several times.

- Each time you read it, experiment with a different speed. See if it is helpful to place the emphasis in different parts of the reading. Does a change of stress on a particular phrase, or a pause between sections of the reading, help it come across more clearly?
- Read the same passage again from another translation of the Bible. Does reading a different translation bring out any new perspectives on the text?
- Repeat the exercise using the other biblical texts.
- You may find it helpful to get someone to listen to you reading and ask them for some feedback.

Performing biblical texts	
In your reading you might try to express something of the dramatic way the storm is described. How can you best convey the contrast between the despair of the sailors caught up in the storm, and the calm that descends when they reach their desired haven?	Psalm 107.23–32
As you read this passage, how will you convey the disciples' fear in the midst of the storm?	Mark 4.35–41
What tone of voice will you use when Jesus says: 'Woman, what concern is that to you and to me'?	John 2.1–11
How will you express the pain in Jesus' cry of dereliction; and in contrast to this, what note will you strike when it comes to the confession of the centurion?	Mark 15.33–39
What is the best way of reading out the apostle's series of rhetorical questions here? How can you best convey the confidence of the closing verses?	Romans 8.31–39

Performing your sermon script

Having created and edited your *oral script*, it is helpful to practise *performing* it. If there is a long gap between when you prepared the sermon script and actually preaching it, you will find it helpful to re-read it to remind yourself of what you have prepared. Reading your *oral script* out quietly to yourself will help you notice any points where the language needs further editing.

In the early years of ministry I sometimes went to church early on a Sunday morning and preached the sermon to an empty church. This gave me time to revisit the material and a chance to test out the acoustics and find out what my voice sounded like in that larger setting.

Doing that meant I was able to check whether or not I could see my sermon notes clearly while standing by the lectern, and find out the best way of turning over the pages of my script without getting into an unholy muddle.

There is no one correct way of doing this. Those who feel most comfortable using a tablet computer will develop a consistent way of scrolling through their material. Preachers using sheets of paper need to find a comfortable way of moving through the pages of their script in an unobtrusive way.

I carried on with that practice for only a short time until I settled into the rhythm of preaching regularly in a new context. Clearly not everyone will be able to practise performing their sermon in an empty church or hall. Where it is possible it adds another dimension to the preparation process, because in this larger space there is scope to experiment with the process of projecting your voice as you *perform* the sermon.

Making yourself heard

> Nancy didn't go any more herself, except to funerals sometimes. She thought about resuming her old habit, ingrained since childhood, of going to morning service but then she remembered how it had depressed her for years before she gave up. So few people there, lost in the echoing place, coughing and shuffling, hardly one of them able to sing a hymn. And the vicar was pathetic, his sermons mumbled with head down, barely audible and without meaning.[6]

Having prepared a coherent sermon, it is vital to speak clearly and confidently. No matter how good the material, if people cannot hear the sermon clearly then everyone is left dissatisfied.

It is tempting to assume that if a PA system is being used, it is not necessary to speak clearly and loudly. However, it is still important to make the effort to project your voice and to speak with some energy and enthusiasm. There are various kinds of microphones and it is helpful to make friends with whichever kind you are being asked to use.

> In general, unless you are preaching to a congregation of many hundreds, the PA will be acting as *sound reinforcement*. As the name suggests, the amplified sound is used to support the sound of the unamplified voice. Thus, the amplified sound of the preacher's voice is meant to be heard in *addition* to the voice itself.
>
> Key rule 1: *Don't speak more quietly just because there is a PA system. Unless you need to make a particular point with the way your voice sounds, speak as if the system was not there.*[7]

Learning from others

In conversation with a poet who revels in giving poetry readings, I asked him: 'What can preachers learn from poets?' Around the same time, I met a stand-up comic and asked her the same question. It was interesting to discover that they both gave me the same answer: '*Eye contact* and *timing*'.

Some may wonder if working from an *oral script* or a set of notes might make it more difficult to establish good eye contact with people in the congregation. One practical way of overcoming this potential issue is to ensure that the sermon script is easily visible. If sermon notes are positioned at your eye level on the lectern it will be possible both to preach from the sermon script and to look at the congregation. The *oral script* is there to remind you of the things you want to say. Where you have woven stories and illustrations into the sermon, it is often easy to retell those stories without needing to refer to the script very much.

There is something amusing witnessing young children who are learning to tell jokes, for they often have little sense of comic timing and rush on to deliver the punchline without giving their hearers time to say: 'I don't know. Why did the chicken cross the road?'

In preaching it is important to have the confidence to pause at certain points rather than rush headlong to the end of the sermon. For example, in this extract from a sermon on the temptations of Jesus in Luke 4, it was important to insert the briefest of pauses in among a series of questions about how the second Adam would fare when faced with temptation.

'Then the devil led him up and showed him in an instant all the kingdoms of the world. And the devil said to him, "To you I will give their glory and all this authority; for it has been given over to me, and I give it to anyone I please. If you, then, will worship me, it will all be yours."'

All authority on heaven and earth will one day be in the hands of Jesus ...
But will he use the world's methods to gain the upper hand? *[pause]*
Will he seek power in the way the world seeks power? *[pause]*
Or will he overcome evil in God's way? *[pause]*
Will he overcome evil with suffering love? *[pause]*

And the good news is that Jesus comes through this test as well, for:
'Jesus answered him, "It is written, 'Worship the Lord your God, and serve only him.'"'

Variations on a theme

'Monotonous'

1 Of a sound or utterance: continuing on or repeating the same note; having little or no variation in tone, pitch, or cadence. Also, of a musical instrument: able to produce sounds at only one pitch.
2 In extended use: lacking in variety; uninteresting or tedious through continued sameness or repetitiveness; lifeless, plain, prosaic, routine.[8]

Offering feedback to people starting on their preaching journey, one of my regular comments is about the need to introduce more variety into the delivery of sermons. If the person speaks with a constant tone, pitch or cadence all the way through, then it is difficult to retain people's interest. In performing a sermon, it is important along the way to vary the pace and the volume, and the emotional intensity.

For example, in the sermon commented on in Appendix 8 there is one section that relates the story of a preacher who took a phone call from his doctor that moved him from the kingdom of the well into the kingdom of the sick. The tone in which that part of the sermon was told had to be rather different from the opening section, which mentioned watching a recent television programme.

This is another reason why it can sometimes be helpful to have a trial run at preaching sermons, in order to get in touch with those points at which it would be good to change gear, be that by slowing down or by raising your voice.

PAUSE FOR THOUGHT

- Find a way to record one of your sermons. This could mean using a video camera on a smartphone or tablet, or you may have friends happy to make a video for you.
- As you watch and listen to the recording, what do you notice?
- Can you be heard clearly?
- If a microphone was available, how well did you use it?
- Do you speak at a constant pace or is there some variety in your pace of speaking?
- Do you tend to get quieter at the end of sentences?
- To what extent is there good eye contact with the congregation?
- Can you notice any distracting mannerisms (adjusting your glasses, jingling a set of keys etc.)?
- In what ways might you improve the delivery of your sermon?

Performing a sermon using PowerPoint

This Studyguide has argued that preaching should not be evaluated primarily through an educational lens. A sermon is different from a lecture, where the communication of information may play a larger part. A sermon involves delivering a message from God rather than providing every possible bit of information about a particular biblical text. As discussed in Chapter 4, it can be helpful to use PowerPoint slides, providing they can complement and support the kind of sermon you wish to deliver. PowerPoint works in a linear, step-by-step manner. That underlying operating philosophy is probably not what is required for sermons held together not by linear logic but by some form of a *homiletical plot*. Where PowerPoint can be used to support a sermon's own inner logic, there are guidelines worth noting.

Ten Commandments for PowerPoint[9]	**Reflections on those Ten Commandments for preachers**
1 Talk to your audience, not to the screen.	If eye contact is one of the key aspects of effective person-to-person communication, it is undermined by continually looking over your shoulder to check which PowerPoint slide is on the screen. If you are preaching with PowerPoint, you will need to have a computer or monitor in front of you that you can see without turning away from the congregation. It is preferable for the preacher to be in charge of moving slides on in sync with the sermon, perhaps using a hand-held remote control or wireless presenter. Continually having to say 'Next' to the PA operator at the back interrupts the flow of the sermon.

2 Do not read your slides.	There is little benefit in simply reading verbatim all the material on the screen. Unless there are visibility problems, people will be able to read that information quickly for themselves.
3 Keep text to a minimum – think visually instead (but beware clipart).	Even for a formal lecture it is possible to put far too much material on the screen. PowerPoint can support preaching by putting a picture on the screen consonant with the message. Simply having a funny picture on the screen adds little to a sermon. Sometimes the danger is that the picture on the screen is actually in conflict with the message being proclaimed. For example, one preacher I listened to utilized a template for all his PowerPoint slides that had a picture of a snowy mountain in the background. It was a pleasant enough picture, but for a sermon on Ezekiel 47 that image conflicted with the vision that holds that biblical passage together, which is of the river of life flowing across a dry, barren desert.
4 Use a font style that is simple, large (at least 24 points) and is commonly found on all computers.	Another reason why it is important to keep text to a minimum is that it needs to be in large enough letters to be easily readable. Large print works happily for sermon headings but not for long quotations.
5 Keep the number of bullet points to 3–5 per slide.	A list of bullet points is compatible with a style of preaching that focuses on conveying a series of propositions. However, if the sermon is held together by a story or an image, a series of bullet points is going against the grain of the sermon.

6 Avoid 'exciting' animations.	While some viewers may be fascinated by text that moves around on the screen, it is likely to distract attention from the message the preacher is seeking to convey.
7 Aim to take an average of 3–5 minutes per slide.	If there is a picture on the screen that is helping to give shape to the sermon, there can be value in leaving it on view for a little longer. For example, I once put on the screen one of the famous pictures of land near Ypres laid waste by war during the First World War.[10] This remained on the screen while I talked about verses from Habakkuk 3.17–18, where the prophet declares his enduring faith in God even if the land he lives in experiences total devastation.
8 Use a small number of colours that have high contrast (e.g. yellow on blue).	At times it feels attractive to experiment with alternative colour schemes, but it is worth finding one of the classic, contrasting colour combinations that works clearly in your specific context.
9 Allow the audience time to absorb complex information (e.g. from a graph or chart).	This is less applicable in the context of preaching a sermon, but is another reminder not to overload the information on the screen at any one time.
10 Have a backup plan in case the presentation doesn't work.	This reminds me of occasions when I wish I had had a backup plan in place!

David Day sums things up in a characteristically pithy fashion. He suggests that: 'PowerPoint, like marriage, is "not to be taken in hand, unadvisedly, lightly or wantonly, to satisfy carnal lusts and appetites, like brute beasts that have no understanding." On the other hand, think carefully about a call to absolute celibacy.'[11]

Seeking feedback

It is helpful to be proactive in seeking feedback on your preaching, especially in the early stages of your preaching journey. As 'for everything there is a season and a time for every matter under heaven', there are more and less appropriate times to get feedback on your most recent sermon. Immediately after the service, when you have invested everything into performing the sermon and are feeling emotionally drained, is definitely not the best time to sit down with your friends so that they can offer you constructive criticism. It is much better to find some space during the week when everyone has had time to reflect on things, and you are also able to view them with more critical distance. One helpful resource, both for you and for those who listen, is a booklet produced by The College of Preachers entitled *What Did You Make of Your Sermon?*[12] A useful list of questions from that booklet for sermon listeners can be found in Appendix 9.

It's not rocket science …

This chapter has focused on some of the communication skills involved in *performing* a sermon. Having been on the receiving end of both good and bad examples of communication, we probably have an instinctive awareness of some of the things that aid effective communication. The homiletical skills hinted at in this chapter can be developed with regular practice, and by those who are willing to take on board regular feedback from those who listen. In the next and final chapter of this Studyguide, it will be appropriate to conclude by offering some reflections on the person behind the sermon.

Further reading

David Day, *Embodying the Word: A Preacher's Guide* (London: SPCK, 2005); see ch. 15, 'Powerful or Pointless? Preaching with PowerPoint'.

Robert May, 'Preaching Without Notes', in Ian Stackhouse and Oliver D. Crisp (eds), *Text Message: The Centrality of Scripture in Preaching* (Eugene, OR: Wipf & Stock, 2014), pp. 166–80.

Geoffrey Stevenson, 'The Act of Delivery', in Geoffrey Stevenson and Stephen Wright, *Preaching with Humanity: A Practical Guide for Today's Church* (London: Church House Publishing, 2008), pp. 82–93.

The College of Preachers, *What Did You Make of Your Sermon? Some Questions to Help You Take Stock of Your Own Preaching*.

Joseph M. Webb, *Preaching Without Notes* (Nashville, TN: Abingdon Press, 2001).

Notes

1 Revd Mark Burbridge.
2 Kate Bruce, *Igniting the Heart: Preaching and the Imagination* (London: SCM Press, 2015), pp. 131–4.
3 Bruce, *Igniting the Heart*, p. 131.
4 Donald A. Hagner, *Matthew 1—13*. Word Biblical Commentary, Vol. 33a (Dallas, TX: Word, 1998), p. 139.
5 Geoffrey Stevenson provides practical advice in the chapter 'The Act of Delivery', in Geoffrey Stevenson and Stephen Wright, *Preaching with Humanity: A Practical Guide for Today's Church* (London: Church House Publishing, 2008).
6 Margaret Forster, *How to Measure a Cow* (London: Chatto & Windus, 2016), p. 41.
7 Revd Ed Kaneen, 'The Proper Use of Microphones', lecture given at South Wales Baptist College, 2014.
8 *Oxford English Dictionary*, www.oed.com.
9 Revd Ed Kaneen. 'Making and Delivering Effective Presentations', lecture given at South Wales Baptist College, 2015.
10 See e.g. pictures of countryside near Ypres devastated by war in the Imperial War Museum Collections: www.iwm.org.uk/collections/item/object/205246381.
11 David Day, *Embodying the Word: A Preacher's Guide* (London: SPCK, 2005), p. 148.
12 See www.collegeofpreachers.co.uk.

Part 5

The Preaching Life

11

The Fully-Alive Preacher

For a video introduction to Chapter 11 visit studyguidepreaching.
hymnsam.co.uk

In 1956 the ageing John Ames starts writing a letter to his young son, reflecting on many long years of Christian ministry. It is a letter his son will eventually read when he is grown up, some time after his father's death. Among other things, in her acclaimed novel *Gilead* Marilynne Robinson paints a moving picture of the elderly minister reflecting back over his life and the vocation of preaching that has shaped it. As he reflects back on preaching 50 sermons annually for each of the last 45 years, he wonders about the value of his sermons, and of a life shaped so powerfully by the work of preaching.

> My father always preached from notes, and I wrote my sermons out word for word. There are boxes of them in the attic, a few recent years of them in stacks in the closet. I've never gone back to them to see if they were worth anything, if I actually said anything. Pretty nearly my whole life's work is in those boxes, which is an amazing thing to reflect on.[1]

As time progresses, he begins to wonder if there might be an alternative use for those old sermon notes.

> I'll just ask your mother to have those old sermons of mine burned. The deacons could arrange it. There are enough to make a good fire. I'm thinking here of hot dogs and marshmallows, something to celebrate the first snow. Of course she can set by any of them she might want to keep, but I don't want her to waste much effort on them. They mattered or they didn't and that's the end of it.[2]

In a poignant way, John Ames raises some searching questions about our preaching. At the end of the day, are our sermons and sermon notes only fit for the fire, or can they be ignited by the fire of God's Spirit to fan faith into flame?

Ultimately, of course, the preacher is not in control of the Spirit's holy fire. However, preachers take the risk of speaking to others, relying on God to take our meagre, limited human words and use them to mediate his love to others. If a prime element of the preaching life is to discover a message from above for the people of God, this underlines the spiritual dimensions of the task and reminds us of the need for a healthy spirituality.

> The sermon itself is the main thing: its matter, its aim, and the spirit in which it is brought before the people, *the sacred anointing upon the preacher*, and the divine power applying the truth to the hearer: these are infinitely more important than any details of manner.[3]

The fully-alive preacher

The title for these concluding reflections is drawn from a book by Mike Graves.[4] Alongside offering stimulating advice about the preaching process, Graves deliberately concentrates on the spirituality of the preacher. He examines what he calls 'Ten Sacraments of Renewal', suggesting that they are some of the ways God can inspire and sustain weary preachers.

At the heart of this approach is Irenaeus' vision that 'the glory of God is a human being fully alive',[5] and in a variety of ways, that is what Graves encourages preachers to become. Different personality types may find some of his practical suggestions more helpful than others. That does not in any way diminish the challenge he presents, that preachers are called to be people fully alive to God and to others; people continually seeking to be renewed spiritually.

This poses the challenging question: 'To what extent is relevant and effective preaching simply one of the by-products of that process whereby Christians are becoming human beings who are fully alive, filled and empowered by the Holy Spirit?'[6]

Life practices

In an article that begins by stating 'I never intended to preach', Barbara Shires Blaisdell writes about the weekly routine she follows to sustain a regular preaching ministry. Alongside the work she does on interpreting the Bible and preparing her sermon, she talks about a number of 'life practices' that help sustain her Christian spirituality.

> In addition to a weekly routine, there are four life practices that aid my writing when I do them, and hinder my work when I don't. I read constantly. I see a lot of movies. I get daily physical exercise. I write three pages of whatever junk is in my head and on my heart every morning as a prayer to God. In order to keep my mind stimulated enough to produce eight to ten pages of creative material every week, I need to read constantly: theology and Biblical scholarship, of course. But I also find that good novels and writing that is honest about the human condition give me insight and perspective, even if I never use them in a sermon illustration.[7]

PAUSE FOR THOUGHT

- What life practices help you develop and sustain your faith and spirituality?
- What other life practices, or spiritual disciplines, might help you sustain both your faith and your preaching?

For me preaching is like …

With a number of groups, I have invited students to complete the sentence, '*For me preaching is like …*', and some of their answers have appeared earlier in this book. The following response to that question provides a fitting conclusion to this exploration into preaching. It acknowledges the reality that preaching is a costly and painful business. But it also affirms that preaching is ultimately worthwhile, because by the grace of God, it is life-giving.

> For me preaching is like ... having a baby. The process is uncomfortable and sometimes painful; it changes your image of yourself and how the world sees you. You work hard to produce something that you will be proud of and which will make the world a better place, but ultimately you have little control over how it is received and you just have to leave it in God's hands to do with what he sees best.[8]

The enormous privilege of preaching is to be invited by God to share in this life-giving process.

Notes

1   Marilynne Robinson, *Gilead* (London: Virago, 2009), p. 21.
2   Robinson, *Gilead*, p. 280.
3   C. H. Spurgeon, *Lectures to my Students: New Edition Containing Selected Lectures from Series 1, 2 and 3* (London: Marshall, Morgan & Scott, 1954), p. 272; emphasis added.
4   Mike Graves, *The Fully Alive Preacher: Recovering from Homiletical Burnout* (Louisville, KY: Westminster John Knox Press, 2006), p. 4.
5   Irenaeus, *Adversus Haereses*, 4.XX.7.
6   Peter K. Stevenson, 'Is There Any Word from the Lord? Connecting Relevant Preaching with Effective Leadership', in John Nelson (ed.), *How to Become a Creative Church Leader* (Norwich: Canterbury Press, 2008), pp. 95–104 (103).
7   Barbara Shires Blaisdell, 'Mother to Mother: Centered in a Circle of Need', in Jana Childers (ed.), *Birthing the Sermon: Women Preachers on the Creative Process* (St. Louis, MO: Chalice Press, 2001), pp. 4–5.
8   Revd Lisa Kerry.

Appendix 1

Extract from Service Broadcast on BBC Radio Wales on Sunday 6 July 2014

Sermon Part 1 – Come to me

Bible reading: Matthew 11.25–30

At this time of the morning it's maybe a bit risky to start talking about sleep and rest – especially as most of us aren't getting as much *of it* as we need. Indeed a few months ago one research project suggested that a lack of sleep could perhaps cause a permanent loss of brain cells.[1]

Apparently the average person gets about six-and-a-half hours' sleep a night. But over the years the average amount we get has gone slowly down, which leaves some scientists wondering about the long-term impact on our health.[2]

And if that wasn't troubling enough, it turns out that our love affair with using our smartphones, laptops and tablet computers late into the evening makes matters worse, because the blue glow from their screens disrupts our body clocks and stops us *from heading off into the land of nod.*[3]

Now whether it's a lack of sleep, or an overly busy schedule during the day, many of us do end up weary and longing for more rest.

And so our ears prick up when we hear the voice of Jesus saying: '*Come to me, all you that are weary and are carrying heavy burdens, and I will give you rest.*'[4]

Now that sounds a very attractive offer for busy people, but I have to explain that the 'rest' that Jesus has in mind isn't really about our lack of sleep, or our need for rest and relaxation.

It's much more about offering rest to people who're exhausted by a destructive form of religion that tires folk out with an endless list of demands.

For in the days of Jesus some well-intentioned religious teachers put impossible demands on people's shoulders. They'd turned faith in God into a massive burden, by adding over 600 rules and regulations on top of the core commands to love God with all your heart, soul and strength, and to love your neighbour as yourself. And Jesus says that such teachers *'Tie up heavy burdens, hard to bear, and lay them on the shoulders of others; but they themselves are unwilling to lift a finger to move them.'*[5]

But Jesus does much more than just lift a finger to help, because he intervenes to remove the heavy burdens of legalism that cut people off from God. He cuts through the red tape, gets to the heart of the matter, and invites people to an authentic, living and warming experience of God by saying *'Come to me, all you that are weary and are carrying heavy burdens, and I will give you rest.'*

- Free membership at the health club …
- Cheap internet and TV package …
- Luxury foods direct to your front door – 50 per cent off your first order.

I'm sure I'm not the only one to receive lots of invitations and free offers through the letter box or in my email.

And some of them look really good – well at least for a while, until you start reading the terms and conditions. And so often buried in the small print, you discover that what seemed to be too good to be true – really is too good to be true.

Because 50 per cent off the first order is still more expensive than the meat we normally buy …

And that cheap internet package isn't all that competitive when the line rental's added on, and you see what it's going to cost after the first three months …

And if your month's free exertions at the gym aren't enough to make your eyes water – then the regular monthly bill just might …

With those kinds of experience in the memory banks, it's not surprising if we hear a little voice deep down inside us saying: 'So – what's the catch with this great free offer that Jesus makes?'

Well there's no small print and no nasty surprises here, for as soon as Jesus says '*Come to me, all you that are weary and are carrying heavy burdens, and I will give you rest*', he goes on to say '*Take my yoke upon you, and learn from me; for I am gentle and humble in heart, and you will find rest for your souls.*'[6]

And those words echo an earlier Jewish book in which the divine Wisdom urges people to come and learn the wisdom that's needed for life in all its fullness.

You see, Jesus is God's Wisdom come down to earth, in person; and the invitation he makes for us to take the yoke of discipleship on our shoulders echoes that older invitation where God's Wisdom says:

> Acquire wisdom for yourselves without money.
> Put your neck under her yoke,
> and let your souls receive instruction;
> it is to be found close by.[7]

So when Jesus invites people to take his yoke on them, he's inviting them to change direction and submit:

> to a life of obedience –
> to a life of discipleship –
> to a lifetime of learning what true Wisdom really involves.

Over the last couple of months, students across Wales and the UK have been busy sitting exams and submitting all sorts and sizes of assignments.

And over the last couple of months, teachers and tutors have been busy reading and marking those essays and exam papers. That structured approach to education, which we're all familiar with, is one important and valuable form of learning.

But there's a much more intimate and personal kind of learning in view when Jesus goes on to say '*Take my yoke upon you, and **learn from me**.*'

For those words invite us to be closely yoked together with Jesus; to be harnessed up alongside him, so that we can learn to walk with him, step by step, day by day.

You see in this extract from Matthew's Gospel, what we find is nothing less than Jesus issuing the same call to discipleship that he made when he said to the fishermen by the sea of Galilee: '*Come follow me.*'

So when Jesus says:

Come to me
Take my yoke upon you
    Learn from me

- it's an invitation to follow him;
- it's an invitation to obedience;
- it's an invitation to a life-time of learning from Christ.

It's an invitation to learn about keeping in step with the living Christ, and allowing him to set our priorities and determine the shape and course of our lives.

But as I say that, I'm painfully aware that any idea of surrendering our freedom of choice goes totally against the grain in a society like ours that prizes individualism and insists that happiness is found by doing exactly what I want to do.

I don't want anyone telling **me** what to do …

So why should I pay the slightest bit of notice to the Jesus who says:

Come to me …
Take my yoke upon you …
    Learn from me?

Sermon Part 2 – Come to me

Bible reading: John 1.1–4 and 1.14–18

At times as I was growing up, I heard people saying: '*Sticks and stones can break my bones but words can never hurt me.*'

As I got older, and hopefully a wee bit wiser, I realized how wrong that old proverb is. For we know that words are powerful things. We know that words have the power to praise and encourage others, but they can also be used to humiliate and destroy people.

And one aspect of their power is that our words reveal all sorts of things about us.

For the words we say – *and the way we say them* – reveal a lot about the people we are.

Perhaps they reveal something about the place we've come from, or give a hint, maybe, about the place we wish we'd come from.

And that idea of words revealing things stands out clearly in the reading from the opening of John's Gospel.

> *In the beginning was the Word, and the Word was with God, and the Word was God … And the Word became flesh and lived among us … No one has ever seen God. It is God the only Son, who is close to the Father's heart, who has made him known.*[8]

No one has ever seen God, which could leave us all scrambling around in the darkness wondering what God is like. Is he to be loved or is he to be feared? But the good news is that we're not left in the dark, because the divine Word has come to earth in the person of Jesus Christ to reveal the loving character of God.

And across the centuries, Christians have affirmed that the Word who became flesh is the very Son of God, the one who's both fully divine and fully human. And because he is fully divine and fully human, he's able both to reveal the truth about God and the truth about human life as God intended it to be.

And this isn't a message that's found only in John's Gospel, for we find a similar theme in that reading from Matthew's Gospel we heard earlier.

For in that passage we hear Jesus making this startling declaration:

> *All things have been handed over to me by my Father; and no one knows the Son except the Father, and no one knows the Father except the Son and anyone to whom the Son chooses to reveal him.*[9]

For you see the reason Jesus can cut through all the rules and regulations … the reason Jesus can set people free from the burden of destructive, legalistic religion … is because the eternal Son knows the eternal Father …

And because the divine Son knows the eternal Father intimately, he's the one who's fully equipped to reveal the truth about God.

> *No one knows the Son except the Father, and no one knows the Father except the Son and anyone to whom the Son chooses to reveal him.*

And this morning we *Celebrate* that the eternal Son chooses to reveal a God of love, who longs for us prodigal children to return home.

So why should I pay the slightest bit of notice to the Jesus who says:

Come to me …
Take my yoke upon you …
    Learn from me?

Well – if it was just somebody like me saying *come to me, submit to my guidance, let me direct the whole course of your life* – then there's no good reason to pay any attention to me at all.

But it's because Jesus Christ is the eternal Son of God who knows the Father and reveals God to us – that's why we should begin to sit up and take notice when he says:

Come to me …
Take my yoke upon you …
    Learn from me.

Notes

1 www.bbc.co.uk/news/health-26630647.
2 www.bbc.co.uk/news/magazine-24444634.
3 www.bbc.co.uk/news/health-27406987.
4 Matthew 11.28.
5 Matthew 23.4.
6 Matthew 11.29.
7 Sirach 51.25–26.
8 John 1.1, 14, 18.
9 Matthew 11.27.

Appendix 2

Guidelines for *Lectio Divina*

The following framework is drawn from materials available on the Bible Society website: www.biblesociety.org.uk/explore-the-bible/lectio-divina.

A parallel set of resources are provided online by the American Bible Society: www.americanbible.org/resources/lectio-divina/012515.

History

Lectio divina dates back to the early Church Fathers around 300 AD. The four steps were first recorded by a monk, Guigo Cartujo, in 1173. These steps: Lectio (Reading), Meditatio (Meditation), Oratio (Prayer) and Contemplatio (Contemplation) remain central today although methods differ.

Overview

In essence *lectio divina* is a simple way to meet with the Lord through reflection and prayer based on Holy Scripture. It is not a study method. Background knowledge can be helpful but is not essential.

Used in groups a structure is necessary but for individuals the steps need not be followed rigidly. Our aim is meeting God, not just completing the steps themselves. So when the Lord impresses something on us we need to stop and wait. We can always come back to the steps another time. We don't want to lose what God is saying to us.

1 *Lectio* – reading

Reading the Scripture passage humbly and prayerfully is the foundation for everything else that follows and cannot be rushed. So begin with a prayer and ask the Holy Spirit to 'lead you into all the truth' (John 16:13).

Read the passage slowly and carefully. Avoid being tempted to look at the Lectio comments or any of the other steps at this stage.

Have a notebook and pencil ready. Underline, or make a note of, any words or phrases that stand out to you. Write down any questions that occur to you. Read the passage several times and read it aloud. Give yourself time to understand and appreciate what is being said. ...

2 *Meditatio* – meditation

Meditation deepens our appreciation of the passage and helps us to explore its riches. We read in 2 Timothy 3:16 that 'All Scripture is inspired by God and is useful for teaching the truth, rebuking error, correcting faults, and giving instructions for right living ...' So approach Scripture in faith expecting God to speak to you. He may reveal something of himself to you. He might highlight an attitude or behaviour of yours that needs to change. He might show you a promise to encourage and strengthen you.

Here are some suggested approaches you may find helpful

- Use your imagination. Picture the passage; put yourself into the scene and become part of the story. See things through the eyes of the other characters, listen to what they say, watch their reactions, imagine how they feel. Keep coming back to Jesus. Get to know him; delight yourself and become fascinated by him, his words, his actions, the way he responds – everything about him.
- Ask questions. Use your own questions and the questions given to think more deeply about the passage and what God wants to say to you. Ask Jesus why he

did and said what he did. Try to understand his reasons and intentions. Allow time to be quiet, to listen and hear his answer.

- Let the Word be a mirror for you. As we read the Bible it shows us more of what the Christian life looks like and where ours needs to change. We see how God's Word applies to our daily life, as an individual, and as part of our community and society. We will find promises and encouragement, challenges and demands. If we are willing God will nurture and free us to be more fully human and fully alive.

3 *Oratio* – prayer

Prayer opens up a conversation between God and us. In the Psalms we see how the writers pour out their feelings to God, often mixing hopes and fears side by side. God values our honesty. We can't hide anything from him anyway. Using the words of the responsorial psalm can help us but we can also use our own words to have a heart-to-heart conversation with a very special friend.

Through prayer we make our response to the light God's Word has shed on how we are living our lives. Now we can bring what is happening in our own life and in our community before God. We speak and listen, listen and reflect – it is a conversation with God.

4 *Contemplatio* – contemplation

To help us interpret the Gospel reading the Liturgy provides two further Scripture readings. Reflecting on these can both enrich our understanding of the text and bring into focus a response we may need to make to the Lord.

Contemplation gives us the opportunity for an intimate time of communion with God. Be still before God and invite him in. Few words, if any, are necessary here. Enjoy time in his presence. Just be with him and let him love you. Let him refresh your soul.

Review

After you have finished your time of reading, meditation, prayer and contemplation you may want to jot down in a notebook any experiences or thoughts that particularly impressed you. You may find it helpful to look back at these later.[1]

Note

1 www.biblesociety.org.uk/explore-the-bible/lectio-divina.

Appendix 3

Funeral Sermon 1

Bible readings: Romans 8.35–39 and Revelation 21.1–5

After I'd spoken at a meeting in another church, a lady came up to me whose husband had died just a few months earlier. And she told me of something that had brought her comfort and hope.

She explained that her life felt like a jigsaw puzzle that'd been dashed to pieces – but she believed that God had promised to help her gradually put the jigsaw back together again. The picture would never be exactly the same as before, because some of the major pieces were missing. But God's love and care provided the outline, and the framework, for a new picture. And in time he would help her put the pieces back together.

And that image seems to fit this painful occasion, because after our sister's death last week, it feels for many people here as if everything's been knocked for six.

It's as if the pieces of life's jigsaw have been scattered all over the place. Things can never be exactly the same again and we hardly know where to start picking up the pieces and begin putting the jigsaw back together again.

But we're not alone in this difficult task, because God is here – he shares in our sadness and says:

> *I am with you – in this sad and painful situation – and I will help you to pick up the pieces and to put things back together.*
>
> *The picture can never be exactly the same as before because such a major piece is missing. But my love provides an outline for a new picture.*
>
> *My love provides a framework for the future. Let me help you in the slow and difficult process of rebuilding.*

But why do I say that?

What basis have we for believing in that kind of God?

As Christians, we can only say things like that because of Jesus Christ:

- who died and was buried;
- who was raised to new life.

His death shows us how much God loves us – 'Yet the proof of God's amazing love is this: that it was while we were sinners that Christ died for us' (Romans 5.8 PHILLIPS).

The death of Jesus Christ on the cross reveals that God is not immune to suffering. He's not so far away from us that none of life's pain and tragedy ever gets through to him.

This God has been through the mill as well.

He carries the scars of suffering – bears the mark of the cross.

This God shared with our sister in her time of suffering.

He shares in our pain and grief today.

But that's not all – because the Jesus who died and was buried is the one who was raised to new life on the third day. His empty tomb demonstrates that God's love and power are greater and stronger than death. That nothing in life or death, nothing in all creation can separate our sister, or us, from the love of God in Christ Jesus our Lord.

Because of Good Friday and Easter we know that Jesus Christ is alive. He is Lord of the living and the dead. And he is here today to help us find new life and new hope.

This living, loving God is here today to help us begin the slow and painful process of picking up life's broken pieces.

Helping us to rebuild.
Helping us to live again.
God is here:

And so on this painful day we look to 'the God and Father of our Lord Jesus Christ! By his great mercy he has given us a new birth into a living hope through the resurrection of Jesus Christ from the dead' (1 Peter 1.3).

Funeral Sermon 2

Bible reading: Luke 24.1–12

That Bible reading is appropriate for today, not just because we have just celebrated Easter but also because it mentions people who were broken-hearted because the Jesus they loved had died.

His death had shattered all their hopes.

The burden of grief weighed heavily on their shoulders.

And so they came sadly and quietly to the grave to pay their last respects to the dead body of Jesus.

But to their surprise the tomb was empty – the body was gone – and they heard the message: 'He is not here; he has been raised.'

Now, it took them some time to sort out what it all meant, but as they looked at the empty tomb, and later as they met the risen Christ, they found new hope and new reason for living.

They came to the tomb in grief and sorrow, and were surprised to find that God's love was stronger than death; that God had broken death's power and death's grip on people.

And what those women discovered long ago speaks to our situation today: we also come in sorrow because someone close to us has died, and their dying affects all of us in one way or another. Like those women who went to the tomb, we come, as it were, to pay our last respects.

It's never easy to come to terms with someone's death, for as well as our own sorrow we are brought face to face with our own mortality.

Death and suffering stir up deep and painful emotions within us – such as grief, regret and anger.

We can feel angry at God – at others – at ourselves – and sometimes even angry that the person who has died has left us.

And a voice within cries out:

- Why has this happened?
- What have we done to deserve this?

Or that voice might whisper, 'If only …'

- If only we could have done this or that …
- If only things had been different … tragedy could've been avoided and our loved one would still be alive and with us.

And those painful feelings are very natural and normal emotions at a time like this. They are natural expressions of grief that we need to acknowledge and work with.

For those grieving women mentioned in Luke's Gospel, it was discovering for themselves that Jesus was alive that gave them new hope and helped them begin to start living again.

And for us today, hope can still be found in that same Jesus who was raised from the dead and who is alive and active today. For the living Christ is the one who wants to comfort us, and offer us hope, as we begin on the next stage of the journey.

Now, discovering for yourself that Jesus Christ is alive, and relying on him, isn't an instant answer – isn't an instant painkiller. Our grief and our problems won't disappear overnight. But knowing the risen Lord is something that can bring us new life and hope, and can help us find a new reason for living. And that's what all of us need as we are confronted by the stark reality of death again today.

Because of Jesus Christ crucified and risen, the Church dares to believe that there is nothing in life or death that can separate us from the love of God in Christ Jesus our Lord. Because of him we can experience the love of God, which can bring us comfort in our sorrow and the strength we need to face a challenging future.

> Love to comfort us;
> Strength to face the future;
>   And a living hope.

This is what we all need.
   This is what the living Christ promises and provides.

Appendix 4

Sermon Preached at an Ordination Service in August 2009

Bible readings: Isaiah 6.1–8 and Colossians 3.12–17

News was released this week about an attack on a man in east London at the end of July, which left him needing open-heart surgery. He'd gone to Barking to buy a car he'd seen advertised on the internet. But when he got there he got much more than he'd bargained for, because he was ambushed, then beaten, kicked and stabbed in the heart, lungs and abdomen. And then to add insult to injury, the £5,000 he'd brought to pay for the car was stolen from him. The attack took place in broad daylight in a busy place and police are desperate to find witnesses.[1]

We're disturbed by such violence on the streets of our city.

And we're left wondering …
Where will it end?

We live in one of the world's richest nations, and we expect to be secure. But with the global financial crisis, and people losing their jobs, many are starting to worry about paying their bills and wonder if there'll be any kind of pension to look forward to.

Financially we're left wondering …
Where will it end?

Day by day the death toll in Afghanistan continues to rise. And as we hear about roadside bombs and suicide bombers, we're aware that violence scars so many parts of the globe.

As we listen to the news we're left wondering ...
Where will it end?

We live in a time of uncertainty, and our Bible reading today takes us back to another *time of uncertainty*, for Isaiah 6 talks about the year King Uzziah died.

King Uzziah had been around for a long, long time. In fact he'd been on the throne for no less than 52 years (2 Chronicles 26.1–3). So the death of a king who'd been around for such a long time would have been a time of uncertainty that stirred up all sorts of questions.

And during that time of uncertainty a young man called Isaiah went into the Temple to pray. And as he prayed he was given a vision of God.

In the year that King Uzziah died, I saw the Lord, high and exalted, seated on a throne; and the train of his robe filled the temple. Above him were seraphs, each with six wings: With two wings they covered their faces, with two they covered their feet, and with two they were flying. And they were calling to one another:

'Holy, holy, holy is the LORD Almighty;
the whole earth is full of his glory.'

At the sound of their voices the doorposts and thresholds shook and the temple was filled with smoke. (Isaiah 6.1–4)

And this vision reveals a number of important things about the God we come to worship today.

To begin with, it tells us about *The Lord who reigns.*

It may've been a time of uncertainty but Isaiah sees something significant, for he says: '*I saw the Lord seated on a throne.*'

In other words, in spite of all that's happening, the good news Isaiah discovers is that:

- God is still on the throne;
- God is still King;
- God is still at work.

So often as we look at our world it seems as if:

- chaos reigns;
- evil reigns;
- injustice reigns;
- death reigns.

But because of the death and resurrection of Jesus:

- we know that God is stronger than evil;
- we know that God's love is stronger than death.

Because of Jesus, we know that *our God reigns.*

> God is still at work
> ... building his Church
> ... working out his purposes.

And we know that the day is coming when God will wipe every tear from our eyes and put an end to mourning and crying and pain.

Yes we live in a dangerous, fragile world, but we can face the future with faith rather than fear because we worship:

The God who's on the throne.
The Lord who reigns.

And there's another thing this vision reveals, for as we look carefully at this passage, we see *The Lord whose glory fills the whole earth.*

Holy, holy, holy is the LORD Almighty;
the whole earth is full of his glory.

I wonder if you noticed an advert that was on BBC not so long ago. A man and a woman were walking through a shopping centre carrying some bags of shopping. When the woman stepped into a little red circle on the floor, classical music started playing. And when she stepped out of that red circle, the classical music stopped.

The advert invited us to *Step into our world* – which was the world of Radio 3 – the world of classical music.

Now, some people think there's just a small part of the world where you can hear the music of God's love.

Some people feel there's this little circle called '*the spiritual life*' where you can find God, but that outside that little spiritual circle, the rest is what's called 'secular'. Some people feel that every place outside the spiritual circle is a place from which God is absent.

And sometimes we betray this way of looking at the world when we say: 'Oh such and such a place is a godforsaken place.' That district, that part of the city is just too hard for God and for the gospel.

Now the message of the Bible is very clear. The Bible says there's no god-forsaken place anywhere on this planet, because as this passage tells us, '*the whole earth is full of his glory*'. God's glory fills the whole of this earth.

And that message crops up in other parts of the Bible too. Listen to how the psalmist puts it in Psalm 139.7–13:

Where can I go from your Spirit?
Where can I flee from your presence?
If I go up to the heavens, you are there;
if I make my bed in the depths, you are there.
If I rise on the wings of the dawn,
if I settle on the far side of the sea,
even there your hand will guide me,
your right hand will hold me fast.
If I say, 'Surely the darkness will hide me
and the light become night around me,'
even the darkness will not be dark to you;
the night will shine like the day,
for darkness is as light to you.
For you created my inmost being;
you knit me together in my mother's womb.

And in the New Testament the same message comes through in John 1.14, which tells us that '*The Word became flesh and made his dwelling among us.*'

God came in the person of Jesus Christ – the divine Word became flesh.

And when we say that the divine Word became flesh we're saying that:

- God took an ordinary human life;
- God took ordinary human flesh and blood;
- God took the stuff of ordinary everyday life and used that ordinary stuff to reveal his love and to carry out his saving work.

And that's what we see happening over and over again when we share in Holy Communion. We see the living God taking ordinary things like bread and wine and using them to communicate his presence and his love.

You see, incarnation means that God stepped into the little circle that is the life of this world, and he made it his circle. And that means that all of life belongs to him, and because the whole earth is full of his glory, it means that he can meet us in every part of life. And it means he can take the ordinary, everyday bits of this world, and the ordinary stuff of our lives, and use them to bless us and to bless others.

Now there's something else that Isaiah 6 makes clear, for as we read about Isaiah's experience in the Temple, it's clear that he encounters *The Lord who calls people to serve him.*

> *Then I heard the voice of the Lord saying, 'Whom shall I send, and who will go for us?' And I said, 'Here am I; send me!'* (Isaiah 6.8)

Now, we sort of expect to hear those words being read out at an ordination service like today. Often when we read those verses from Isaiah 6 we assume that it's talking about the way God calls some people to serve as ministers in his Church; or about the God who calls some people to work as mission partners in another land.

And yes, God has spoken through this passage to many people in that way. But in addition to that, God speaks through this passage to call everyone to take the ordinary raw material of life and use it to serve God and to serve others.

For many years my mother was a primary school teacher. She saw that work as a vocation, as a calling from God, to help shape the lives of generations of children.

Now her experience is just one example – for God is calling you, whoever you are, and whatever you do, to see it as a calling from God.

God calls you to use the everyday, down-to-earth, raw material of your life as a way of serving God and serving others.

For some that means that God is calling you to serve him:

By caring for the family.
By working as a nurse or social worker.
By doing a good job in your office.
By supporting someone in need.
By using your IT skills.
By being a good neighbour.

In one way or another to use the life God has given you in order to serve him.

Ah, Peter – you're diluting this down too much.
Surely, God's not really interested in …

Oh, yes he is.
Listen to the evidence of another passage from the New Testament:

Therefore, as God's chosen people, holy and dearly loved, clothe yourselves with compassion, kindness, humility, gentleness and patience. Bear with each other and forgive one another if any of you has a grievance against someone. Forgive as the Lord forgave you. And over all these virtues put on love, which binds them all together in perfect unity. (Colossians 3.12–14)

It's very practical – it's saying that how you deal with people in very ordinary situations matters to God; and it goes on to say:

And whatever you do, whether in word or deed, do it all in the name of the Lord Jesus, giving thanks to God the Father through him. (Colossians 3.17)

So as one writer puts it, what we have here is:

an exhortation that is universal in scope, covering every aspect of life … There are few exhortations in the NT which are as comprehensive as this one … Every activity is to be done in obedience to the Lord Jesus and accompanied by the giving of thanks to God through him.[2]

So whoever you are and whatever situation you find yourself in, you're called to use the everyday, ordinary, raw material of your life to serve God, to reveal his love and to share in his work.

Questions about the possible further privatization of the Royal Mail generate heated discussion.[3]

But for today I am more concerned about the privatization of Christian faith. For you see, many Christians say that faith is a very private matter. It's something private between me and God.

And yes it's true that faith must be personal, but that's very different from faith being a very private matter. For you see, Christian faith should affect how we use our:

time,
money,
life.

Christian faith is concerned about the way you treat others – how you speak to people and how you speak *about* people.

Christianity is concerned about the way you vote and the way you work. It covers every aspect of life and every aspect of life is a place where you can:

Meet God
Experience God
Serve God.

The God whose glory fills the whole earth,
the God who calls people to serve him.

This is the God who wants to meet you in the midst of your ordinary, everyday life so that he can enable you to use those ordinary, everyday bits of life to serve him and to serve others.

Sisters and brothers, today we've come to commission our [brother] for the work of Christian ministry in this church and congregation. We rejoice that [he] has responded to the God who asks 'Whom shall I send, and who will go for us?'

And at the same time we're all of us called to respond to *the Lord who calls people to serve him.*

So sisters and brothers, your mission if you choose to accept it is this:

whatever you do, whether in word or deed, do it all in the name of the Lord Jesus, giving thanks to God the Father through him. (Colossians 3.17)

Notes

1 Story from BBC News: http://news.bbc.co.uk/go/pr/fr/-/1/hi/england/london/8222087.stm.
2 Peter T. O'Brien, *Colossians—Philemon*. Word Biblical Commentary, Vol. 44 (Dallas, TX: Word, 2002).
3 This is not intended as an 'up-to-date' sermon in terms of current affairs – as the heading states, it was given in 2009 – but as an example of something that can be evaluated using a particular grid. In fact the British government sold its final share in the Royal Mail in 2015.

Appendix 5

Identifying the 'Slides' that form one of the 'Moves' in the Sermon on Isaiah 6

Biblical Slide 1

And there's another thing this vision reveals, for as we look carefully at this passage we see *The Lord whose glory fills the whole earth.*

> Holy, holy, holy is the Lord Almighty;
> the whole earth is full of his glory.

Illustrative Slide 2

I wonder if you noticed an advert that was on BBC not so long ago. A man and a woman were walking through a shopping centre carrying some bags of shopping. When the woman stepped into a little red circle on the floor, classical music started playing. And when she stepped out of that red circle, the classical music stopped.

The advert invited us to *Step into our world* – which was the world of Radio 3 – the world of classical music.

Theological Slide 3

Now, some people think there's just a small part of the world where you can hear the music of God's love.

Theological Slide 4

Some people feel that there's this little circle called '*the spiritual life*' where you can find God, but that outside that little spiritual circle, the rest is what's called 'secular'. Some people feel that every place outside the spiritual circle is a place from which God is absent.

And sometimes we betray this way of looking at the world when we say: 'Oh such and such a place is a godforsaken place.' That district, that part of the city is just too hard for God and for the gospel.

Biblical (although we could equally label this as 'Theological') Slide 5

Now the message of the Bible is very clear. The Bible says there's no godforsaken place anywhere on this planet, because as this passage tells us, '*the whole earth is full of his glory*'. God's glory fills the whole of this earth.

Biblical Slide 6

And that message crops up in other parts of the Bible too. Listen to how the psalmist puts it in Psalm 139.7–13:

> *Where can I go from your Spirit?*
> *Where can I flee from your presence?*
> *If I go up to the heavens, you are there;*
> *if I make my bed in the depths, you are there.*
> *If I rise on the wings of the dawn,*
> *if I settle on the far side of the sea,*

even there your hand will guide me,
your right hand will hold me fast.
If I say, 'Surely the darkness will hide me
and the light become night around me,'
even the darkness will not be dark to you;
the night will shine like the day,
for darkness is as light to you.
For you created my inmost being;
you knit me together in my mother's womb.

And in the New Testament the same message comes through in John 1.14, which tells us that *'The Word became flesh and made his dwelling among us.'*

Theological Slide 7

God came in the person of Jesus Christ – the divine Word became flesh.
    And when we say that the divine Word became flesh we're saying that:

God took an ordinary human life;
God took ordinary human flesh and blood;
God took the stuff of ordinary everyday life and used that ordinary stuff to
    reveal his love and to carry out his saving work.

And that's what we see happening over and over again when we share in Holy Communion. We see the living God taking ordinary things like bread and wine and using them to communicate his presence and his love.

Application Slide 8

You see, incarnation means that God stepped into the little circle that is the life of this world, and he made it his circle. And that means that all of life belongs to him, and because the whole earth is full of his glory, it means that he can meet us in every part of life. And it means he can take the ordinary, everyday bits of this world, and the ordinary stuff of our lives, and use them to bless us and to bless others.

Appendix 6

Using the Plot in Nehemiah 4 in a Sermon

In preparing to preach on Nehemiah 4, the process of identifying the stages of the plot within the passage proved a useful exercise. Looking at the passage from this particular angle highlighted a lot of useful material for a sermon that illustrates one possible way of working through the stages of the *homiletical plot*.

The following notes try to summarize the aim of each section and contain some of the material from the sermon.

Upsetting the equilibrium

The opening section of this sermon began by upsetting the equilibrium, or comfort, of the hearers by reminding them of recent violent attacks on Israeli tourists.

Those attacks, which attracted international media attention, provided a point of contact with the story of Nehemiah. While he worked at a much earlier time in history, back then the people of Israel living in Jerusalem were also surrounded by hostile neighbours. So the initial situation facing Nehemiah's contemporaries was to some extent analogous to the tensions surrounding Israeli settlers today.

Since the setting up of the modern state of Israel in 1948, Israel has been surrounded by suspicious and often hostile neighbours. So as we pick up the story of Nehemiah at chapter 4, we go back in time to another occasion when the people of God in Jerusalem ended up being totally surrounded by hostile neighbours.

Analysing the discrepancy

The next stage of the sermon provided a more detailed description of the situation facing Nehemiah and his contemporaries. It made use of the ideas listed in the Complication *section of the reflections on Nehemiah 4 in Chapter 7 above. To some extent this section of the sermon was a way of 'running the story'[1] that unfolds in Nehemiah 4.*

When Nehemiah arrived in Jerusalem, the walls of the city lay in ruins. They'd been in ruins for almost 150 years since that time when foreign armies invaded and destroyed the city. Soon he organized people to share with him in rebuilding the city walls, but virtually straight away Nehemiah ran into trouble.

The trouble came initially from a couple of men called Sanballat and Tobiah. Sanballat was possibly the Governor of Samaria and it's possible he'd been a sort of acting Governor for Jerusalem as well. Perhaps he was afraid of losing power and influence. Maybe – but what is clear is that he did his best to stir up all sorts of trouble for Nehemiah …

Now when Sanballat and Tobiah ridiculed the Jews, they were trying to impress their friends and associates and demoralize the Jews living in Jerusalem. And in terms of demoralizing the Jews they did a pretty good job, because in verse 10 we begin to hear a lament from the people of Judah, who say: '*The strength of the labourers is giving out, and there is so much rubble that we cannot rebuild the wall.*'

And that note of lament comes through clearly in the Good News Bible, which puts it like this:

The people of Judah had a song they sang:
'We grow weak carrying burdens;
There's so much rubble to take away.
How can we build the wall today?'
Nehemiah 4.10 (GNB)

With the project only at the half-way stage, the builders say the work is so hard and so big that we'll never get it finished. And as if that wasn't enough, there are some people who want to get out of town before the enemy tanks and armoured cars start arriving on the streets of Jerusalem … The fear was that people had become so demoralized that they would give up entirely and the city walls would never ever be completed.

Disclosing the clue to resolution

On a human level the 'Transforming action' that helped to change the atmosphere was the decisive and positive leadership offered by Nehemiah (see the comments on this passage in Chapter 7).

Although many sermons and books focus on Nehemiah as an example of spiritual leadership, what ultimately transformed the situation was the presence and activity of God, who is the prime mover in this story.

If God is for us, who can be against us? It is that trust and confidence in God that provides the fundamental theological perspective that helps to shed new light on a very difficult situation.

When it comes to electing Presidents or Prime Ministers, people ask questions about who's the best person to handle a crisis. Well, the story that unfolds in Nehemiah 4 gives us the impression Nehemiah would be a good guy to have around in a crisis. For we see him addressing people's fears and taking practical steps to provide guards and defences. And we see him appealing to their past history and reminding them of the way God has fought for them in the past.

Now I am sure that any leader can gain much from reflecting on Nehemiah's leadership style. But I'm equally sure the key character in this episode is not Nehemiah, for Nehemiah's name means something like '*Yahweh has given comfort*', and what is happening here is that Yahweh the Lord God is giving comfort to his people through the work of Nehemiah.

* It was God who had frustrated the plans of people like Sanballat.
* It was God who had inspired the people to press on in the face of trouble from their neighbours.
* It was God who would help them succeed.
* It was God who would grant them success.

Those troublesome neighbours Sanballat and Tobiah were still close at hand, and real dangers were still there. But in spite of that they were able to carry on building because the people were beginning to realize that God was stronger than their enemies and that God was bigger than their fears.

Experiencing the gospel

God's presence in this context makes all the difference, and as we reflected on some contemporary examples, the hope was that people could feel encouraged by the reality of God's presence with us.

The aim here was that the cumulative impact of several scenarios might help hearers sense and feel that God is present in the real world of today, in the world we inhabit.

As I read this passage I am struck by the many differences between then and now. The challenges and difficulties may be different. God may not take the problems away but the good news is that we can continue to work with God because we have discovered that *God is stronger than our enemies and that God is bigger than our fears.* And that should come as no surprise because we follow one who said: '*I will build my church and the gates of hades will not overcome it.*'

… Many of our neighbours in this land have little or no idea about God. Most of them aren't aggressive towards the Church but they react to the gospel with apathy and indifference. And it's not always easy to know how best to reach out and make Christ known to such people. But we press ahead and we can seek to make Christ known because we believe that *God is stronger than any difficulty and that God is bigger than our fears.* We can press ahead because we believe with Nehemiah that '*The God of heaven will give us success.*'

I don't know what difficulties or challenges face you as you engage in mission. But as you engage in mission, as you reach out to the community, don't be surprised if you encounter difficulties, for if you seek to follow Christ and to go in God's direction, you'll be going against the stream.

So as you follow Christ, don't be surprised if you encounter difficulties; but don't be afraid, because the good news is that *God is stronger than any difficulty and that God is bigger than our fears.* We can press ahead because we believe with Nehemiah that '*The God of heaven will give us success.*'

Anticipating the consequences

In this final section the sermon invited its hearers to consider some of the implications of this passage for thinking about leadership and faith today.

In some ways Nehemiah may be a good role model for Christian leaders. In others perhaps we would be better off not following his lead. For example, Christian mission does not focus on building defensive walls to keep others out.

Remembering the theocentric nature of Hebrew narrative, the sermon finishes by repeating a phrase, used throughout the sermon, that affirms our faith in the 'God (who) is stronger than any difficulty and ... bigger than our fears'.

While there is much that we can learn about leadership from Nehemiah, it is also important to notice some significant differences between his situation and the ones we have to face.

1   *We admire him as a man of prayer* ... but there's a note of anger in the way he prayed when he cried out 'Hear us, our God, for we are despised. Turn their insults back on their own heads. Give them over as plunder in a land of captivity. Do not cover up their guilt or blot out their sins from your sight, for they have thrown insults in the face of the builders.' We can understand that anger, but that kind of prayer falls short of the standard Christ sets when he says 'Love your enemies and pray for those who persecute you.'

2   *We admire him as a leader but it's vital to remember that he's not your average religious leader.* For you see, Nehemiah was the official ambassador sent by King Artaxerxes I, and as the story unfolds it becomes clear that King Artaxerxes had sent some military backup along to help him. That's what's in the background in Nehemiah 4 verses 16 to 18. The evidence clearly suggests that Nehemiah was supported by a well-armed troop of soldiers. And those soldiers were not only there to defend the city, they were also around to persuade people not to desert the cause by running away. With that in mind we can begin to appreciate that Nehemiah was exercising his leadership in a very different context – because most churches don't pro-

vide well-armed, military backup to reinforce the 'leadership' offered by Christian leaders!

3   *Finally we see Nehemiah building walls to defend the community against the outsiders.* So here is another big difference, because in our God-given mission, Christians are not called to defend themselves against outsiders. In contrast we're called to build communities that welcome the outsider. So we can suggest that Christian leadership involves leading God's people to play their part in breaking down the walls that keep groups of people apart.

The key thing, however, is that copying Nehemiah as a role model isn't the main point of this passage. The key note this passage sounds has to do with the God who is at work in the midst of this complicated human situation, for this episode reminds us that *God is stronger than any difficulty and that God is bigger than our fears*. All of which means that even in these challenging times we can press on with the task of building for God's kingdom and doing God's work, confident, as Nehemiah was, that in due time '*The God of heaven will give us success*.'

Note

1   Eugene L. Lowry, *How to Preach a Parable: Designs for Narrative Sermons* (Nashville, TN: Abingdon Press, 1989), pp. 42–78.

Appendix 7

Finding the Plot in Ruth 2

Without seeking to disconnect this chapter from the overall plot of the book of Ruth, it may be possible to detect the shape of a narrative plot unfolding with this section of the story. The following suggestions seek to place Ruth 2 in the larger context of the book as a whole. Although God is not mentioned on many occasions here, it is clear that this narrative assumes that God is providentially at work behind the scenes.

| *Initial situation (or exposition)* The circumstances of the action (setting, characters), if need be a shortage of something is indicated (sickness, difficulty, ignorance); the narrative will show an attempt to remove it. | The opening chapter of this book mentions the famine that prompted Elimelech and Naomi, plus their two sons, to migrate to Moab. With the death of her husband and the loss of her two sons, Naomi was left in a precarious situation, because in a male-dominated society a widow without a husband to protect and provide for her was very vulnerable. Without any benefits to live on she returns, with her daughter-in-law Ruth, to Bethlehem, hoping for better times. |

Complication An element that sets off the narrative, introducing narrative tension (a lack of equilibrium in the initial state or complication in the quest).	To make matters worse, Ruth is a Moabite (2.6) and she describes herself as 'a foreigner' (2.10). 'As perhaps the only foreigner in a field of Bethlehemites, did she feel very much like the outsider (the foreman calls her "the Moabitess", 2.6)? Was it her accent, skin, colour, dress, demeanour? Had she been shunned? Had the young men been acting inappropriately?'[1] Ruth's vulnerability is perhaps being hinted at when Boaz says that he 'has ordered the young men not to bother' her (2.9). Suspicion of foreign migrants is nothing new, and for Ruth, being such a migrant worker made her plight all the more precarious.
Transforming action The outcome of the quest, reversing the initial situation: the transforming action is either at a pragmatic (action) or a cognitive (evaluation) level.	It is with the arrival of Boaz (2.4) that Ruth's situation begins to change for the better.
Denouement (or resolution) Removal of the tension by the application of the transforming action to the subject.	Boaz offers her food and drink, not to mention organizing some protection from the unwanted attention of some of the young men (2.9). Things continue to improve as Boaz generously arranges for Ruth to glean and collect food through the harvest season.

Final situation	
Statement of the new state attained by the subject following the transformation. Structurally this moment corresponds to the reversal of the initial situation by the elimination of the shortage.	At the start of this episode the spectre of famine hangs over both Naomi and Ruth. By the end of chapter, the outlook is brighter because there is the promise of food to sustain them through the coming months. They can begin to hope for a better future; and the nature of that better future becomes clearer in the succeeding episodes.

Note

1   M. Daniel Carroll R., 'Once a Stranger? Immigration, Assimilation, and the Book of Ruth', *International Journal of Missionary Research* 39:4 (2015), p. 186.

Appendix 8

Dismantling a Sermon?

It may be helpful to review the *oral script* of a sermon in order to highlight a number of things mentioned in previous chapters. The sermon integrates a mixture of the ideas explored in this Studyguide. I did not set out to preach a particular style of sermon, but having wrestled with the text, the following sermon began to emerge. Looking back on it, in a much more detailed way than usual, I suspect it could be described as an example of episodic preaching, because there is a sense in which the sermon works through a number of 'moves'.[1]

At the same time the sermon is based on a narrative passage from the Gospels and, not surprisingly, exhibits a number of narrative features. To some extent it is an example of a method described by Eugene Lowry as *'running the story'*, where 'the forward motion of the text became the forward motion of the sermon'.[2]

As a visiting preacher at a neighbouring church in north Cardiff I was asked to preach on the episode in Mark 5.21–43, where Jesus transforms the desperate situation of two women.[3] The sermon was part of a series focusing on *Encounters with Jesus*. Having visited this congregation on several occasions, I had a reasonable idea of the congregational culture and knew that people would be expecting a biblically based sermon lasting about 20 to 25 minutes.

Reflection	Oral script
The introduction for this sermon was provided by talking about a recent series of TV programmes. As some of the episodes from the series were mentioned, there were nods of recognition from some members of the congregation who had seen the programmes. Referring to a television programme was not simply an icebreaker to help me connect with the congregation. This section merits the description 'introduction' because it helped to introduce what follows in the sermon, by highlighting the changing roles of women in society during recent decades.	A little while back Susan and I watched a programme on BBC called *Back in Time for the Weekend*. It focused on a family who'd agreed to spend a summer finding out what it might have been like living in the 1950s, 60s, 70s etc. And watching their experiences revisiting the 60s and 70s was at times like seeing episodes from my life flashing before my eyes as they relived the sights and sounds of each decade. It was interesting to see new gadgets appearing year by year (e.g. video players in the 1980s). And one of the things that stood out clearly in those programmes was the dramatic changes that have taken place in the role of women. The family who were featured in the programme included a Mum who goes out to work and a Dad who's a stay-at-home Dad, plus a son and a daughter. But in the programme there needed to be a role reversal when they revisited the 50s and 60s as the man went out to work and his partner stayed at home doing all the housework. And that role reversal reflected life in Britain in the 50s and 60s, when many women worked full time at home doing housework, without being paid – and a much smaller number of women went out for paid employment. I was a bit surprised to hear that such a high percentage of women in the 1950s were working as full-time housewives, partly because I grew up in a family where my mother was a teacher who worked full time in the 50s, 60s and right through to her retirement in the 1970s. Thinking back to my childhood, my mother was possibly the only woman out of the 22 mothers in our street who went out to work full time.

The next stage of the introduction involves a story that moved from the world of television to the real world, in which women face the injustice of discrimination. Hearing about someone who was not permitted to apply for such a post, within the fairly recent past, evoked some interest and reaction. The purpose of this story was not to arouse sympathy for an individual. The hope was that getting in touch with some of the feelings stirred up by one woman's story would help people enter more imaginatively into the difficulties faced by the women described in this passage of Mark's Gospel.	In the early 1960s the head teacher retired at the primary school where my mum worked, and the school authorities began the process of seeking a new head. As deputy head, my mother was well qualified to do the job, but sadly she never got the chance – indeed she never even got the chance to put in an application – because the school authorities decided that only men would be allowed to apply for the post of head teacher. Thankfully nowadays there are laws that try to make sure there's greater equality – so that men and women are treated equally and fairly. And yet we also know that in many ways barriers still exist, and at times there's still a 'glass ceiling' stopping some women rising to the top jobs.
The introductory reflections on the changing role of women in society provide a basis for understanding the setting or the scene against which this narrative unfolds. The social setting of the Israel of Jesus' day, which is an essential dimension of **the world behind the text**, was one in which women were treated as second-class citizens. The final sentence in this section functions as a 'connector' (see pp. 184–5) because it is helping the sermon to move from the difficulties facing women in Israel in general, to the plight of this particular woman who was suffering from a chronic illness.	Our Bible reading this morning from Mark chapter 5 takes us back to the world of first-century Palestine, which was very definitely a world in which women were second-class citizens. For women were denied education … And when it came to religious practice, some teachers even claimed that *'It is better to burn the law than teach it to a woman.'* Women were viewed as unreliable witnesses – who couldn't be taken seriously in a court of law. And when it came to marriage, a wife was viewed as a piece of property belonging to her husband. A man could divorce his wife, sometimes on the flimsiest of reasons, but a wife simply could never divorce her husband. And the woman who encounters Jesus in this passage is someone who was suffering from even greater disadvantage because of serious illness.

At this point I read out these verses from the story. I did not say 'In verses 25 and 26 we hear about a woman suffering from a chronic condition.' Rather than describing or summarizing these verses, I wove them into the sermon by reading them out with feeling, thus allowing the actual words of the text to speak for themselves.	Mark 5.25–26
At this point I did not need to explain in the sermon who this 'one writer' was. The reference at the end of the quotation was for my own use. If anyone asked where the quotation came from, I would have been able to point them to its source. In my original script I highlighted this quotation and a number of others, in order to catch my eye because there were specific words in these quotes that I wanted to stress.	One writer says that historical accounts of medical treatments in those days suggest that the comment about this lady suffering a great deal under the care of many doctors has a ring of truth about it. For 'the treatments prescribed often involved drinking vile-tasting mixtures and doing other such things, many of them even more strange, and none of them likely to do any good, judged by modern medical knowledge' (Larry Hurtado, *Mark*, p. 91).
	With such a medical condition there was little hope of having a family, and if she was married there was a high possibility of her being divorced and abandoned by her husband. Her money had run out and this chronic condition that she'd been struggling with for 12 years meant she was regarded as being **unclean** – and that was one of her biggest problems.
I did not quote chapter and verse from Leviticus 15, but would have been able to point people to the specific passage if someone asked about it afterwards.	For the regulations laid out in the book of Leviticus (in chapter 15.25–30) meant that anything or anybody she touched would also have been regarded as being unclean. And that's why one writer says that: 'This woman was not only defiled, she defiled anything and anyone she touched. Her illness had left her personally, socially and spiritually cut off.'[4]
	So the woman who encountered Jesus that day was someone who was:

• Cut off from family and friends;
• Cut off from fellowship and worship at the synagogue;
• Cut off from trading in the market;
• Cut off from all normal human contacts and conversation. |

In between these two sentences I have deliberately left a bit of space, perhaps to remind me to pause for a moment after the phrase 'except for one thing ...' The pause is functioning as a kind of 'connector', which helps to provide a way of moving into the next phase of the story where this person encounters Jesus.	Medically and socially her outlook was hopeless except for one thing ... And the one hopeful thing was that 'she had heard about Jesus'.
If I was marking this as part of an essay I would look for a more formal written style. But as Chapter 9 explains, an oral script is 'something consciously written for the ear rather than designed for the eye' and is deliberately more conversational in style. This section also draws on the social and religious setting behind the text. Understanding something of how people understood purity, and the problems associated with being 'unclean', helps paint a clearer picture of the risky and courageous – maybe desperate – step this lady took in approaching Jesus.	She'd heard about Jesus healing people – maybe she'd heard how he'd healed that hopeless demoniac, nicknamed Legion, who lived on the other side of the sea of Galilee. And so she comes up behind Jesus in the crowd and touched his cloak. You see, she couldn't come up to him face to face, because in such a large crowd of people that would be a risky thing to do – because no one in the crowd would want to bump into her accidentally and end up being ceremonially unclean. It was a risky thing for her to do because there was the danger that the crowd might turn on her and drive her away. And so she approaches Jesus from behind – hoping against hope that it might help – and reaches out to touch his cloak – to touch the hem of his garment. For she said: 'If I but touch his clothes, I will be made well.'

The call to have faith is one of the notes that is present in this passage (see verses 34 and 36). This section reflects on what kind of faith is evident in this episode. Again the references for the quotations are for my benefit.	Now this desperate lady wouldn't have been able to recite the Apostles' Creed or define the doctrine of the Trinity – but deep down inside she's got a small seed of faith because she's got confidence in the power of Jesus to help her. And so one writer asks 'Is her faith superstitious? It is.
	But there is something else here. She bets everything on a desperate gamble. That is faith. That is the only faith she has. It is sheer audacity.' (Theodore Jennings, *The Insurrection of the Crucified*, p. 76)
	Or as another writer puts it, what we see here is:
	'A little craftiness, a little modesty, a little shyness due to her own uncleanness and through it all an unlimited confidence in him.' (Ernest Lohmeyer, cited in Eduard Schweitzer, *Good News According to Mark*, p. 118)
Again, reading out or performing these verses rather than simply referring to them.	Mark 5.27–29

Another 'connector' preparing the way to ask some questions about what Jesus did.

Each term at college we've some sessions exploring what's involved in offering effective pastoral care to people who're in different situations.

But when we hear what Jesus did next we'd wonder if this was the most appropriate thing to do pastorally.

Mark 5.29–34

At this point the verses that tell of Jesus' conversation with the woman after her healing were read out. This was followed by a series of questions that changed the pace and tone of the delivery, in the hope that listeners would be encouraged to think more deeply about the text. These questions helped to prepare the way for considering the larger significance of this encounter with Jesus.

It seems as if that whole conversation takes place in public in front of the crowd.

Couldn't Jesus have been more sensitive?

Couldn't Jesus just've taken her off to the side and had a quiet word with the lady out of public view?

Didn't Jesus know that he'd embarrass the woman by calling out and encouraging her to come out into the open where everyone else could see her?

So why did he make this lady come out and make her confess in public what she'd done?

Well, Jesus wanted to help the woman to see that her healing was not something magical but was because her faith and confidence was placed in him.

And maybe he also wanted to acknowledge publicly that she'd been healed; because such a public declaration of her healing would've been the first step in a process that would make it possible for this isolated person to be restored back into normal society.

For you see, this encounter with Jesus was much, much more than just a physical healing. It was a total transformation of every aspect of her life, physically, emotionally, socially and spiritually.

And so this nameless woman who'd been in such a hopeless state that had robbed her of her sense of dignity and self-worth, hears the precious words 'Daughter, your faith has made you well, go in peace and be healed of your disease.'

And those words 'Go in peace' imply that this lady can go back to her community, and back to normal life as someone who's been 'restored to a proper relationship with God' (Schweizer, p. 118).

As this person has written publicly about his situation, it was appropriate to refer to him by name. For the full article, see Guy Sayles, 'Never Sure to Preach Again: Cancer and Easter Hope', *Journal for Preachers* 39:3 (2016), pp. 11–16.

A few weeks ago I was reading an article about a Baptist preacher from North Carolina, who refers to the seventeenth-century Puritan preacher Richard Baxter. Baxter spoke about his ministry like this: 'I preached as never sure to preach again and as a dying man to dying men.'

This preacher, Guy Sayles, explains that because of being diagnosed with a serious illness, he feels a similar urgency about life and preaching because he's become unavoidably aware of his mortality.

He writes movingly about the evening in December 2013 when he took a short phone call during which the doctor explained that he was suffering with multiple myeloma. He said that the telephone call lasted less than five minutes, but the news it bore moved his primary residence from what Susan Sontag called 'the kingdom of the well' to the 'kingdom of the sick'.

Within sermons that employ a series of stories, rather than a set of ideas, to communicate a message, the repetition of key phrases is one of the things that can help to hold the sermon together. These phrases about moving from 'the kingdom of the well' into 'the kingdom of the sick' emerged as useful catchphrases that helped the sermon move forward.

Our Bible reading this morning tells us about not one but two women who'd moved from the kingdom of the well to the kingdom of the sick.

Thinking about **the world within the text**, it is worth noting that:

the evangelist Mark is the champion of inserting plots, which is also known as the 'sandwich' … The story of the raising of Jairus' daughter (Mark 5) begins with the father coming to Jesus and asking for the master to come and lay hands on her (5.21–23). Jesus complies with the request and goes with him, followed by a large crowd (v. 24). The complication is brought about by someone from Jairus' house saying, 'Your daughter is dead, why trouble the master further?' (v. 35). In the meantime another episode has taken place with its own plot (vv. 25–34): a woman who has been afflicted with a loss of blood for 12 years has come up to Jesus on the way, touched him and has been cured, and when the Lord asks her questions she has thrown herself at his feet to tell him 'the whole truth'. But from v. 35 on the plot of the first narrative resumes with the arrival of the people from Jairus' house; it continues with the arrival of the group at the home of the leader of the synagogue, the revival of the girl ('Little girl, I tell you, awake') and Jesus' command to keep silent about this miracle.[5]

Because the healing of this nameless woman who'd suffered for 12 long years is sandwiched in the middle of a story about a young woman just 12 years old, who's got to that age at which she'd be regarded as old enough to get married.

She's the daughter of a leading member of the community – one of the leaders of the local synagogue called Jairus.

And she's also in the kingdom of the sick – indeed she's on the verge of dying before her adult life has really begun.

And her loving father pleads with Jesus to come and lay hands on her so that she might be healed.

Mark 5.21–23

The story of the woman, which is sandwiched into the story of Jesus coming to heal Jairus' daughter, complicates the plot by adding to the tension. The series of questions in the sermon used sensory language to help us identify with one of the significant characters in this story. By using this language I was inviting people to imagine how Jairus might have felt about Jesus' being delayed by the crowds and by the woman who'd been ill for 12 years.	And maybe Jairus' hopes are raised as he walks along the road with Jesus? And maybe Jairus gets anxious again as the crowd gathers around Jesus? And maybe Jairus gets anxious and angry – as Jesus' progress is slowed down by this unclean woman who shouldn't be mixing with the public? And Jairus' hopes must have evaporated as he got closer to his home and heard the news that his beloved little girl had died. Mark 5.36–42
The reference to civil war in Syria is a connector that marks a change of direction, for it indicates the start of another 'move' in the sermon that sought to establish connections between **the world behind the text** and the tragic dimensions of **the world in front of the text**, which is the everyday world we all inhabit. John's Gospel describes the miracles of Jesus as 'signs'. Although that language is not so clearly applied to the miracles recorded in the Synoptic Gospels, it is still appropriate to see them as signs, for the Gospels see the healing ministry of Jesus as visible evidence that the power of the kingdom of God is at work in the here and now. The healings Jesus brings are also signs that point forward to the final victory of God's kingdom.	The ongoing civil war in Syria, which is killing many people, is just one reminder among many that we live in a violent world. And when we think of all the suffering from the five years of civil war in Syria (not to mention all the other tragedies around our world), the story of Jesus healing two women in Mark's Gospel may sound rather small beer. But the healing of the nameless woman who'd suffered for 12 years and the raising up from death of this 12-year-old girl were not just life-changing events for them. They're of much wider significance, because like all the other miracles in the Gospels, they're signs and evidence of the power of the kingdom of God at work in and through Jesus. They're signs that God's kingdom is at work, tackling the destructive power of evil. And the healing and raising up of this little 12-year-old girl is a sign of a greater resurrection that is to come – for it's a sign of that great resurrection of Jesus from the dead on Easter morning. It's a sign pointing forward to the resurrection of Jesus, which itself is a sign of the ultimate victory of God's kingdom on that day when he wipes every tear from our eyes and puts an end to mourning and sorrow and pain.

A brief pause combined with the references to fears about the Zika virus provide the connector that signals that another 'move' in the sermon is getting under way. Current ideas about disease and infection help us get some idea of the ideas of purity and uncleanness that were woven into the social and religious fabric of the world behind the text.

Over the last few weeks we've started to hear about the destructive impact of the Zika virus in places like Brazil.

And scientists all around the world are wondering how best to fight this disease and prevent the spread of the infection.

Well, in first-century Palestine, people thought about purity and uncleanness in a similar way to how we think about infectious diseases. And as most people understood things, it worked like this:

- If Jesus was touched by a woman whose disease made her unclean – that should make him unclean.
- If Jesus touches the body of a 12-year-old girl who has just died – that should make him unclean.

But far from Jesus being infected or contaminated by their disease or impurity, the opposite happens, for what we see here is that Jesus' love and power and healing and holiness proved to be contagious and infectious in the other direction.

His love and power and healing and holiness proves contagious and effective in driving out sin and disease and death.

One writer puts it like this, saying that Jesus:

'literally reaches out to those whose touch is supposed to render unclean, and power flows in the opposite direction: they do not pollute him – he cleanses them'. (William Placher, *Mark*, p. 88)

The quotation from Henri Nouwen signals that the final 'move' of the sermon is getting under way. The sermon is moving towards an ending.

I was not totally happy with this way of concluding the sermon and tried to edit things a bit as I went along. I was happy to depart from the script in an attempt to get across the heart of this final section using fewer words.

The catchphrase about moving from 'the kingdom of the sick' to 'the kingdom of the well' proved useful in this final phase of the sermon.

One Christian writer reflecting on his life and work said this:

> 'You know ... my whole life I have been complaining that my work was constantly interrupted, until I discovered that my interruptions were my work.' (Henri Nouwen, *Reaching Out*, p. 36)

While he is on the way to Jairus' house to bring healing to Jairus' 12-year-old daughter, Jesus is interrupted by the woman who's suffered from chronic bleeding for 12 years.

But far from treating that needy, nameless woman as a nuisance – as an inconvenient interruption – he reaches out in love and healing to move her from the kingdom of the sick to the kingdom of the well.

And it's important to remember that this nameless woman, who'd spent all her money in an unsuccessful attempt to be healed, was not an influential member of her community. She wasn't one of society's movers and shakers.

Indeed, one of the early Church Fathers, John Chrysostom, picks up this idea and notes that the person society would have dismissed as less important, indeed despised, gets Jesus' first attention and a welcome into his symbolic family:

> 'Do you see how the woman is superior to the ruler of the synagogue? She did not detain Him, she took no hold of Him, she just touched Him with the end of her fingers, and, though she came later, she went away healed first.' (Chrysostom, *Homilies on the Gospel of St Matthew*, cited in Placher, *Mark*, p. 83)

As we focus on this encounter with Jesus, we begin to see how Jesus notices and reaches out to those people who were regarded as second-class citizens.

The sermon does not spell out in detail which groups of people today are treated as 'second-class citizens', but the hope is that it prompts the congregation to think about those they believe to be marginalized today.	And that not only encourages us to believe the good news that the living Jesus continues to notice and reach out to us – it also encourages us to follow his example in noticing and reaching out to those people today who many dismiss as second-class citizens. And the living Jesus who reaches out to us longs for us to open our eyes to see and notice people society ignores. The living Jesus still is able to move people from the kingdom of the sick to the kingdom of the well; he calls us to see – to notice – and to reach out in love to those people who're excluded and ignored by our society.
Immediately after the sermon there was a time of quiet prayer, to create space for people to reflect on the implications of the sermon for their own lives.	

Notes

1 See Chapter 6, 'Creating a Sequence'.
2 See Eugene Lowry, *How to Preach a Parable: Designs for Narrative Sermons* (Nashville, TN: Abingdon Press, 1989), p. 49.
3 Sermon preached at Ararat Baptist Church, Whitchurch, Cardiff, on 28 February 2016.
4 R. A. Guelich, *Mark 1—8:26*. Word Biblical Commentary, Vol. 34a (Dallas, TX: Word, 1998), p. 296.
5 Daniel Marguerat and Yvan Bourquin, *How to Read Bible Stories: An Introduction to Narrative Criticism* (London: SCM Press, 1999), p. 53.

Appendix 9

Questions for Sermon Listeners

A good sermon energizes the listeners and invites them to think or behave differently through the hearing of God's Word. Ask a friend or friends to assess your next sermon by answering the following questions. To talk these through you will need about 15 minutes – perhaps longer – within a few days of the sermon.

1 What did you hear as the central message in the sermon? How did the message reach you – through a story, an image or a persuasive argument?
2 In what ways did God speak to you through this sermon? Did the sermon help you understand the passage(s) of Scripture afresh?
3 How did the sermon unfold? Did it keep your interest? In what ways?
4 How did the sermon lead you to explore new connections with Scripture and the world?
5 What feelings did the sermon stir within you, and what was it that sparked them off?
6 What did the preacher reveal about their personality in the sermon, and how did their Christian experience come through?
7 If the preacher were to preach this sermon again, where could it be improved?
8 What will you take from this sermon into the future?

These questions for sermon listeners have been drawn from the booklet *What Did You Make of Your Sermon? Some Questions to Help You Take Stock of Your Own Preaching*. Copies can be obtained from The College of Preachers via their website:
www.collegeofpreachers.co.uk/home.html.

Bibliography

Core texts on preaching

Bruce, Kate, *Igniting the Heart: Preaching and the Imagination* (London: SCM Press, 2015).

Day, David, *Embodying the Word: A Preacher's Guide* (London: SPCK, 2005).

Heywood, David, *Transforming Preaching: The Sermon as a Channel for God's Word* (London: SPCK, 2013).

Long, Thomas G., *The Witness of Preaching*, 3rd edn (Louisville, KY: Westminster John Knox Press, 2016).

Other useful books

Aldred, J., *Preaching with Power: Sermons by Black Preachers* (London: Cassell, 1998).

Anderson, Kenton C., *Choosing to Preach: A Comprehensive Introduction to Sermon Options and Structures* (Grand Rapids, MI: Zondervan, 2006).

Bartlett, David L. and Barbara Brown Taylor, *Feasting on the Word: Preaching the Revised Common Lectionary* (12 vols) (Louisville, KY: Westminster John Knox Press, 2008–10).

Brown, Rosalind, *Can Words Express our Wonder? Preaching in the Church Today* (Norwich: Canterbury Press, 2009).

Bruce, Kate, *Igniting the Heart: Preaching and the Imagination* (London: SCM Press, 2015).

Brueggemann, W., *Finally Comes the Poet: Daring Speech for Proclamation* (Minneapolis, MN: Fortress Press, 1989).

Brueggemann, W., *Subversive Obedience: Truth Telling and the Art of Preaching* (London: SCM Press, 2011).

Brueggemann, Walter, 'Psalms and the Life of Faith: A Suggested Typology of Function', *Journal for the Study of the Old Testament* 17 (1980), pp. 3–32.

Brueggemann, Walter, *The Message of the Psalms: A Theological Commentary* (Minneapolis, MN: Augsburg Publishing House, 1984).

Childers, J. (ed.), *Birthing the Sermon: Women Preachers on the Creative Process* (St. Louis, MO: Chalice Press, 2001).

Craddock, Fred B., *Preaching* (Nashville, TN: Abingdon Press, 1985).

Craddock, Fred B., *As One Without Authority*, 2nd edn (St. Louis, MO: Chalice Press, 2001).

Davis, Ellen F. and Richard B. Hays, 'Learning to Read the Bible Again', *Christian Century*, 20 April 2004, pp. 23–34.

Day, David, *A Preaching Workbook* (London: SPCK, 2004).

Day, David, *Embodying the Word: A Preacher's Guide* (London: SPCK, 2005).

Day, David, J. Astley and L. J. Francis (eds), *A Reader on Preaching* (Aldershot: Ashgate, 2005).

Durber, Susan, *Preaching Like a Woman* (London: SPCK, 2007).

Florence, Anna Carter, *Preaching as Testimony* (Louisville, KY: Westminster John Knox Press, 2007).

Francis, Leslie J. and Andrew Village, *Preaching with All Our Souls: A Study in Hermeneutics and Psychological Type* (London: Continuum, 2008).

George, Timothy, James Earl Massey and Robert Smith, Jr. (eds), *Our Sufficiency Is of God: Essays on Preaching in Honor of Gardner C. Taylor* (Macon, GA: Mercer University Press, 2010).

Graves, Mike, *The Fully Alive Preacher: Recovering from Homiletical Burnout* (Louisville, KY: Westminster John Knox Press, 2006).

Graves, Mike and David J. Schlafer (eds), *What's the Shape of Narrative Preaching?* (St. Louis, MO: Chalice Press, 2008).

Heywood. David, *Transforming Preaching: The Sermon as a Channel for God's Word* (London: SPCK, 2013).

Jensen, Richard A., *Thinking in Story: Preaching in a Post-Literate Age* (Lima, OH: CCS Publishing, 1993).

Jones, Kirk Byron, *The Jazz of Preaching: How to Preach with Great Freedom and Joy* (Nashville, TN: Abingdon Press, 2004).

Kent, Grenville J. R., Paul J. Kissling and Laurence A. Turner (eds), *'He Began With Moses …': Preaching the Old Testament Today* (Nottingham: InterVarsity Press, 2010).

LaRue, Cleophus J., *The Heart of Black Preaching* (Louisville, KY: Westminster John Knox Press, 2000).

LaRue, Cleophus J., *I Believe I'll Testify: The Art of African American Preaching* (Louisville, KY: Westminster John Knox Press, 2011).

Lischer, Richard, *The Company of Preachers: Wisdom on Preaching, Augustine to the Present* (Grand Rapids, MI: Eerdmans, 2002).

Long, Thomas G., *Accompany Them with Singing: The Christian Funeral* (Louisville, KY: Westminster John Knox Press, 2009).

Long, Thomas G., *Preaching from Memory to Hope* (Louisville, KY: Westminster John Knox Press, 2009).

Long, Thomas G., *The Witness of Preaching*, 3rd edn (Louisville, KY: Westminster John Knox Press, 2016).

Lowry, E. L., *How to Preach a Parable: Designs for Narrative Sermons* (Nashville, TN: Abingdon Press, 1989).

Lowry, E. L., *The Sermon: Dancing the Edge of Mystery* (Nashville, TN: Abingdon Press, 1997).

Lowry, E. L., *The Homiletical Plot: The Sermon as Narrative Art Form*, 2nd edn (Louisville, KY: Westminster John Knox Press, 2001).

Lowry, E. L., *The Homiletical Beat: Why All Sermons Are Narrative* (Nashville, TN: Abingdon Press, 2012).

McClure, John S., *Preaching Words: 144 Key Terms in Homiletics* (Louisville, KY: Westminster John Knox Press, 2007).

Mitchell, Jolyon P., *Visually Speaking: Radio and the Renaissance of Preaching* (Edinburgh: T. & T. Clark, 1999).

Paul, Ian and David Wenham (eds), *Preaching the New Testament* (Downers Grove, IL: InterVarsity Press Academic, 2013).

Quicke, Michael J., *360-Degree Leadership: Preaching to Transform Congregations* (Grand Rapids, MI: Baker Books, 2006).

Quicke, Michael J., *Preaching as Worship: An Integrative Approach to Formation in Your Church* (Grand Rapids, MI: Baker Books, 2011).

Robinson, Haddon W., *Expository Preaching* (Nottingham: InterVarsity Press, 1980 and 2001).

Schlafer, D. J., *Surviving the Sermon: A Guide to Preaching for Those Who Have to Listen* (Cambridge, MA: Cowley, 1992).

Stackhouse, Ian and Oliver D. Crisp (eds), *Text Message: The Centrality of Scripture in Preaching* (Eugene, OR: Wipf & Stock, 2014).

Standing, Roger, *Finding the Plot: Preaching in a Narrative Style* (Carlisle: Paternoster Press, 2004).

Stevenson, Geoffrey and Stephen I. Wright, *Preaching with Humanity: A Practical Guide for Today's Church* (London: Church House Publishing, 2008).

Stevenson, Peter K. and Stephen I. Wright, *Preaching the Atonement* (London: T. & T. Clark, 2005; Louisville, KY: Westminster John Knox Press, 2009).

Stevenson, Peter K. and Stephen I. Wright, *Preaching the Incarnation* (Louisville, KY: Westminster John Knox Press, 2010).

Thompson, James W., *Preaching Like Paul: Homiletical Wisdom for Today* (Louisville, KY: Westminster John Knox Press, 2001).

Troeger, Thomas H. and Leonora Tubbs Tisdale, *A Sermon Workbook: Exercises in the Art and Craft of Preaching* (Nashville, TN: Abingdon Press, 2013).

Webb, Joseph M., *Preaching Without Notes* (Nashville, TN: Abingdon Press, 2001).

Willimon, William H., *How Odd of God: Chosen for the Curious Vocation of Preaching* (Louisville, KY: Westminster John Knox Press, 2015).

Willimon, W. H. and Lischer, R., *Concise Encyclopedia of Preaching* (Louisville, KY: Westminster John Knox Press, 1995).

Wilson, P. S., *The Four Pages of the Sermon: A Guide to Biblical Preaching* (Nashville, TN: Abingdon Press, 1999).

Wilson, P. S., *The Practice of Preaching*, rev. edn (Nashville, TN: Abingdon Press, 2007).

Wilson, P. S., Jana Childers, Cleophus LaRue, John M. Rottman, John F. Kutsko and Robert A. Ratcliff (eds), *The New Interpreter's Handbook of Preaching* (Nashville, TN: Abingdon Press, 2008).

Wright, Stephen I., *Alive to the Word: A Practical Theology of Preaching for the Whole Church* (London: SCM Press, 2010).

Index of Bible References

Index of Names and Subjects